To Yes,
Happy Christmas 2

# A Dual
# Perspective

# A Dual Perspective

## The German in an English Judge

Konrad
Schiemann

First published in Great Britain in 2022
by Sir Konrad Schiemann
In partnership with whitefox publishing

Copyright © Sir Konrad Schiemann, 2022

www.wearewhitefox.com

ISBN 978-1-915036-66-7

Also available as an eBook
ISBN: 978-1-915036-73-5

Designed and typeset by seagulls.net
Cover design by Tomás Almeida
Project management by whitefox

Printed and bound by CPI Group (UK) Ltd, Croydon CR0 4YY

# Contents

# *Introduction*

'What on earth persuaded you, who are clearly enjoying life here, to leave that life and be a judge in the European Court of Justice in Luxembourg instead?' A number of my colleagues in the Court of Appeal in London asked me this in 2003.

The question which came so naturally to them was one which none of my continental colleagues, friends and family ever asked. For such people, as for me, to play a part in the construction of Europe was both a duty and an honour. Various members of my family had in different ways been engaged on this task for more than 150 years. In some sense my whole life had been a preparation for doing the same.

At a dinner party in Hampstead some years ago I was asked about my origins and replied that I had spent most of my life aping the manners of an English gentleman but had never been able to conceal my incompetence at cricket, riding, tennis, golf or at talking knowledgeably about sport or the weather.[1] There was an immediate outcry at the suggestion that I should have been guided by the concept of a 'gentleman', which was mocked as ludicrous. I had to apologise to my hosts for having innocently provoked in Hampstead a disturbance which I thought would not have occurred in Kensington. I explained that I owed it to my upbringing in England, which involved learning English by reading P. G. Wodehouse aloud to a clergyman born in the nineteenth century. I added that in the Germany in which I had been brought up the concept of an English gentleman was much admired.

My evasive reply is one which I often repeated when others have asked me the same question. I, having come to England from Germany just after the Second World War as an orphan, was anxious, as schoolboys tend to be, to try and fit in with the behaviour of my fellows. This tendency has never really left me.

I had spent some of the war being bombed by the British. My contemporaries had spent some of it being bombed by the Germans. In the 1940s and 1950s to say you were German was to risk abuse rather than encourage friendship. To say you had lost your parents invited explanations and further questions. 'What did your parents do during the war?' was a question which I did not want to be posed and, so far as I can recollect, was not posed for most of my life. I was

---

[1] I once asked a French ambassador what he thought were the relative strengths of our foreign services and he replied that undoubtedly the English had a cultural advantage. This sounded an odd start from a Frenchman, and I asked him to explain. He said that a Frenchman, when introduced to someone, immediately tried to slip into the conversation what interesting things he had been doing, had read or what interesting people he had met, and generally to give the impression of being well connected. It was easy to tell the genuine article from the imposter, which was important for an ambassador. He knew that in England this self-exhibitionism was regarded as ungentlemanly and that instead people talked of cricket and the weather. 'I never know whether I am talking to a genuine idiot or someone who is merely doing this out of politeness. That puts me at a disadvantage.'

leading a busy and fulfilling life here in England and was not myself at that point interested in my antecedents.

Why then come clean now? A number of factors have come together.

Now that Germany has been generally accepted once more as part of the civilised world, it is easier to be pleased with the fact that my heritage is German than it was at a time when the best course was to forget it.

Since I retired as a judge in the European Court of Justice, my days are no longer filled by a very busy agenda compiled by others as they had been throughout my previous life. So there is time at my disposal. I have always been interested in history, and on my shelves among the unread books were several written by or about my ancestors who had played some part in European history. So I got round to reading them.

My interest in them had been stimulated by my attending a celebration by the German government and leaders of the German judiciary in memory of my great-great-grandfather Eduard von Simson. Much was made of his Jewish origins. This surprised me, because I had come across no trace of specifically Jewish beliefs or practices in my upbringing. Yet personally I had long been fascinated by Judaism, as my bookshelves witness. So I had been very pleased to be invited by my Jewish friends to a seder, a bar mitzvah, the synagogue and even a ritual circumcision.

In the attic there was a large collection of letters written in the 1930s and 1940s which had been given to me as people died and which I had not bothered to read before. Many were written in old German cursive handwritten script, which I then had to try to learn. The handwriting was moreover not always perfect. Fortunately others had been typed.

I read of the friendship between the last German Kaiser and my great-grandfather Professor Theodor Schiemann. I read with astonishment a letter written in 1930 by his son, my grandfather, to my father explaining why he had joined the Nazi Party. I realised for the first time that my mother had expected to be shot for her friendship with Berthold Count Stauffenberg, who with his brother Claus had planned what should be the consequences of an assassination of Hitler. The assassination attempt failed in July 1944. I had been aware that my family lost many friends in the subsequent revenge taken by Hitler but, as I read this, all became so much more immediate.

I stumbled across a wonderful collection of letters by Helmuth James, Count von Moltke to his wife[2] and recalled that my uncle had mentioned him. I saw that he had become a member of my Inn in the 1930s and had been executed on Hitler's orders in 1945. So I arranged a service in his memory in the Temple Church to which many came. The more I read about him the more I saw that he had been the centre of a group – some politicians of various political convictions, some Christians of various confessions – who together had tried to work out how Europe could best be organised after the fall of Hitler. In due course their ideas played a part in the creation of the European Community after the war.

I was invited to receive from the Israeli ambassador to Germany a medal on behalf of my great-aunt Elisabeth Schiemann, who had been declared one of the Righteous among the Nations for helping the Jews during the war, and so I started to look at her life story.

I was largely brought up by a von Simson uncle who left Germany for England in 1939. I became increasingly conscious of the fact that my Schiemann family past had not been mentioned

---

[2] *Letters to Freya 1939–1945* (Collins Harvill, 1991).

much and I had not asked any questions about it. Nor had there been much talk of the von Simson family past. Nor did I question those who might have been able to tell me more.

When the Covid pandemic arrived there were no other distractions, and it seemed natural to record and try to make sense of what I was discovering and to try to see how my present has been formed by my family past. For the first time this started to interest me, and I devoted time to finding out.

Then members of my family started asking me questions to which I did not know the answer. It became increasingly clear that I should have found out more from people who were alive at the relevant time. It was easier for me than for anyone else to try and find out more.

All these factors came together to provide the impetus for these pages. So here is what I have been able to find out.

*Eduard von Simson, President of the Reichsgericht.*
*Painting by Lenbach*

I

# The Family Before
# the First World War

## Eduard von Simson: President of Parliaments
## and of the Supreme Court[3]

Not long before I became a judge in England, I received a very grand
invitation to attend the festivities in Karlsruhe on 10 November
1985 in honour of the 175th birthday of Eduard von Simson, who
was described as a great parliamentarian and judge. Of course I
accepted. I was gripped by what I had heard of Eduard's values, of
which my own were an echo.

At the festivities the then President of the Federal Republic,
Richard von Weizsäcker, opened his speech with these words:

---

[3] In Germany he is often referred to as 'Chorführer der Deutschen' (Chorus
Leader of the Germans). In German as in English the term for the leader of the
chorus in Greek tragedy is used in an extended sense to embrace the leader of or
speaker for any movement.

In the reception room of the Villa Hammerschmidt, my official residence in Bonn, two pictures hang opposite one another. On one side, a dark painting of Bismark by Lenbach. Opposite, smaller but striking by reason of the lively, clever eyes, the radiant Jupiter head and the dark red of the judicial robe, Eduard von Simson.

The President referred to Eduard von Simson's remarkable gifts which included: his astonishingly early development – a doctorate at eighteen, a professorship at twenty-five; the steadily increasing and uninterrupted continuity of his authority, which led him to the presidency of five German Parliaments and of the Reichsgericht (Germany's supreme court); his teaching abilities and his gifts as a speaker, of which one contemporary said that he combined the clarity of Goethe with the sweep of Schiller ('Simson speaks music', said another); and the steady nobility of his character and his dignified appearance. The President also mentioned the development of his relationship with Bismarck, which was tense at the start: as a young liberal Simson was sceptical of the rights of the *junker* landowners, a group Bismarck championed. However, as the years went by, Simson developed some regard for Bismarck's political *nous*, describing the politician's manoeuvres as resembling the daring game of a rope dancer. Despite their very different origins, both men respected each other.

The President concluded:

I believe that Simson, like most representatives of the people, was not prepared to abandon either freedom or unity. He hoped that democratic freedom would follow unity of the nation. The words of the preamble to the German Basic Law (i.e. the German Constitution)... can be regarded as the legacy of Eduard von Simson. This Königsberger of Jewish origins played in the nineteenth century a formative and essential role in the road to freedom and unity of all Germans.[4]

Helmut Kohl, the German Chancellor, followed him. He stressed that throughout his political life Eduard had been imbued with a strong sense of justice and a sensitivity to injustice which no doubt was connected with the history of his Jewish origins. This had given him a sensitivity to any inequality before the law and the importance of law in the safeguarding of human rights and the dignity inherent in man. He knew that only a free state with constitution and law could provide an adequate defence against private and governmental power. He wished to create a catalogue of human rights to act as a sure beacon for the state.

Kohl also stressed the way Simson's values had found their way from the 1849 discussions about human rights through to the current German constitution. In 1849 the Assembly over which Simson presided resolved that 'The work on the constitution upon which we are now embarking should become the foundation of the unity and freedom of Germany and the long-term welfare of the citizen.'

Kohl stressed that, drawing on that nineteenth-century foundation, the Basic Law starts with the obligation to safeguard human rights and provides a legal basis for challenging the actions of the state in which this safeguarding can become a reality.

---

[4] This speech was delivered at a time when the reunification of Germany had not yet been achieved and when serious political attempts were being made to restore the Jews to the important role they had had for centuries in German life.

He was followed by the President of the Federal Parliament,[5] Philipp Jenninger, who praised Simson's work as a President of various Parliaments who had established traditions of parliamentary conduct that were still observed – a point made by all the speakers. He stressed that Simson represented the best of nineteenth-century German *Bildungsbürgertum* – the comfortably off social class of those brought up in a culture of classical civilisation in which were joined moral values and demanding political ends. He described Simson as a person who was at once academic, politician, sensitive to the fine arts, contemplative and yet a practical politician; who had combined academic, judicial and political careers; not an opportunist; interested in theology; a realist who was ready to compromise; an ascetic armed with a certain scepticism.

The President of the Federal Court of Justice, Gerd Pfeiffer, made a speech which made a particular impression on me at the time and to a degree has shaped my life since:

History shows us that there have been many states and alliances which have broken up. In the long term, political entities made up of several independent states can only continue with a certain unity in the applicable law. This is evidenced not merely by the supersession of the many sovereign entities in nineteenth-century Germany, but also in Italy and above all in Switzerland with its varied cantons and its multilingual nature. If one wishes to understand the development of human institutions one must remember the maxim that an ounce of history is worth more than a pound of theory. We should also take this into account when we consider Europe.

---

[5] In the British tradition the President is known as the Speaker.

Two frightful wars took place on our continent and left behind terrible disturbances and deep wounds. In common, generous, working together these rifts have been overcome as first six, then ten and now twelve states have voluntarily come together in the European Community jointly to work for the peace and wellbeing of their peoples.

The thought of a United Europe is gradually becoming a reality. We are concerned with a continuing process of unified action in politics, the economy and law. The unification of Europe has by no means ended.

I quote this at length because not only did these words move me but they were spoken at a time when Germany was still divided into two by the Iron Curtain.

Pfeiffer went on:

The thought of European unity must be carried by the slow and difficult process of unification of law. In this context one thing is clear: just as in the national unification movements specific local priorities and interests had to yield to national ones, so at the end of the day national interests must give way to supranational ones.

A unified law, a unified method of making law and a unified judicature will in the future be the most effective way to a unified Europe. It is a consequence of the voluntary growing together of the states in the European Community that yielding to this law reflect the dignity and self-understanding of the states.

The more the law becomes unified, the greater the consciousness of a unified legislative and judicial order, the greater the sensitivity to common legal conceptions, the more will be the general willingness to work for the freedom and dignity of the individual in a unified Europe.

Simson's influence is to be seen in this context. He stands at the beginning of a great historical process as an important link in the unending chain of history.

As I have grown older, I have increasingly seen myself as a link in this chain, a chain to which more links are being added. My own influence on history has been significantly less than Simson's, but I have visited some of his pastures and must have inherited some of his genes. I share his joy in the use of language, his ecumenical outlook, his pleasure in trying to create a unity among people who started off with conflicting views, his desire to create a state ruled by law, his interest in politics and how authoritarianism can be controlled, and his consciousness that a complete life involves more than concentrating on the day job, important as that is, and should involve reading and the arts.[6]

Eduard's father Zacharias Jacob Simson was a practising Jew, grew up in very modest circumstances in Königsberg at the time of the Napoleonic wars and had no formal education, teaching himself to read and write. He married Marianne Friedländer, who came from a family which had already made its name. Marianne's grandfather, Joachim Moses Friedländer, had moved to Königsberg in 1739. A descendant of his became Chief Rabbi in the UK and wrote a friendly letter to me after an address[7] I gave in the Temple

---

6 When talking with aspirant judges I used to encourage them to be conscious of the inevitably restricted breadth of their personal experiences and therefore to read widely so that they might acquire a better insight into the feelings and thought processes of those appearing in front of them.

7 See Appendix, p. 375.

Church in the 1990s. I knew his daughter Michal, who is currently the curator of the Jewish Museum in Berlin and was a friend of our daughter Juliet.

In 1823, Zacharias and Marianne decided to christen their children.[8] Eduard converted to Christianity in his teens and some years later his parents followed him. He never sought to hide his Jewish origins, even in the fairly anti-Semitic environment prevalent at the time. Indeed the spirit of toleration of religious difference was strong in him throughout his life and this has been passed on down the generations to me. It is evident in the several constitutions which he had a hand in drafting and which themselves influenced the current German constitution and the European Convention on Human Rights. Because of his Jewish origins the streets named after him were renamed in Nazi times. Now, however, one finds them again in Berlin, Leipzig, Karlsruhe, Frankfurt and no doubt elsewhere.

As a young boy Eduard was precocious but, according to his teachers, not as clever as he thought he was and given to talking too much in class – a tradition carried on in my family. Nonetheless, he became a Doctor of Laws aged eighteen and because of his outstanding achievements was awarded a travel bursary, which he used for journeys to Berlin, Weimar, Bonn, Paris and Heidelberg.

On 31 August 1829, on the occasion of Goethe's eightieth birthday, he paid the poet a visit in Weimar, bringing greetings from Goethe's close friend, Karl Zelter. Zelter it was who rediscovered Bach's Matthew Passion, which was conducted by Mendelssohn at about that time. Goethe evidently conversed amiably with the young

---

[8] At a celebratory lunch after my mother's confirmation her father made a speech in which he quoted at length from a letter written by Abraham Mendelssohn at a time when his Jewish daughter was confirmed a Christian. It gives an insight into the mindset of the assimilating Jews. See Appendix, p.375.

man, who, in due course, became the first president of the Goethe Gesellschaft, which was founded in 1885. Eduard's son Bernhard wrote of his father: 'He had sixty volumes of Goethe and read them, I do not know how often, from beginning to end. Nothing in them had escaped him. The margins of innumerable pages are annotated in his handwriting.' I fear that the originals have got lost or destroyed but I do have the complete works on my shelves for easy reference.

Eduard married Klara Warschauer in 1834. Their long marriage produced nine children. In 1847, he journeyed to England and wrote home to his wife of his doings there. I shall quote from one of his letters because it refers to the influence for the good which he saw as coming from England to Germany. It was a time when the death penalty was still in force in England, and it is arresting to see how Eduard's social life was combined with capital trials. He visited the Central Criminal Court in Old Bailey several times, where he sat on the bench to the right of the presiding judge.

On 30 October he wrote to Eduard's wife:

Now I come to the most remarkable day of my visit ... Since two murder cases were on the list the President of the Exchequer the Lord Chief Baron, Sir Frederick Pollock, presided. At his request the Sheriff showed him my letter of introduction and my card. This had the result that we talked to one another frequently during the day. After I had accepted the invitation of the Sheriff to lunch he said he was sorry not to be able to join us but his lady was unwell. Round about 6 p.m. the Lord Mayor appeared on the Bench; about 6.30 pm the hearing was finished and we went to table led by the Under Sheriffs with their white wands. Magnificent room, Lord Mayor in the Chair, 25 people, mostly in robes and wigs etc. Grace by the chaplain of Newgate; I was introduced to the remaining judge from Westminster Hall, Baron Cresswell, a most agreeable man hardly older than I. At table the Lord Mayor, Baron Cresswell etc., etc. wish to take a little wine with me; gratefully accepted; I suppose half a bottle of the heavy sherry descended down my throat, which, as you will shortly see, was just as well. Another grace when the tablecloth was removed; then the Lord Mayor proposed the usual toasts, Church and Queen, Army and Navy, etc. Then he proposed a toast to My Lord from Westminster Hall, who thanked him and wished the Lord Mayor a long life.

Now, pay attention! After yet another toast the Lord Mayor proposed the health of Dr Simson the learned Prussian justice; at this point Dr Simson rose and, carried by the sherry, gave thanks in English for the honour shown to him by the acceptance by the company of the toast of the Lord Mayor. He said that Germany owed England the growth of its own literature; the assembled spirits of Lessing, Goethe, Schiller having all been inspired by the genius of Shakespeare; Prussia owed the beginnings of its own constitution to the completion of that of England; that he (Dr Simson) would not wish to be thought a false prophet if he said that Germany would give thanks for the refreshment of its criminal process by that of Albion in order to see which he had forsaken wife and child. So he, as a Prussian patriot, would propose 'the immortal institutions of this imperial kingdom'. Applause after each sentence, at the end loud cheers and clapping of hands and stamping of feet and more compliments for his speech then he – Dr S – had ever earned in Germany. I have to tell you that everything went *comme il faut* and I returned home in high spirits.

His wife and child were not told the result of the capital trials. When I read this letter I cannot get out of my head Pope's couplet:

*The hungry judges soon the sentence sign*
*And wretches hang that Jurymen may dine.*[9]

Nonetheless, in later years I gladly accepted the Sheriff's invitation to lunch at the Central Criminal Court and remembered this piece of family history. I gave the court a translation of the letter written in 1847.

In 1849 Eduard was elected President of the National Assembly in Frankfurt, the first modern German attempt at a Parliament. This was at a time when what became the German state was still a collection of smaller sovereign entities – kingdoms, cities and so on. There he helped prepare an all-German constitution. This included a whole chapter devoted to the dignity of the individual and what we would now call fundamental rights. As Helmuth Kohl pointed out, subsequent German constitutions, including the present one, reflect much of its thinking. So does the European Convention on Human Rights.

Eduard was sent by the Assembly to head a delegation offering an imperial crown of Germany to the King of Prussia, Frederick William IV, who, however, refused to accept it unless it was offered by the various German princes. He did not accept that the Frankfurt Assembly had any authority from anyone to prepare such a constitution, still less to offer him the imperial crown.

This was a bitter blow to Eduard. The Assembly in effect dissolved.

---

[9] 'The Rape of the Lock'.

*Reception of the delegation in 1849 by Prince William of Prussia.*
*Illustration in Meinhardt, Günther: Eduard von Simson (R. Habelt: 1981)*

At the dinner after the audience with the King, Eduard said to the Crown Prince (the future William I) that one of the members of the Assembly had said that no one will rule Germany who has not been anointed with a drop of democratic oil. To this the Crown Prince replied, 'I entirely agree, with a drop. But here we have a whole bottle full.'

Thereafter, Eduard, as was then possible, combined political, academic and judicial work. In England, this used to be possible but only for the Lord Chancellor. But as I describe later, that possibility has now been removed. Yet when Lord Hailsham said to me at my

*Eduard von Simson*

swearing-in that he wished me to concentrate on judicial review I, the latest link in the family chain constituted through the generations, was very pleased. He opened the door to what is perhaps the nearest one can nowadays get to combining these three avocations.

Something of Simson's style can be gleaned from a debate in one of the houses of the Prussian Parliament on 10 February 1866 about freedom of the press and freedom of speech. A regulation had been promulgated which purported to regulate the press, and a judgement had been given against two Members of Parliament for things that they had said. He took the view that these restrictions on the freedom of speech inhibited any constitutional control of government. In the course of his speech he said:

> And now that I must say a word in conclusion, there comes
> into my mind the day when I attacked before you the press

regulation of 1 June 1863. On that occasion, gentlemen, some three and a half years ago, I shared with you my conviction that there was no stopping on the road on which the government had embarked; that this type of regulation – which is so far from the concept of freedom – was intolerable whatever personally noble and patriotic motives may have driven them to enact this measure, as to which I know nothing. Our Ministers are unable to govern (much as they might wish to) with a free press; they are unable to govern without influencing the composition of courts, even if this leads to the loss of all respect in this country for justice; they cannot govern without interfering in elections even if as a consequence an apparent result is achieved which is contrary to that which the nation desires in its heart; they cannot govern with free local government; finally they cannot rule with a House in which the freedom of speech which is envisaged by article 84 can be enjoyed.

I know of course that the liberty of thought and action of these bodies is not formally restricted by the current general regulations: but in the nation at large the idea will spread abroad that speech is only free in outer appearance, that one cannot know what in truth is in the speaker's heart but has been swallowed by him for fear of prosecution. The government cannot pursue its policies without interfering with the essential and irreplaceable safety valve of these bodies.

I cannot believe that in order to achieve government policy it is necessary, not merely for the brief time of our lives but for the whole of the continuing life of the nation, to squander for an ounce of the present, untold tons of the future. To act thus is to fight against the moral and spiritual powers of the present age.

Sooner or later you will need give way to these powers whose strength you underestimate and if I am not much mistaken the judgement of the court dated 29 January 1866 which you have secured will be the first step in this direction.

The problem with which Eduard was here dealing was the legality of a regulation restricting, as he saw it, freedom of speech. He was commenting as a politician on a judgement which had held the regulation lawful. The lawfulness of a regulation is just the sort of problem which I encountered in many judicial review cases in England and in the European Court of Justice.

In December 1870, when Simson was president of the Norddeutscher Reichstag (the North German Parliament), he once more presided over the preparation of a constitution. With this in due course the southern German states agreed.

Meanwhile, the French had declared war on Prussia and launched an invasion. The Prussians countered by sending in their troops, who overran much of France. The Prussian King installed himself at Versailles.

At the request of the Reichstag, Simson led a delegation which went to Versailles and, in what Bismarck described as one of history's jokes, once more offered the imperial crown to the then King of Prussia, William I. The King, like his elder brother Frederick William IV in 1849, considered that accepting the crown would in effect destroy Prussia. He was reluctant to accept an imperial crown until all the German princes agreed, which they eventually did. He regarded the Assembly as a subsidiary actor.

The Crown Prince, the future Kaiser Friedrich III, recorded in his diary that Eduard's speech brought tears to his eyes and indeed that no eye remained dry.

Between 1871 and 1873 Simson presided over the first all-German Reichstag and the preparation of the new German Constitution. Then he retired as President but continued in parliament as President of the Justice Commission which was occupied preparing an all-German law and judicial system. When the first German Supreme Court – the Reichsgericht – was set up and it came to choosing its first President, the Emperor and Bismarck agreed that Simson was the man, and he agreed to take the post. So it came about that he laid the foundation stone of the Reichsgericht in Leipzig.

The building, much restored after bombing and enlarged, is now used by the Federal Administrative Court. I went there as part of a visiting delegation from the ECJ and was greeted by the then-President of that court with the words 'Welcome home' which I thought very charming of her. She had a picture of Eduard behind her desk.

In 1888, by the award of the order of the Black Eagle, Eduard was taken into the hereditary German nobility by Kaiser Friedrich III.

Eduard's very long obituary in *The Times* of London of 4 May 1899 included the following:

His career forms in itself an epitome of the progress of Germany through the struggles of the century towards the unity which was proclaimed in the Salle des Armes at Versailles on January 18, 1871 ...

The moderate attitude of von Simson gave his speeches all the greater weight. The student and disciple of Goethe was a master of literary form, and his statements of the policy of the Opposition gave it the impress of an authoritative exposition of the will of the nation.

He belonged to an intellectual race of Germans of which there are few survivors, and he formed a link between the spirit and teaching of Goethe, whom in his youth he had visited at Weimar, and the political ideals of modern Germany. As one of his biographers says of him, 'he still cherished in some measure the dream of the eighteenth century that mankind could be educated for liberty by reason and philosophy, by art and beauty'.

It is a dream I also cherish.

## Theodor Schiemann: adviser and friend of the Emperor William II

The Schiemanns had settled in Königsberg in 1604, before the Simsons. They were pastors and practising lawyers, judges, doctors and so on. I have a 1730 mezzotint of my great-great-great-great grandfather[10] wearing what looks remarkably like an English bob wig such as I used to wear at the Bar.

My great-grandfather Theodor Schiemann was born in 1847, not in Königsberg but in Courland further east. Courland at the time was part of the Russian Empire and is now in Latvia. During his early life this part of the Baltic, which had been under German influence, came increasingly under the sway of Russia. He read, translated and spoke Russian but disapproved of the Russification of the Baltic, which he thought of as essentially German. As a consequence, at the age of forty he moved to Germany and settled in Berlin. His influence was through his writings, both academic and as article writer for the *Kreuz Zeitung*, a leading conservative German newspaper of the time.

It was through these articles that Theodor came to the attention of the last German Kaiser, William II, the grandson of William

---

10 Alexander Friedrich Schiemann.

*Alexander Friedrich Schiemann*

I, the first German Kaiser in modern times, to whom Eduard Simson had conveyed the offer of becoming Emperor. He belonged to a group known as the *Kaisertreuen* (those faithful to William II), who distrusted the Chancellor, Bernhard von Bülow, and told the Kaiser so. This came to the ears of von Bülow who, in his memoirs, makes clear that he in turn thought nothing of Schiemann, whom he regarded as a sycophant.[11]

The Kaiser in his memoirs written in 1922 wrote:[12]

Professor Schiemann enjoyed my particular confidence. An upright man, a native of the Baltic Provinces, a champion of

---

[11] Bülow in his memoir levels this criticism against a number of those whom he regarded as responsible for his downfall. He himself can also be accused of sycophancy to the Kaiser. The fact is that it was common at the time to praise the Emperor in terms that would now be regarded as over the top.

[12] Wilhelm II, *The Kaiser's Memoirs* (gutenberg.org/ebooks/43522), p. 200.

the Germanic idea against Slavic arrogance, a clear-sighted politician and brilliant historian and writer, Schiemann was constantly asked by me for advice on political and historical questions. To him I owe much good counsel, especially regarding the East. He was often at my home and often accompanied me on journeys – as, for instance, to Tangier – and he heard from me in our talks much important confidential matter not yet known to others on political questions. His unshakable capacity for keeping his mouth shut justified my trust in him.

*Great-grandfather Schiemann wearing the Kaiser's cravat pin*

At the beginning of the first decade of the last century, the professor was of the opinion that war with England could be avoided. This, however, proved difficult, given the insistence of the Kaiser that there should be equality between Germany and England in the size of their fleets and, on the other hand, the unwillingness of the English to concede that equality. For the majority of those in power in England at the time the idea of equality between the British and German Empires was simply unthinkable.

Theodor translated into German a book by Sir Roger Casement, whose theme was that Germany was essentially in the right and that Irish Nationalists were its natural allies. He drew this to the attention of the Kaiser, and it helped to convince the latter that the English would be bound to lose any war and therefore would not enter into one. By this time the professor had been in contact with Casement for a number of years. Schiemann considered British politics in relation to Germany misguided and published in 1915 a pamphlet entitled 'How England Hindered an Understanding with Germany'.

*The Times* of London obituary of him, which appeared on 28 January 1921, included the following:

Dr Schiemann was for many years Professor of history at the University of Berlin, and wrote voluminously on the West European States. For a considerable period he combined the functions of historical writer and teacher with those of a political journalist and spy for the ex-Emperor Wilhelm II.

He visited England immediately before the European war broke out in 1914, when the Ulster controversy was at its height, and was piloted through the mazes of Irish politics by his friend and colleague the notorious Professor Kuno Meyer. He was during that time the honoured guest of the

German Embassy in London, and reported his impressions to the ex-Kaiser on his return to Germany. It is considered possible that Dr. Schiemann's information upon the imminence of civil war in Ireland may have helped to determine Wilhelm's decision to urge Austria into war with Serbia. In any case, it was authoritatively stated that Wilhelm's letter of encouragement to the emperor Francis Joseph to sanction the ultimatum was shown to the Professor-intriguer Schiemann before dispatch.

Dr Schiemann's pamphlet on Ireland as the 'Achilles' heel' of England was published in Berlin in 1915; it was a direct and vehement appeal to the Irish to arm and revolt in the German cause.

I have not come across anything which suggests that he was a spy in the accepted sense of the word.

Theodor's will, written in early 1918, includes various personal wishes, including 'Give the Emperor my decorations. Tell him then that I accompanied him in loyalty and love and thank him for all the favour, the friendship and trust that he reposed in me.'

There is an addendum dated 8 July 1920 to the will which evidences the unchanging character of the professor. 'The important thing is this that we are true to ourselves and hold high the honour of our German name until our last breath.' He was a national romantic and thought about Germany in much the same way as General de Gaulle thought about France and some of those who campaigned for the exit of the United Kingdom from the European Union thought about England.

In Gordon Brook-Shepherd's book *November 1918* I came across a description of Berlin at the end of the First World War when the monarchy was replaced by a new political order and the Kaiser had fled to Holland. He writes:

Ironically the most blatant public demonstration of loyalty to that absent monarch on the streets of Berlin had come from a civilian. On the afternoon of 9 November, as crowds of workers were flooding down the broad *Unter den Linden*, shouting their republican slogans, a small well-dressed gentleman kept pace with them on the pavement, and was observed to lift his black top hat at regular intervals, crying out as he did so, 'Long live the Emperor!' His name was Professor Schiemann [and he was not even a German, but a Balt].

His conception of loyalty to the state, then represented in his eyes by the Kaiser, was impregnated in his children, but they reacted in different ways. My grandfather Thor entered the Nazi Party because, as he explained in a letter to which we shall come, he saw it as being the best available tool for running an orderly state. His sister, my great-aunt Elisabeth, a determined opponent of Hitler, nonetheless retained a deep loyalty to what she regarded as the underlying German state.

Theodor remained friendly with and true to the Kaiser to his dying day. We have a photograph of him wearing a cravat pin with the letter 'W' in diamonds given to him by the Kaiser.

The Kaiser in 1921, at this point in exile in Holland, sent a wreath to Theodor's grave.

### Paul Schiemann: politician

This is an appropriate place to mention Theodor's nephew, Paul Schiemann. I include him because I find that my ideas on the subject of the nation state and of sovereignty, although developed before I had read anything about or by him, echo Paul's articulated nearly a century ago.[13]

Paul was a German Balt born at a time of Russian suzerainty in what is now Latvia. He served in the Tsar's army during the First World War and was a prominent politician in Latvia between the wars. Latvia had been ruled for years by the German nobility under the purely nominal suzerainty of the Tsars. But people of German origins and culture were a minority in the Baltic countries. In due course the Tsars became more active. The German nobility struggled for years to maintain their privileges but this became impossible after the First World War.

Paul sought to develop a political philosophy which diverged from the idea of nation states in which minorities were either in control or oppressed and moved towards a philosophy based on individual rights and cultures, recognised and exercised peacefully within multicultural states or alliances of states. This idea did not chime with his father or his uncle, the professor, with whom he corresponded about it and who thought the Germans should rule in the Baltic. Indeed, Paul's political views were out of tune with the generally accepted ideas of the time. The concept of a national sovereign state, all powerful within its own territory, underlay the establishment of both the League of Nations and the United Nations. In subsequent decades the tension between national sovereignty and minority and individual rights has, as will appear below, occupied me and many others. Paul's ideas became more fashionable in the late 1940s.

He was a famous Latvian journalist and politician of a liberal bent supporting Latvian nationalists and insisting that the Germans

---

[13] See John Hiden's book *Defender of Minorities* (Hurst and Company, 2004).

must learn to live as a minority. Theodor strongly disagreed with Paul's support for the Latvian nationalists all his life until November 1918. However, then Theodor wrote to him: 'My dear Paul. I have read your letter with its enclosures and have been convinced by it that you are right and I am wrong. Until now I had no such detailed insight into the actual realities. Best thanks. Uncle Theodor.'

I came across a plaque to him in Riga and I remember my Latvian colleague[14] in the ECJ introducing me to some visitors as a relative of the famous Paul. Of course I was pleased.

Paul sheltered a Jewish lady during the early 1940s, and it was this which led to him being recognised in the World's Holocaust Remembrance Centre in Jerusalem as one of the Righteous among the Nations,[15] an honour which he shares with Theodor's daughter, my great-aunt Elisabeth. She looked after me when my parents died and I write more of her later.

## My Schiemann grandparents

My grandfather Thor was born in 1880. He married another Balt, Hertha Johannsen, who was seven years his junior. One of her grandmothers was a Scot called Eliza Ann Nicoll, who had married a merchant from the Baltic. In so far as I can claim any British blood in my veins it is hers, very much diluted, and I have never worn a kilt or trews.

Thor was handsome and a good rider but not academically inclined.

---

[14] Egil Levits, now president of Latvia.
[15] On 1 January 2020 there were 27,712. Some were saintly by any definition, others had manifest character faults despite which they acted heroically.

Instead, he joined the Kaiser's army as a cadet before the First World War from which, after having been decorated for bravery, he emerged as a major. He and Hertha had three children: my father Helmuth and his two sisters, Gerda and Thora.

They lived in a village then called Altschlage, now in Poland, where they owned a house and farm of some 200 acres of pretty poor land. My father went to the Joachimsthalsches Gymnasium in Templin, a famous school for the children of nobility, officers and civil servants near Berlin, where he met my mother's brother, Werner von Simson, and his twin brother Dettloff. They often spent holidays together in Altschlage, and my grandparents were very fond of them.

*Hertha Schiemann at the time of her marriage*

*Thor Schiemann as a young officer*

*Thor and Hertha*

My grandfather taught them to shoot with guns and pistols but drew the line at their shooting his stags. Werner, who in effect became my father when I moved to England, told me that my grandmother always arranged for hot milk to be brought to him in his bedroom in the morning. He hated hot milk but used it for shaving.

## My Simson grandparents

My grandfather Hermann von Simson was born in 1880, the same year as my grandfather Thor. Like Thor, he became an officer in the Kaiser's forces, in his case the navy.

Since the theme of this book is the repeated connections in my family between Germany and England, I pause for a few words on Hermann's father August, himself the son of Eduard von Simson. August was another lawyer.

Just as his father had done in 1847, August made a trip to England in 1863. There he saw various judges, Baron Bramwell, the Lord Chief Justice, and Thomas Erskine May[16] who looked after him on 24 June. He describes a visit to the Temple Church to which I so often go. This was followed by a visit to Scotland after which he returned to England and saw his friend Mr Justice Mellor on circuit.

On 6 October 1864 he married Beate Jonas, the daughter of the Berlin preacher Ludwig Jonas – so far as I know the only one of my ancestors to have fought in the battle of Waterloo.[17] The pair moved to Berlin, where he became pastor at the Nicolaikirche. They had ten children of whom the youngest was called Beate, after whom

---

[16] Erskine May wrote the bible on Parliamentary procedure which bears his name and is still in use.

[17] Ludwig Jonas (1797–1858). Although born into a Jewish family, he became an important Protestant theologian. There is a family foundation – the Jonas Stiftung – which still organises annual weekends for his descendants.

my mother was named. They lived in the baroque Nicolaihaus. The house in the Brüderstrasse is still there near the rebuilt Berlin Schloss.

August worked as chairman of the Supervisory Board of Friedr. Krupp and, along with the Kaiser, was a guest at the wedding in 1907 of Bertha Krupp and Gustaf von Bohlen. It was this Bertha after whom the huge German guns in the First World War were named.

But back to Hermann, my grandfather. He married Marianne Rauhaus in 1906, and they had four sons – including my uncle Werner, who became a father to me. They also had three daughters who remained in Germany during the Second World War. The eldest was my mother, Beate.

During the First World War Hermann was appointed Legation Secretary to the German Embassy in Switzerland. His task was to entertain prominent people, hear what he could, and report back. Thus he spent the First World War with his children in a relatively carefree life.

*Hermann von Simson*

*Ludwig Jonas*

The Simsons lost most of their possessions during the hyper-inflation in Germany of the early 1920s, followed by the 1930s financial crash. I was told by my uncle Werner that at this time all the family turned to the most experienced banker among them and asked for advice on what to do in this unprecedented situation. The banker refused to advise any of them, saying that he simply did not know. As it turned out, he was the only member of the family who managed to save something and indeed he did quite well. Admirably, he then divided this among the rest of the family. In the event, compared with those who had been injured during the war and the poor and out of work, of which there were very many, the Simsons were comfortably off.

Hermann entered commerce and lived with his family in an agreeable house in Charlottenburg in Berlin during the 1920s and '30s. He was a competent pianist, and his wife was remembered as having a beautiful soprano voice. Werner's twin Dettloff wrote in his memoirs:

In those days one was expected at home to have a much higher degree of competence on a piano. What one can now approach effortlessly on tapes and records had in my youth to be brought alive through piano transcriptions. So it was that we got to know in my parents' home symphonies, overtures, and quartets through piano transcriptions which we played with four hands. This was an undoubted advantage when one came to hear a concert performance and also gave one a certain competence in reading music from the page.

Their happiness, however, was blighted by the fact that Hermann's wife in the course of giving birth to their seven children had repeatedly been given opium and had become an addict. The children's life was overshadowed by this. At Christmas 1932 she took her own life.

Alongside this private grief there was a much larger one.

*Helmuth and Beate Schiemann at the time of their marriage*

# II

# *The Growth of Nazism*

## A historical reminder

1933 was a momentous year for both Germany and my parents who, having entered it as an engaged couple, married in November.

On 30 January Hitler was appointed Reich Chancellor. In February repressive measures started being formally imposed, and an Emergency Decree was issued which took away various basic rights of freedom of speech, assembly and so on. Opposition Members of Parliament were arrested and opposition newspapers and electioneering activities were massively disrupted. The SA and the SS unleashed a systematic campaign of terror against political opponents. Elections followed in March from which the NSDAP ('the Nazis') emerged as the largest party, albeit with less than 50 per cent of the vote. By mid-March, 10,000 people had been arrested in Prussia alone. The Enabling Act, which deprived Parliament of all its powers and abolished the system of parliamentary democracy, was passed. By April Jews were regularly and openly attacked in the streets and there was a three-day boycott of Jewish shopkeepers, lawyers and doctors. On 7 April the Law for the Restoration of the Professional Civil Service came into force. This forced all officials of non-Aryan descent to retire. The law did not define the term 'non-Aryan', but four days later a regulation was issued which attempted to define this elusive concept. Month by month the exclusion of non-Aryans was widened.

Whereas my father was impeccably (if that's the word) Aryan, the Simsons were not. The reader may recall that my great-great-grandfather Eduard von Simson was born into a practising Jewish family. He and his parents had embraced Christianity 100 years before the Nazis came to power. But in Nazi eyes this ancestry was an indelible stain. The ideology of the Party was summed up in a document, sitting here in front of me, known as an *Ahnenpass* or ancestor pass. It opens with these words:

> The idea that it is the first duty of a people to keep its blood pure of foreign influences and to extirpate the foreign blood which has forced its way into the body of the people is deeply rooted in National Socialist thinking and rests on academic studies of heredity and racial research.

The Law for the Restoration of the Professional Civil Service of 7 April 1933 and similar legislation for other occupations required that for certain posts and professions an Aryan ancestry was a prerequisite. The *Ahnenpass* was intended to demonstrate that none of the subject's parents or grandparents had non-Aryan blood. This in turn involved showing that the great-grandparents were Aryan. In due course, further laws were enacted forbidding marriage between Aryans and Jews because this was regarded as 'shaming the race'.

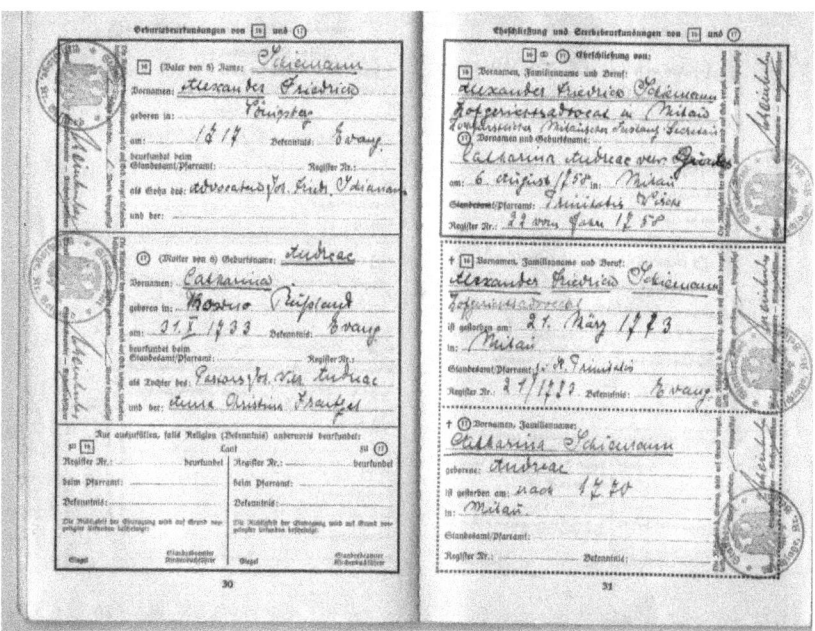

*A page in the Ahnenpass referring to Alexander Schiemann.*

This racial theory was a development of ideas earlier propagated by Houston Stewart Chamberlain (1855–1927), who, although born in England, settled in Germany, was admired by the Kaiser and became an early admirer of Hitler. Nowadays it is surprising that these racial ideas had such purchase and one asks how they were ever taken seriously. But they were, and by no means only in Germany.

My uncle Werner von Simson described the advent of the Nazi regime when he was living with my parents in Berlin in a short piece which he wrote for his university sixty years later.[18]

How was this possible? is often asked nowadays and the answer is that we too, until reality dawned, did not think it possible and certainly had no idea what traits the new regime

---

[18] 'Erzählte Erfahrung', *Freiburger Universitätsblätter*, 114 (1991), pp. 22ff.

39

would betray. It came to power precisely because no one could imagine its real nature. Hitler always lived from the weaknesses of others which, with the nose and instincts of a jackal, he knew how to find and use. The weakness of the Weimar republic was that no one believed in it. No one believed in the values which a democracy should protect. The moment these values – freedom and the willingness not to insist on being right all the time – were seen as not immediately useful, but rather as standing in the way of the newly promoted aims and dreams of national power, they revealed themselves as dispensable. Even today [1990] the central tenets of democracy are not the roots of any belief because here they are not rooted in any tradition and only appeal to reason …

Hitler by contrast brought a faith. He was able to portray his beliefs as a mission which had been given to him by the people. However full of lies, vulgar and stupid these beliefs were, they brought hope to many who were at their wits' end and gave to those who were looking for it a purpose to their existence. For those who did not have enough, those with feelings of inferiority or hatred, this new learning gave them something which before had been denied them. They could be someone – if only they cooperated. They had something to say and something to contribute. Moreover, without the idea having occurred to them, they belonged to an eternally superior race … The many flags, the eye and the voice of the Führer, the fear in the eyes of the Jews, after all one of the oldest and most honourable people in world history, somehow compensated for their previous shortcomings. A degradation without equal. We suspected but tried not to think about what a terrible price would be exacted.

He wrote that the question essentially was not 'Why did people put up with it and simply look at what was going on?' but rather 'Why did they have to put up with it; why did they have simply to look on?'

The answer is that a small minority organised itself, managed to terrorise their own organisation and succeeded in being seen as the saviour of a hopeless situation and in having a number of astonishing successes. Those who had brought them to power could see no escape but thought that they would be able to control this minority and moderate their extreme ideas. They did not take their slogans seriously, partly because they were manifestly so idiotic and partly because they would soon collapse by reason of lack of success. By the time it had become clear that they had become a ghastly reality, resistance was no longer possible. The army believed that it could not be responsible for a civil war. Whoever tried to resist was sent to the concentration camps or the gallows. The country was in the hands of hooligans. Everyone saw this but no one wanted to say so. Practically everyone sought simply to organise their private life in such a way as not to be involved more than was unavoidable.

The explanation makes sense but, as we shall see, Werner's own failure openly to oppose the regime clearly haunted him all his life. As will appear, years later, when I was in the Court of Appeal each judge was faced with an official request to declare whether or not he was a freemason. Because of my consciousness of what had happened in Nazi Germany and simply as a matter of principle, I refused to make the declaration sought.

## Nazism and my parents

It was clear to everyone in 1933 that for the Aryan Helmuth to marry the non-Aryan Beate posed problems which, unless Hitler were deposed, would only get worse.

In 1933, two weeks after the Law for the Restoration of the Civil Service, Thor wrote:

My dear Helmuth,

Today I must give you some news which will undoubtedly amaze you. I have asked to join the NSDAP (National Socialist German Workers Party). This is a step which, as you can imagine, I only took after considerable struggles within my conscience. It was preceded by 'differences of view' within the co-operative which caused me to ask myself whether I should either join the Party or resign as chairman of the cooperative, which would have had the result that I would be replaced by an inferior character from the Party. However, this decision was not pressing whilst the Party was prepared to let me continue. Decisive was a conversation with Neindorf [a military contemporary of Thor's who later became a general and fell in Russia]. He had advised me a fortnight earlier not to apply to join the Party. However today he asked me to join because now the unreliable masses were joining, and all the best people were standing aside because they hesitated to appear as opportunist followers of the crowd. But it was just these people who ought to be in the Party. I made no secret of the fact that I was by no means 100 per cent behind the aims of the Party. What attracts me is caused by my loyalty to the nation and its leader whatever his views. Moreover I have the firm conviction that the German National Party [which he had supported] will shortly be dissolved. The Stahlhelm [a veterans' association of which Thor was a member] has already recognised Hitler as the supreme leader. So the fortunate situation will arise when there will only be the NSDAP and no more political parties.

If one does not take the decisive step now then one must reckon with the consequence that one will be excluded from all business activity. I hope I don't think too highly of myself if I consider that I will be able to render more service to the Fatherland by being in this movement than by sulking critically on the sidelines. I do hope, dear boy, that you will understand and agree with the step I have taken. Then consider your own position and ask yourself whether the considerations which have moved me might not equally move you as a young man with his whole life in front of him. Mama has not so far been able to agree with me. Since she has only fourteen days ago maintained her position publicly in the Women's Institute it is more difficult for her than for me ...

So putting all things together: my position is that these days one cannot withdraw from the factual power of the Hitler movement and thus finds oneself with the choice of either working with others to make a success of things or of standing impotently aside, secure in the knowledge that one has not sacrificed one's convictions. So consider. Whatever you decide I will understand. No more applications will be entertained after 1 May.

On 2 May 1933 he wrote:

The recent developments in relation to the Stahlhelm have strengthened my opinion that the evolution into a National Socialist state cannot be stopped and that one can approve of the basic ideas of the movement. I therefore consider it right no longer to stand aside but to work together with the movement. A constitution or a party of which one approves 100 per cent will never exist. You write that you are no socialist and in consequence could never belong to the party. Heaven knows that I am no socialist in the old sense of the word but I believe that anarchic socialism is not and will never be present in the new state. Put in its place 'social understanding and empathy' then you have arrived at the convictions in which you have been brought up and which I think you still have and so the bridge to National Socialism has been built. What have up till now kept me from the party are traditional convictions with which you as a young man are not burdened. What should draw you into the movement – despite its excesses – is the enthusiasm by which it is inspired. It is after all precisely your generation which is faced with the task of building up a new state. It is precisely the leadership principle, the value of which one must acknowledge, which provides the only way out of the morass of the past. As a convinced monarchist, my decision was made easier by the closeness which the new state has to a monarchical constitution. Once you accept the idea that one must follow the leader of the nation then it is an inherent part of this that one accepts that one's own ideas must take a backseat without being disloyal to those ideas. Even if this involves carrying out laws made by the Leader

(Monarch) with which one does not personally agree. It's the old soldier's maxim: Obedience!

So my boy I don't think you need have any worries in this regard. There remains the objection that you are just joining the crowd. I however regard it as a crime against yourself and your future family if you for reasons of machismo refuse to take a part in the construction of the new state (or its economic life). It is my firm view that if you stand aside you will ruin your future or at least significantly harm it. Because this state knows no compromise and indeed cannot know compromise without breaking its backbone. Therein lies its strength and also the danger if decent people play no part. But if this state collapses then Germany is faced with communism. There is no halfway house. Moreover I am of the view that the many derailments which came with the first days of the revolution will be set aside within the foreseeable future. So think it over and don't be pig-headed.

Added to this letter was a comment by my grandmother Hertha:

Dear Helmuth,

I'm continuing this letter ...

By and large I agree with Papa. I agree that further kicking against the pricks is of no use. I entirely understand your point of view but consider it unwise in the context of your joint future. I myself for reasons similar to yours have not entered the Party, although Papa naturally wanted this. Such a course would in my case currently have been motivated solely by personal egotistical considerations. As things stand, I can continue such part of my work as I consider important.

I do not know whether Helmuth replied in writing but I can imagine his unhappiness on receiving these letters. Reading them ninety years later, I also was at first shaken. My grandfather had never mentioned to me that he had joined the Party and never gave the slightest impression that he was proud of what the Party had done. Yet trying to understand the mindset of those in 1933 who had lived through the politically and economically disastrous previous decade I now have a better comprehension of his position. My granddaughter would be horrified. To me the letters are of interest as showing the varied reactions at the time of essentially decent people to the advent of the Nazis.

The letters give one a feel of the tensions in 1933. I have not come across any evidence that Thor tried to discourage my parents' wedding. However, he clearly and understandably took the view that Helmuth would not prosper in Nazi Germany with such a wife. Helmuth, who could not dispute this, wanted to marry her just the same, and indeed my parents married in November 1933 in the Twelve Apostles Church in Berlin. The pastor was Adolf Kurz, himself married to a Jew.

Thor, encouraged by his wife, accepted this, and there was no family row so far as I can tell from the correspondence. Indeed, my grandmother was clearly very fond of Beate as a teenager, although they were very different people. I get the impression that my mother was never wholly at ease in Altschlage. The fact is that her whole urban cultural background and circle of acquaintances, dominated by a love of what is now broadly called classical music, was totally different from her father-in-law's country friends interested in hunting, shooting and fishing. I do not know but imagine that her knowledge that my grandfather was a member of the Party must have made her uneasy.

## Tensions

Throughout Hitler's Germany families were full of tensions and compromises of this sort. People had different points of view which sometimes overlapped and they often moved from one position to another. There were tensions within many families between those who were enthusiastic Nazis and supported everything that was done by them, those who thought that the Nazi Party was the best political party in the poor field available in post-First World War Germany, those who just did not want to know and tried to keep their heads down and lead as normal a life as possible, and those who were prepared to risk their lives because of their intense opposition to Nazism.

Then there were tensions between those who felt it was their patriotic duty to stay in Germany and adopt one or other of the courses outlined above and those who felt that in the circumstances they should leave Germany. No-one in my family was so far as I know an enthusiastic Nazi but examples can be found in these pages of each of the other courses of action I have described.

The Schiemanns remained behind, but quite a number of the Simsons emigrated.

My mother's uncle Ernst von Simson was forced to resign all his offices by reason of his Jewish ancestry. He was one of August's children who became a lawyer and practised first in the German Foreign Office, then in industry and then in private practice. He was a lifelong friend of Felix Mendelssohn's grandson Albrecht and was a regular visitor at the Mendelssohn house. I have in the course of my life innocently led people to believe that I was a distant relation of Felix. However, before writing this memoir I did some research and discovered that, if my British blood is very thin, my connection with the composer is even more tenuous. It seems that Felix Mendelssohn's grandfather was the great-great-grandfather of Ernst's von Simson's wife Martha.

Ernst himself became a leading person in the German Foreign Ministry from 1918 to 1922 and his signature and seal can be seen on the German ratification of the Versailles Treaty formally ending the First World War. However, he was not safe because of his Jewish background and came to England in 1933. He died in Oxford in 1941.

Another emigrant was his son, Otto von Simson, the renowned architectural historian who wrote *The Gothic Cathedral*. He seems to have had a penchant for marrying exotically named aristocrats. First, Aloysia Alexandra Prinzessin von Schönburg-Hartenstein and, after her death, Marie-Anne Altgräfin zu Salm-Reifferscheidt-Krautheim und Dyck. Giving their maiden names over the telephone would clearly have presented a challenge but I have no reason to suppose that this played any part in their willingness to marry Otto. My mother's four brothers also emigrated and all married foreigners. The three sisters, however, remained in Germany, as did their father.

The Schiemanns who remained had different opinions. Thor's sister Elisabeth took a different view from his. She was resolute in her opposition to the Party from the beginning and, before I move on, I should give a glimpse of her life, which illustrates the Germany of that time.

### Great-aunt Elisabeth

She was born in 1881 in Estonia. At the time it was under Russian suzerainty. She was admitted to Berlin University at the age of

*Professor Elisabeth Schiemann*

twenty-seven as one of its first women. She obtained her doctorate in 1912. I suppose being a woman slowed down her academic advancement, and she did not qualify as a professor till 1931. Even so because of her political views she was not made a full professor until 1946.

She was an eminent botanist whose successful academic career was interrupted because she was openly opposed to the Nazis. She was a believing and practising Christian and an admirer of Dietrich Bonhoeffer.[19] She was on the side of the Confessing Church rather

---

[19] Dietrich Bonhoeffer (1906–45), a Lutheran pastor, founding member of the Confessing Church and an important theologian, who was imprisoned and murdered by the Nazis along with Admiral Canaris, the head of the Abwehr. There is a statue to him as a modern martyr above the west door of Westminster Abbey. Before his imprisonment he travelled and made contact with various persons from the West including George Bell, Bishop of Chichester, trying to see whether there was a possibility of a negotiated peace.

than the German Evangelical Church. The latter did not think it right to be an open opponent of the Nazis. In 1935, the majority of the Confessing Church tried to protect those Jews and their offspring who had converted to Christianity. They, however, considered that to act on behalf of all Jews, whether converted or not, would be to play a bigger political role than was appropriate for the Church. Elisabeth and Bonhoeffer went further and sought to persuade the Confessing Church also to protect from the Nazis even non-Christians of Jewish heritage. She based her life on a theory of natural human rights which adhered to people because they were human and which the Church should recognise as such. This was an attitude which Eduard von Simson would have shared.

One of her former students recalled that during a meeting organised by students 'only Schiemann got up and stated with a clear although slightly breaking voice – as was her wont in times of great stress and passion – that we should acknowledge the contribution of different peoples to German culture and science – French, Italian, and "Yes, let us say it clearly, the Jews."'

Before the war she wrote openly to Lutz, Count Schwerin von Krosigk, a Nazi Finance Minister, protesting against the treatment of the Jews:

6 December 1938

Minister,

Thousands of Germans of Jewish descent are ready to emigrate. Hundreds of mothers and wives, whose sons and husbands are sitting in concentration camps, must try these days to get together the necessary paperwork.

As I found out this morning, there exists an official Emigration Bureau at no. 15 Linkstrasse.

My journey to work carried me to the Wannsee station. As I came out, I saw an old lady with uncertain gait who was puzzling over a piece of paper in her hand and was hesitating about crossing the road.

When I asked her, 'Can I help you?' I discovered that she was looking for the Emigration Bureau in the Linkstrasse in order to obtain a passport for her son. The old lady was manifestly suffering from heart trouble – she later told me she was sixty-two – and so I accompanied her to her destination and through the first stages of her quest.

Minister! Just take a look at this place!!! Perhaps you will say that you have no time. Then let your wife, as a woman and a human being, have a look. One can surely spare this time from Christmas preparations.

A small old-Berlin backyard, with a hut in the middle: that is where the first preliminary step involves handing out two bits of paper for the 'prisoners' (which I suppose means those in concentration camps) to those who get to the front of a queue of some fifty people waiting. After we had obtained these, we were then told to wait till the stairs became clear.

Waiting meant standing in a queue in the open in an overcrowded yard. As the door opened for the next person, she, who was more than sixty years old, was allowed on to the stairs, where others helped her. That is, people squeezed together to let her through. At this point I saw how difficult she found the steps.

'Minister! It was dark even at midday. Circular stairs, two storeys high, with every step filled. This in order to fill in the papers at the top when it must be in the interest of the office to let things progress more quickly.

... that, faced with these poor and helpless creatures who have been sentenced by us to losing their home and are thus anxious, one should mistreat them to the uttermost discomfort that a sadist could invent! That one should choose the smallest and least suitable place for innumerable ill people and half children ... Minister, this is unworthy and sticks in one's throat.

Once I knew that the old lady was being helped by her fellow sufferers, I left to go to work but not before I had tried to persuade an unknown official, whom I took to be the person in charge, to lay before the appropriate authorities measures to ameliorate this situation. He assured me that nothing could be done! ...

In 1919, my father, when he saw injustice wrote an open letter to Ebert [President of Germany at the time] which could be printed everywhere. And today?

A copy of this letter was among Aunt Elisabeth's effects when she died. Ministry files record the original as having arrived, but it has disappeared. No reply was received. None of the normal results of a letter critical of the regime appear to have happened to her immediately. Perhaps one of the people in the office knew her father the professor, knew the normal consequences of such a letter and quietly caused it to disappear.

During the Hitler era, Elisabeth published a monograph in which she stated that Nazi racial theories on miscegenation were misguided, as could be seen by studying the cultivation of various plants which thrived on cross-breeding. On 14 April 1940, she was told she would not be considered for a professorship, and her right to teach expired, as did her income. It seems the final straw was that she had given it as her opinion that it was improper to refuse someone his doctorate in agriculture on the ground that he had a misguided *Weltanschauung* (or worldview, i.e. he was not a supporter of Hitler's political philosophy).

She was, however, allowed to continue to make trips to study botanical specimens, and it seems she used to take parties of a dozen students to the Alps to study flowers. Apparently, she regularly smuggled a couple of Jews in with her group, and they would quietly slip over the border to Switzerland.

Back in Berlin, Elisabeth and her sister Gertrud sheltered two Jewish girls in their flat. As a result of these girls' efforts she, like her cousin Paul Schiemann, is listed in Yad Vashem as one of the Righteous among the Nations, she as a German, he as a Latvian. For her efforts on behalf of the Jews in Berlin during the war, I was presented in 2018 with a medal evidencing this fact by the Israeli Ambassador to Germany at a large public ceremony in Berlin. The medal is now on my mantelpiece.

She was a friend of Lise Meitner, the famous physicist, who fled Germany because of her Jewish background. Letters between them are preserved at Churchill College, Cambridge.

A street in Berlin is named after her. She is buried with her sister in the St Anne churchyard in Berlin Dahlem.

# III

# *The Second World War*

## My grandparents

Thor was called up in 1939 as a major in the reserve. He served in Poland, France and Russia, was promoted to colonel and was awarded the German Cross in Gold for repeated acts of bravery. By December 1943 he was in Altschlage, having been retired from the army because of his age.

During most of the Second World War, my other grandfather, Hermann, who suffered from a heart condition, lived in the lovely Alsatian town of Colmar, which at the time had been reincorporated into Germany. Like many of the inhabitants he spoke both German and French.

In late 1944 he was forced to move from pillar to post and ended up in Bavaria, where my mother and I stayed with him in 1945 after we had left Berlin. My only memory of that time, apart from being fond of him, was the pervasive smell of wood in the sawmill where he lived. This had been provided for him by a relation, Prinz von Leinigen. Conditions were fairly primitive. In a letter written in November 1946 he mentions that he last saw a bath eighteen months earlier.

## My own memories

My own memories of this time consist solely of a few individual flashes. I have no memories of being predominantly happy or unhappy. A small boy's time frame is very short. I spent many of the early years of the war in what is now Poland – either at my Schiemann grandparents' farm in Altschlage in Pomerania or at my aunt Marianne's farm in Siegersdorf in Silesia.

My very sketchy memories of my time in Altschlage are happy ones. Several young cousins were also there, and we were splendidly looked after by our affectionate and competent grandmother of whom more later.

I remember climbing on to a load of hay on a wagon, something strictly forbidden, and enjoying the view from up there. I also recall the swishing of the horse-drawn carriage on skis in which I sat, wrapped up in furs.

I went to the village school but got a bad mark on my arrival by asking the headteacher who was the man with the moustache whose photograph was all over the school. A silly question for a six-year-old in Hitler's Germany.

I recall learning to write on a slate with a slate pencil and I use this as an unconvincing excuse for my handwriting, inelegant to this day. My grandmother claimed that on this first day at school I had unexpectedly walked back home before lunch to announce that there was no point in staying because I knew all the stuff they were teaching. In this respect at least I evidently followed the approach of

*Hertha with her grandchildren*

the young Eduard Simson. So did my grandson. Thus the latest link in the chain carries on the tradition.

I think I remember a Christmas spent as a five-year-old in Altschlage. The cousins were there. We all sang carols. In an extract written by my grandmother to which we shall come later she describes a similar Christmas a year later.

As for Siegersdorf I was also predominantly happy being looked after by my mother's sister Marianne Schwerdtfeger and her mother-in-law the redoubtable Aunt Hilda. I have happy memories of looking at Marianne's daughter Bettina and less happy ones of being bitten in the backside by a goose. Aunt Hilda was English by birth but had married a German army officer before the First World War and remained in Germany thereafter. When I was five she attempted to teach me some English, but I gather that I pointed out that since she spoke good German there was no point in my learning English since we could perfectly well talk in German. Nevertheless she persisted, and her efforts made life easier after the war when I was successful in persuading some English soldiers to give me some chocolate. She was a lady of the old school and expected a certain degree of deference. When a British sergeant in 1945 started shouting at her, she addressed him firmly in English and told him not to talk to a lady in that offensive manner. He, no doubt astonished but accustomed to deference to those who spoke like that, took it in good part and apologised.

**My mother's occupation**

Hermann, my Simson grandfather, was a friend of Admiral Gladisch who was until 30 April 1943 the commissioner for the Prize Court, a court concerned with how enemy and neutral ships and their content should be treated during the war. More significantly for present purposes, Gladisch was in charge of a committee for the development of the law of war. That committee consisted of Helmuth James, Graf von Moltke, Professor Ernst Martin Schmitz, Berthold, Graf Schenk von Stauffenberg and Professor Dr Berthold Widmann. All of these people were out of sympathy with the Nazis. Schmitz died in 1943 in an accident. At Hitler's behest, Berthold was hanged in August 1944 after the failure of his brother Claus' assassination attempt. Moltke was hanged in January 1945 and Canaris, head of the Abwehr, in April of that year. Widmann committed suicide. Gladisch survived.

I suspect that it was Gladisch who arranged for my father to be transferred from the army to the navy and to be allocated to the Prize Court. Undoubtedly Gladisch secured my mother a posting with Widmann who became a significant figure in her life during the years when she was separated from my father by reason of his postings abroad. He was a well-known expert on the law of war, which is why he was recruited to join the committee. She worked as his assistant and, although he was twenty years older than she, clearly became very fond of him and he of her.

## My mother in Berlin

I think I can construct a fairly accurate picture of my parents' very close relationship with each other nourished by a more or less daily correspondence during the war, albeit that my mother's letters in the last couple of years have got lost in the general confusion which reigned at the time of my father's death.

On Christmas Day 1945, just before her death, she wrote a biographical letter to her father to which I shall return from time to time in this story. She wrote of her husband:

> He became the contents of my life. There was no need to consider anything, no fights, which other youngsters perhaps have to endure and through which they grow. It was all self-evident. So self-evident that, from shortly after our marriage I was able to do the university studies which I had wanted to do since childhood until they were concluded. We lived our happiest years together with the last brother [Werner, who remained in Berlin till 1939] and were conscious of being happy in that life together. We did not live in the future. We

enjoyed each day as it came. These years were overshadowed by Helmuth's certainty that there would be a war. But we were too young to let thoughts of the future poison our own present life. Thus we spent four Christmases, each happier than the last. and we were conscious of the gift that we had received in one another.

The letters give a picture of a marriage in wartime which must have been paralleled in all the countries involved. She was clearly not only missing her husband but also obsessed by the feeling that she ought to be bringing babies into the family. Yet they were separated, and on the rare occasions when Helmuth had leave this was followed by a sad letter explaining either that no child had been conceived or that there had been a spontaneous abortion.

The letters also give a picture of her office life, the nature of her relationship with some of those executed for opposition to Hitler and her friendship with her immediate superior, Dr Berthold Widmann. This friendship caused some unease to her father and others, and there were those who thought that it might threaten her marriage. They, of course, could not look at the correspondence. Having done so, I don't have that impression. She was indeed afraid that Helmuth might be jealous and, as the following letters reveal, told him so. There is no indication that he was remotely worried. She was also perturbed that their long separation by reason of the war would result in their growing apart. Helmuth radiated calm.

She wrote to Helmuth in August 1941:

My admiral came back from leave yesterday and brought me an armful of roses into the office which was charming of him … I have taken them home since today is Sunday and I enjoy them very much because they really are lovely and you know what a friend I am to such attentions. I get on all right with Dr Widmann and the other one but the only thing is he drives me mad with his repeatedly asking me how I am. Every morning hours are spent remarking on how I look. Then he asks where and with whom I eat and I always lie because I do not wish him to invite me continually. Then at 5 there is a further discussion as to whether I should not go home after which we work till 6.30. He even helps me with checking the situation reports and I find this so moving that I have never yet told him that I would do it twice as fast if he did not help … I do wish you were here because I cannot easily exchange thoughts with Widmann. Moreover, I want your presence for personal reasons which you can imagine since without you these discussions are not fun … I keep on thinking of people with 6 or more children and then I think that perhaps that ought to be my occupation and that we will now have to wait so long and even then it may not work etc., etc. Were you to come at Christmas you would no doubt think that a baby ought to be there.

Later that month she wrote to him:

I would like to know when you are likely to get leave since it is not reasonable for me to take my leave in September and then take more leave when you come.

It is always a bit difficult for me to talk over such things with W because with him I must start the whole discussion all over … W is as rude as ever if something does not suit him, and my position is that I have to do the work of a referendar while holding the position of a typist ... a position in which the admirals are no help to me at all ...

Things are going well for Konrad, albeit that we both suffer from the almost daily air raids. I think in October I must send him away so that he does not become nervous.

In a long letter written in September about life in the office she says that she ought to learn more about Prize Law and wishes to master it. She continues:

Yesterday I spent the entire day in the naval war command with Stauffenberg reading his papers. I want to see if I can write an overview of the implementation of Prize Law during this war which, if it is good, could be used as a draft for Gladisch's report in the winter ...

In later letters it becomes clear that she is absorbed by the work and that her superiors were happy to let her get on with it. She writes in October 1941 of her work in the committee with Stauffenberg and the others:

Almost the most significant of the men is Stauffenberg, an exceptionally clever fellow who has the characteristic that he never, even in the most complicated discussions, loses sight of the whole picture. It is often astonishing with what superiority he approaches matters. And yet he is apparently without ambition and probably not gifted with a greater desire to work than the rest ... Moltke is quite different with his concentration on the economic impact which he never forgets and so he completes the contributions of the others. I am so very grateful to W that he lets me take part even when he gains nothing whatever from it. He is really very nice and keeps me content with interesting things. In return I do a lot of boring things without ever complaining.

Returning to the question of her relationship with Widmann, she wrote on the 26th October::

My dear, are you against my friendship with Dr W.? If so I would of course give it up. Please answer this. For me it is, since you are not here, naturally lovely to spend as many evenings as possible with him, partly so that I am not alone and secondly because I like talking with him, and thirdly because we get to know each other and become better comrades. So at least as far as the first two points are concerned, there are only advantages for me rather than for him. However, since I cannot assume that he regards himself as having been put into this world for my sole entertainment it must be that he also finds it agreeable. On the other hand, I find it very unfair that naturally the moment you come here you are the only one and if we should thereafter drink beer that will not be a need for me as it is at present when I am alone. I don't know if I have put this well but you are in the habit of understanding me even when I am a muddlehead. The fact is I do not wish to give a third person who is very dear to me the feeling, to put it crudely, that I am using him when you are not there. Of course one can say it was always clear from the beginning but I would love to know what you think.

Then in November she writes:

> Dr W invites me home sometimes after the office to what he calls
> 'sausage vespers', which consists of bread rolls, hard sausage, red
> wine and French cognac. I always love it and then miss you the
> more because it is comfortable and reminds me of earlier times.
> Then I'm always in a good mood at the end of the evening. Pity
> that the sausage is only seldom there. But when it is, he shares
> it fairly with me which I find very touching. You see that I am
> much spoilt but, although I really enjoy it, it is not the same as ...
> well you know all that. Moreover he gives me all his chocolate.
> You should bring him something if you find something suitable.
>
> You need not say that you spoil me with such frequent
> letters ... Firstly, you must in any event spoil me because I like
> it so much. Secondly, I write to you just as often and always
> such loving letters ... You know when you are here I will want
> to sleep in the afternoons and you must sit yourself at the side
> of my sofa and give me a kiss ... I hope you will get used to my
> older-looking face.

It appears that she and Widmann had hatched a plan for them
all to write a history of Prize Law and the courts during the war and
that she thought that the powers that be might transfer Helmuth to
the Prize Court in Berlin. Widmann was clearly putting himself out
to secure such a transfer for him, but it came to nothing. Indeed, he
repeatedly but in vain tried to secure a home posting for Helmuth.
My mother describes the fiftieth birthday party for Widman in
August 1942. She pictures a life in which work is increasingly unfulfilling, and she and I are permanently hungry and cold. Since she
cannot buy any alcohol, she feels she cannot invite people, so she

goes to bed at eight o'clock. She wrote to Helmuth that she does not think she can have any more children for the moment because she thinks that being alone with them throughout the week would kill her. She says that leaving the Prize Court would be regarded by Admiral Gladisch as rats leaving a sinking ship.

She writes sadly to Helmuth that she has a bad conscience so far as he is concerned because he will no doubt be looking forward to coming home but will find that she is different from what he is used to,

> and this is because of something of which in the nature of things you can have only a limited understanding and about which you can do nothing. The worst is my inability to work. I forget everything and when I read something, by the time I get to the second sentence I have forgotten what was in the first sentence. Everyone laughs – they cannot possibly know from where this suddenly comes – when in the middle of a sentence I stop speaking simply because with the best will in the world I cannot remember about what I was talking. I always thought this would improve with time but until it now it has got steadily worse … W. has given me a couple of bottles of brandy, which I shall keep for you … You must not think that I ever drink alone when one of the men gives me a bottle of alcohol: I buy an evening's company with it so that I am not permanently alone.

It is clear from the letters that I knew Widmann and got on well with him but I now have no recollection of him whatever – not even a recollection of ever having had a recollection. Some thought that their relationship may have gone beyond friendship, but I have seen no clear evidence of this. He addressed her with the formal plural to the end.

## The introduction to Stauffenberg

In her biographical letter to her father my mother described how Helmuth was sent to Greece as a naval judge in 1941 while she remained behind in Berlin. She continues:

In August I was offered the chance to work most closely with Widmann, Schmitz and Stauffenberg. I no longer had Helmuth close enough to ask him questions and had to do everything by myself. With the exception of Stauffenberg the men were rough ...

Meanwhile Helmuth had settled down in Piraeus, sent letters and reports and was clearly pleased at my increasingly interesting work about which I wrote to him almost daily. Helmuth and I were not accustomed to appear at work as a married couple. We hardly did that in private if other people were there. Helmuth was if anything too guarded and so in the autumn of 1941 there was only one person who understood his mental and spiritual gifts and that was Stauffi, who was just as reserved as Helmuth. It was Stauffenberg who repeatedly offered me his help if I had to represent Widmann and from whose great wisdom I often sucked honey when the others had no time for the 'pupil'.

When I came back from Siegersdorf I had put in front of me the consent to three weeks' leave for Helmuth, and I hugely looked forward to that ... Six weeks later Helmuth came for the first time after we had been seriously separated without being able to reach one another. The first night we were unable to sleep for excitement at being able to speak to one another again. Just at that time I was unable to get a total holiday so that Helmuth had time to look over the work which I had done and to report on it. The three of us often spent the evenings together, and the two men became good friends. We talked over all sorts of problems and rather like students brought each other home.

In the first few days of 1942 Schmitz, Stauffenberg and Widmann suggested to Helmuth that he should work with them after the war. Fourteen days later, Schmitz died in a plane crash and so far as work was concerned he was irreplaceable. How things generally developed is well known. Our work became more and more pointless. Helmuth left us in November 1942 to go to Wilhelmshaven, where he spent Christmas 1942. In September 1943 he went to Italy. Christmas 1943 both our dwelling and the office were bombed out.

There had indeed been a huge RAF bombing raid on 16 December 1943 centred on Charlottenburg, where our flat was. My father took what turned out to be his last leave and came to Berlin. The flat was so badly damaged that we had to move out suddenly to the house of a relation. As will be seen, a year later, when he could not take leave at Christmas, my father reminded me of how happy we had been the year before. All things are relative.

## What is to be done with Konrad?

My mother's letter to her father continues:

On 9 January 1944 on a wet dark morning at about seven o'clock I took Helmuth to the Anhalter station. The only time

I have ever brought him to a station! I see him even now going off with his hand on his blue cap.

Then I was quite alone. And so afraid. At the Reichskanzlerplatz it was still dark. It suddenly seemed to me impossible to go to the room in which, only two hours before, we had slept. It was raining so hard that I could not remain outside. So I went to Widmann and thought I could perhaps sleep there for a bit. He had already used his last coffee beans and replied to my astonishing question 'And where else should you go now?' [20]Where else indeed should I go.

In the last full year of the war, Berlin would be raided more than 150 times – every other day – with RAF Mosquitos during the day and ASAAF raids at night, making the bombing a round-the-clock torment for those on the ground.[21]

My father was strongly against my remaining in Berlin during the bombing, as were my grandparents. My mother did not wish to be separated from me but at the same time felt that she ought to remain in Berlin.

My parents corresponded almost daily from 1943 to 1945. Sometimes more than once a day. Not all the letters from my father have survived; practically none from my mother. The following extracts give one the flavour of the times. One needs to bear in mind that letters were subject to censorship and that in 1944 my mother knew about the intended assassination attempt on Hitler's life by Stauffenberg. However, she was not able to tell Helmuth about it because he was not there. This fact, my mother's feeling that to leave Berlin amounted to desertion, her friendship with Widmann and

---

[20] Widmann addressed her with the formal *Sie*.
[21] Roger Moorhouse, *Berlin at War* (The Bodley Head, 2010), p. 325.

the fact that I was clearly safer in Altschlage than in Berlin led to a certain amount of misunderstanding between them.

On 17 February 1944 my father wrote to her:

I am keyed up to know what has happened to you since presumably it will by now have been decided whether you are to be released from the Prize Court and what is going to happen to Widmann. I still hope that you will be able to get a release and go somewhere else with Konrad for the duration of the war. It seems to me highly probable that the air raids on Berlin will continue at their present intensity if indeed they do not increase. Living conditions in Berlin will certainly become more and more difficult, and you can be of equal if not greater use to others away from Berlin.

I kiss you in my thoughts and hope that you receive this letter in good health. All the best my love and greet Konrad for me if you can still telephone him.

On 11 March 1944 my grandfather Hermann wrote to Beate:

By reason of my serious concern about you – but in this as you know I share Helmuth's position – I ask you, the more so since your professional duties have fallen away – urgently to arrange your departure from Berlin. Please understand the words 'serious concern' properly. It is not the fear of losing you although, as you know, you are perhaps the most precious thing in my heart. Because if one of my children or sons-in-law falls in the fulfilment of their duty to their country I would hope to be able to bear that loss with proper seemliness. But you no longer have any duty to your country and fellow countrymen in Berlin. In those circumstances concern about your husband and child is your <u>first</u> duty and if you push that backwards after other concerns then you harm not only yourself but also the esteem of your husband. Please let these thoughts go through your mind. I feel myself duty bound to utter them but henceforth will use no word of reproach if you, after mature reflection, are convinced that you are behaving properly and in accordance with your conscience.

It is the beauty of our relationship with one another that we can be frank without endangering this relationship, don't you agree? Farewell my dearest. I hope you got away from Berlin in time.

Because of the slowness of the wartime posts I need to go back a little. On 20 February 1944 my mother had written a letter to Helmuth about Widmann, which unfortunately is missing. It may be fortuitous but it was about this time that she learned about the assassination plot and that both Admiral Canaris and Helmuth James von Moltke were arrested. It is possible that she made a remark which made Helmuth think that her letter ought to be destroyed.

I was touched to read Helmuth's reply:

Your letter of the 20th, my dear girl, shows me that you are still the dear old muddle head whom I love so much. You make things far more difficult for yourself than they are in reality. In particular you have no reason whatever to suppose that that I believe that your friendship with Widmann has any significant impact on our relationship. I have never so much as dreamed of this still less written it and you really should not have believed this possible. I am firmly convinced that our relationship is something unique in each of our lives and you know perfectly well that I would never ask you to part from Widmann just as I know that if I even hinted this you would do so forthwith.

What I was asking for was something totally different, namely, that you could part from Berlin. I thought that this was a possibility even if it involved a separation from Widmann, who is tied to the place. For some time you have not had any significant professional obligations which might cause me to think that you should stay there for reasons of keeping up morale during the war. What I believe is that the human obligations which you have in particular towards Konrad trump any obligations which one might feel towards your, and I may say my, circle of friends. When I took Konrad against your wishes to Altschlage I did so not because I was anxious about him – which of course I am – but because I am convinced that it is our duty, in so far as it is within our power, to bring him through the war mentally and physically sound. This so that he may later so far as possible through these difficult times find a sound existence in so far as this is within our powers. Now that bombing during the day has begun, the time has come – judging by what you thought during my last leave – when he no longer belongs in Berlin and where the relative safety of the night shelter is no longer sufficient to support his continued existence.

But actually I wanted to write less about Konrad than about our relationship with one another. Here I want to add something to what I have already written about Widmann. You, my dear Atchen, inherited from your mother a rare capacity for human relationships. To awaken these feelings in you is not easy and I am happy that our life together enabled me to capture some of them. But I know that my own in many ways totally different tendencies leave me unable to sound some of your strings. I have always seen your friendships and musical life in this light. The idea, that you by these means rob me of something or that your giving to and taking from other people in some way makes me poorer, never went through my head. In time there will grow in me whatever grows in you through these contacts because you yourself grow richer by reason of them. As regards the rest, you are bound in me and I in you so firmly in the things that matter in human life that our relationship with others is on a level which simply cannot touch our relationship with and our feelings for each other. This is how I see you and us, dear Atchen, and my anxieties concerning you are not simply that I know you to be in danger but that, in fulfilling what you see as your duty arising from one set of relationships, you make impossible the fulfilment of your duties arising from what in my view is the more important thing in your life and your further development in this regard.

It is difficult, my dear Atchen, to speak about such things and yet more difficult to write about them since the living word after all conveys more than the written word. I think I ought to write to you once more about these things and perhaps you will understand that which I have incompletely expressed.

One can so easily picture the scene with each anxious about the other and not really knowing what is going on. My father typically being calm, analytical and loving but a little anxious. I can easily see myself writing such a letter. My mother, worried that their relationship would suffer through the war and yet also clearly deeply loving and worried about whether Helmuth would feel threatened by her relationship with Widmann. Whether in truth her relationship with Widmann in any way affected her own feeling for Helmuth I cannot tell. I was a little boy and if there were any tensions they were successfully hidden from me or I have simply forgotten them. Instinctively, perhaps because I am her son, I think she turned to Widmann for comfort in a situation where her husband was away and the world was very frightening. Helmuth seems to understand this well and to be grateful that there was someone there to hold her hand. This must have been such a common situation during the war in all the affected countries.

What of course was a cause for anxiety in them both was where I should go and whether she would be with me.

On 30 March Helmuth wrote:

The only thing we must consider seriously is the question how and where you have your base during the remainder of the war … I think life in Berlin is the worst of all solutions. I am convinced that for Konrad this simply ought not to be regarded as a possibility, because even if there is an invasion in the West, which in my opinion would probably lighten the burden on the homeland, we must still count on continuing terror attacks [the received description of Allied bombing raids] on Berlin. This is a danger to which one ought not to expose Konrad since there is absolutely no guarantee that he would be able during the day to reach a bunker in time. Altogether it seems to me that a life in Berlin, which according to Widmann has become a rotten carcass, is hardly bearable for him. The same is true for you, darling Atchen, and if you have the opportunity to leave Berlin, which seems to be the case, then use it. For Konrad, by reason of the alarms and the food, Altschlage would be a better solution than Hochheim [where a cousin of Beate's lived] not least because of the children with whom he will be able to mix there. However, since you do not wish to live there, life à deux in Hochheim would be better. If that does not work you ought to seriously consider whether you could not live in Siegersdorf. I don't believe that the air quality [a reference to the bombing, I suppose] in Berlin will improve.

By mid-April Beate was back in the flat after some repairs had been carried out. Helmuth wrote on 16 April 1944 about her and my future and the firmness of their relationship:

I thank Widmann and you especially for your two letters. You must not think that I do not understand your links to the ruined Berlin and I shall write no more about it or about a wish that you should leave the town. Since you, in agreement with me, believe that Konrad does not belong in this city of ruins you must yourself decide how you live your life for the rest of the war whether alone in Berlin or with him in the certainly not quiet but probably bearable Hochheim.

Dear Atchen, you are right, this war has hit and changed us all. Its ghastly face is and should remain unforgettable. Yet I am firmly of the view that, after its conclusion, we two or perhaps we three, if that is granted to us, will come together again and that we, despite all outward obstacles, will have the strength together to build a new life. I simply do not believe that we two could become strangers to one another. Of course, currently we are developing differently and in some respects may appear to go in different directions. But I believe this difference, which you feel so strongly, is not as important as you think. If we could live together again and not merely meet once a year for a short leave during which one can be important to one another but cannot say much, being the sort of people we are, then daily life together would show us that the differences do not touch the essential things we have in common. The fact is we both are quite different people and we should welcome this fact.

But, my dear Atchen, I am firmly convinced that we belong together and that it is no mere coincidence but a huge gift that we have found each other. Our task in life in our personal sphere is so to arrange our life together that it is always renewed. We can do this and we will do this. Think on those times, the long years, when we could live together. I think you too had the feeling that our marriage was no mere coincidence but that we, in our very differences, managed to live together a life in which you felt secure. So you must believe as I do. I believe in you and that you are my wife.

Don't be afraid to write. Don't force yourself but, when your heart tells you to, write everything that you want and don't fear that I will not understand. I think you know that this has always been the case and you may believe that it will always be so.

Two days after 6 June 1944, the day of the Normandy landings, Grandfather Hermann wrote to Beate: 'You can imagine with what excitement I follow the developments in the West ... for the moment it seems all goes well.'

On the same day, my father wrote to Hermann:

I think we ought to stop trying to encourage Beate to leave Berlin. I have written to her very seriously about the anxiety which her remaining there causes me but have told her that in future I shall keep them to myself if she, notwithstanding these fears, thinks it right to remain in Berlin. Since she has the feeling that to leave Berlin is a form of deserting the flag one must respect this point of view even if neither of us share it. Moreover, the great attack in the West which has now started has altered the situation somewhat. As long as there are battles there, Germany proper may be left under less pressure from these continual terrorist attacks and instead receive only the occasional one required for prestige purposes. Beate always planned to bring Konrad back to Berlin at this time, but I did not really approve of this plan. Now my mother writes that Konrad has whooping cough and, sad as I am that my mother has to bear this as well, I hear of the combination of invasion and his whooping cough from a purely personal point of view with a sense of relief. We can then wait and see what happens.

The war is clearly gaining in intensity and one can see its likely conclusion more clearly than before. Notwithstanding all the difficulties which will face us on all fronts, the pressures will I think decline. Even in your part of the world there will probably be consequences. I send my birthday wishes to you in the increased hope that the next year will enable us to see one another again.

Unknown to Helmuth but known to his wife, the planned Stauffenberg assassination was becoming imminent. Beate was clearly pressing Helmuth to ask for leave so that she could see him again but on 14 June 1944 he wrote to her:

> The question of leave has gone away. There is a total stoppage of all leave except in the case of death or one's own marriage. The first neither of us wants, and you can hardly divorce me in order to marry me again in order to get leave! Moreover our leave year is from October to October. I have had that leave. If it was fouled up by being bombed that's our personal bad luck. Since I obtained an elongation of the leave by reason of the bombing I really have no claim to a second leave. You must understand that, since I also have the responsibility for overseeing failures to comply with military rules, I cannot conceivably give myself advantages which no one else has.

My own wife, when she read this, said, not entirely approvingly, that's just the approach you would have adopted. She was right.

On 1 July, Helmuth wrote on his birthday to Beate:

> It is a pity that we have to spend so much time separated from one another but perhaps this is nevertheless a birthday of which one can hope that it is the last of this series and that we can spend the next one together. I have had greetings from all parts of our country and I know that people are with me in thought. Above all, of course, I treasure your greetings, my dearest, and send my thoughts to you and embrace you warmly. I thank you for all the love which you have given me and give you my thanks for all the care which you are now taking to restore our home. Perhaps at some time we will actually be able to live there.

Don't worry too much about Konrad's wildness or that he is not unduly troubled by the pale cast of thought. He is only a little chap, and I firmly believe that these holes in his upbringing will be filled in due course when things have progressed to a stage where we can reflect not merely on his bodily welfare but also can take care that he receives an appropriate intellectual grounding … I live in a very attractive hotel room with a bath, albeit that the last is of purely theoretical interest, since the water supply is generally broken.

On 14 July 1944, he wrote to her:

I will try and give you a picture of my life here but I cannot, of course, describe what I am actually doing. In part for local reasons, in part for others. And so the picture is necessarily incomplete because you know that these things are very demanding and apart from the time that they require for their fulfilment give rise to a lot of care and reflections. [He then gives a description of his daily life.] So you see, my love, that my work proceeds much more quietly than yours in Berlin. Its difficulties for me lie in a different aspect, namely, the nature of the work which I have to do.

What this was I do not know. It may, I suppose, have included imposing the death sentence. I recollect asking my grandfather Thor whether he had ever had to sentence a person to death in a court martial. He said he had and that it was his great regret that the sentence had not been carried out. A German soldier had raped a Russian woman. Under the Prussian military code that deserved the death penalty. However, under the Nazis, the defendant, because he was a Party member, was transferred out of my grandfather's regiment and indeed promoted. The colonel found this a breach of military honour and said it made him furious. When we had this conversation, I did not know that after his retirement my grandmother had herself been raped by a Russian soldier.

On 17 July 1944, Hermann wrote once more to my mother about what she should do.

> Naturally in present conditions when you cannot reach Helmuth, circumstances can arise which make it desirable to act otherwise than Helmuth in different circumstances thought desirable. I think you must act in accord with your conscience and your best knowledge of how things seem to stand. If it turns out – one hopes not – that you have made the wrong decisions you must say to yourself that one can only do right in the light of how things seem at the time of the decision.

## The Stauffenberg Plot 1944

I return now to the biographical letter written by my mother to her father. She describes the situation in July 1944. She and perhaps Widmann had been given a new job, namely, fire-watching between 2300 and 0300. She wrote:

> Things became always more and more hopeless. We felt increasingly that something had to happen. I gave up my position [as a legal adviser] after it had become a farce. Night after night we put out fires. I once practically fell asleep up to my knees in water because I was so tired. Night after night we

went in horror through the burning streets hand in hand like children. I wrote to Helmuth daily. He wrote back peacefully and filled with thanks for the past but the 'Swabian Count' [Stauffenberg] no longer had any hope. The landing in France had been a success. We had nothing more to lose. To the questions which I posed in this context the 'Swabian Count' answered with Hamlet's words to Horatio – that I should not ask him but trust him. Since I could not speak I began for the first time in my life to answer this banality with music. I played the chorale from the Matthew Passion: *'Ich will hier bei Dir stehen, verachte mich doch nicht.'*[22]

In the office the atmosphere must have been tense and depressing. Stauffenberg wrote to his wife on 14 July 1944, six days before the attempt, 'The most dreadful thing is to know that it cannot succeed and that yet one must do it for the sake of our country and our children.'[23]

On 17 July 1944 my mother turned up unexpectedly at Altschlage and took me back to Berlin. My father and his parents were amazed that she had done so when he had asked her to keep me away from the bombing of the capital, but he wrote that the decision was hers given that she was on top of

---

[22] The sixth verse of *O Haupt voll Blut und Wunden* – O Sacred Head Sore Wounded:

| | |
|---|---|
| *Ich will hier bei dir stehen,* | I will stand here with you, |
| *Verachte mich doch nich!* | Do not despise me! |
| *Von dir will ich nicht gehen,* | I will not leave you |
| *Wenn dir dein Herze bricht;* | When your heart breaks. |
| *Wenn dein Haupt wird erblaßen* | When your head pales over |
| *Im letzten Todesstoß,* | With your dying breath |
| *Alsdann will ich dich faßen* | Then I will hold you |
| *In meinen Arm und Schoß.* | In my arms and bosom. |

[23] Wolfgang Graf Vitzthum, *'Der Stille Stauffenberg'*, Tübingen, December 2021.

events there rather more than he was. She, of course, had not been able to tell any of them of her knowledge of the plot.

No contemporary letters in my possession describe the preparations for the assassination attempt. She maintained to my grandparents, my father and her father that she had taken me back because a forthcoming travel ban had been announced which would make it impossible for me to return to Berlin and would thus have separated the two of us for a long time. My father accepted that it was impossible to know what it was right to do in such a situation. It seems that my nurse Anna was in our flat with us, but Beate was waiting anxiously with Widmann to see what would happen.

# IV

# The Failure of the Plot: Awaiting Execution

On 20 July 1944 Stauffenberg's attempt to assassinate Hitler failed disastrously. Thousands were arrested and killed in the Führer's revenge. My uncle Max Schwerdtfeger gave what on the face of it was a soldier's reaction in writing to grandfather Hermann: 'You will be interested to know our reaction to the assassination attempt. So I write to you straightaway. We were all equally horrified.'

To this Hermann, once a naval officer, replied:

> I was very pleased to read your opinions, which must be and are also those of the troops. From my point of view it is only necessary to add that an assassination attempt is in all circumstances the most cowardly and miserable crime imaginable. He who employs assassination excludes himself from human society whatever considerations moved him to make the attempt.

Contemporary correspondence was, of course, censored and must be read with that in mind. But it seems to me perfectly possible that each meant exactly what he said. One cannot know. I rather suspect that Grandfather Thor would also have taken the same view. From a conversation which I had with him, not about Stauffenberg but about a communist spy in Germany after the war, I formed the impression that for him betraying one's fatherland was the ultimate crime. He was not someone who had a sophisticated view of what constituted such a betrayal.[24]

Judging by what she wrote to her father in her biographical letter describing the time in July 1944, things seemed different to my mother.

We stayed fourteen days and nights together and barely said a word. For the first time in my life Helmuth could not take part. I could not even write to him, which moved me more than I can say. [It is clear from Helmuth's various replies in my possession that she was in fact writing to him, but no doubt not about the failure of the plot and its possible consequences for her and her friends.] Then Stauffenberg was hanged. We, however, lived and knew that everything was lost, worse than that, even now hardly anyone one understood us.

One reads in memoirs that the conspirators realised that they would be seen as traitors even by people who were not committed Nazis and that this made the whole enterprise seem even more daunting.

---

[24] His father, the professor, by contrast had been more nuanced. In a totally different context – the dismissal by the Kaiser of Bismarck, whom he admired – he wrote on 16 May 1891 to Hugo Jacobi: 'The important question is "How long do you keep your opinions to yourself for reasons of patriotism and when does the moment come when opposition is one's higher duty?"

After having immersed myself in the tense atmosphere of her office, it was chilling for me to read a contemporary Foreign Office minute by John Wheeler-Bennet:[25]

> The Gestapo and the SS have done us an appreciable service in removing a selection of those who would undoubtedly have posed (*sic*) as "good" Germans after the war ... It is to our advantage therefore that the purge should continue, since the killing of Germans by Germans will save us from future embarrassments of many kinds.

This was minuted by Frank Roberts, a subsequent ambassador to Germany, with the words 'It all seems sensible and calls for no special comment.' It received none from anyone so far as I know.

Griff: Things look very different depending on where one is standing. Helmuth wrote to his father-in-law on 11 August:

> I think that the current position is such that it would be better for the boy to go to Altschlage than to stay in Berlin. I have indicated this to Beate and will now see what she does. In the nature of things I cannot play a direct part. It is jolly difficult for me because her letters are very depressed and I would say tired. The eternal night-watching which she has to do in order that, in case of an alarm, she and the boy can get to the shelter must interfere with her health. If she were alone she would need less time and get more sleep since for herself she could rely on the sirens. If work is added to this then things look black. The fact that she seems to do nothing to find a job

---

[25] See Meehan, P., *The Unnecessary War* (Sinclair-Stevenson, 1992), pp. 8–9.

for herself gives rise to thought. That is not typical of her ... Her lack of drive probably fits in with Widmann's approach to life. He is a real pessimist in the philosophical sense who only thinks of life as a necessary evil. Beate, to whom such negative approach to life is totally strange, simply does not believe in it.

By reason of the distance it is impossible to speak a saving word to put things in balance. One can only hope, and this I believe, that the inner buoyancy and healthy life-affirming disposition which is in Beate will in the not too distant future succeed in putting this problem aside. I am grateful that you wrote to me about these things and ask you to continue to do so. You confirm a surmise which only comes from a knowledge of the two people concerned. Beate has written nothing of this to me and has not hinted at it.

## Christmas 1944 in Berlin

My father could not take leave for Christmas 1944 but reminded me in a letter how happily we had spent the previous Christmas:

Do you remember that we all slept together in the dining room of Uncle Konrad and that we then celebrated in his drawing room while he had moved out to be with his family in the country? Was it not lovely? But in wartime we cannot be together every year and we must be happy that you can spend Christmas this year with our dear Mummy. Not by any means all children can do this. I would love to know whether you were able to get a Christmas tree but I think that the broken railways will make this impossible. That is sad.

But listen: the war will not last for ever, and when peace comes we will always be able to have Christmas trees and then we will be able to spend Christmases together again. Next year I expect. But we can't know this. You can only know when a war starts. You do not know when it ends until afterwards, when children learn about it at school. But this year we are still at war and so you must spend Christmas alone with Mummy and I can only think about you. I am afraid Mummy will be a bit sad that I cannot be with you. That is when you must show her that you are now a bigger boy who knows about these things and knows that you must comfort Mummy and help her so that she is not sad. You must tell her that we can be happy, that we all love each other and that this is much more important than spending Christmas together. Then you must give her a kiss and tell her that I am thinking of her at that very moment even though I am far away. So our three thoughts will be together, and that is practically the same as our three bodies being together.

Have you been able to make a present for Mummy? You must write and tell me. You write that for the first time you were in a shelter which was not underground but above ground. Goodness! Do you know there are lots of shelters like that, some round, some four-sided. I knew some near where I worked. They were all very good. Quite a lot of bombs fell all around, which made a dreadful noise inside and shook the place a bit, but otherwise nothing happened ...

Beate concluded her biographical letter to her father as follows:

For Christmas 1944 I did not even have a Christmas letter from Helmuth after a year's separation because the Brenner railway was not functioning. Leave was simply unthinkable. Altschlage and Siegersdorf were lost.

My own memories of wartime Berlin are dominated by bombing and my mother. I used to wake up as she listened to radio announcements that the bombers had got as far as Hanover or Bielefeld. Then she would get me out of bed and put me on the back of her bike, and we would bicycle to the nearest underground shelter, where there were lots of others who had done the same thing. I can't now remember what the shelter was like: I must have been too sleepy to notice or I have simply followed what may already then have been my usual practice of forgetting the disagreeable and remembering the good things.

After an air raid she would then bicycle back with me to see whether the flat was still there. I remember something of the journeys back because there was a strange smell and there were flames in the sky. I thought this exciting. As a seven-year-old, fortunately I did not have the imagination to put myself in the position of those who were suffocating to death under the ruins. In one of her letters my mother records me as pointing out that, if the English would confine themselves to bombing during the day, not only could we sleep at night but so could they. Air Marshall Harris was not attracted to this idea, which seemed eminently sensible to me, and so the raids continued.

For the months following the assassination attempt, my mother lived in our flat with me and my dear nurse Anna, who had come to us when Lise Meitner, who had employed her, emigrated to Sweden. My mother taught me herself, as there were no proper schools at that time in Berlin. All the same, children had to turn up three times a week for *Weltanschauung*, Nazi teaching about world affairs.

Thus there was plenty of time for piano teaching, and Aunt Elisabeth wrote to Lise Meitner that I sat quiet as a mouse and watched the cello as trios were being played. She describes me as 'a dear lad who is hotly attached to his generally absent father' and continues: 'it is touching the way he brings him into all his little adventures and wishes. What Beate has made out of the ruins of her flat – which stands practically alone amidst burnt-out ruins – is astonishing.'

# V

# *What Happened to my Relatives in the East*

Hertha, my Schiemann grandmother, retained her sense of humour in nearly all circumstances and was able to see positive elements in even the most negative circumstances. Because many in her family had served the Tsar she had some command of Russian apart from Polish and French. As will be seen, this may well have served to save my grandparents' lives.

On 20 April 1956, the anniversary of Hitler's birth, she started to write down an account of her experiences eleven years earlier as the war neared its end. It gives a vivid picture of what life was like for my grandparents in the last months of the war. Because of my mother's obduracy she had not taken me to Altschlage, and so I fortunately missed the experience. Coming face to face with the advancing Americans, as I shall shortly describe, was a much gentler experience than what she describes in the following pages.

## Christmas 1944 in the Baltic

In 1944 we were still able to celebrate Christmas properly. In the country we were never really short during the war. Even if you kept strictly to the rules you could manage perfectly well. I had secured what was possible and used the last reserves which we had put aside. Probably out of a desire to make it seem just like previous years. Gerda with her three children had been at Altschlage for practically a year. Ingrid [another grandchild] had been with us all the time since she was six months old.

Gerda's husband Fritz was able to join us. I had a timely letter from Helmuth which sounded optimistic for the first time – at least so far as how long the war would last! He wrote: 'If we should meet again in Altschlage after the end of war that would be luckier than one dares to hope for.'

We were not able to celebrate in the large dining room (7 × 9 metres) because of shortage of firewood. But the beautiful Christmas tree stood in my room which was 7 × 5 m. The tables for the children were placed under the tree or against a wall. Presents for the adults were on the grand piano.

Presents for the French prisoners,[26] Gretchen and Feodosia were given to them in the kitchen. Everyone had his own little tree for their room. After Thor had read the Christmas Gospel, as he did every year of our marriage, Fritz played carols and everyone sang. The children were wildly happy. Inka was given my doll 'Snow White' together with bed. So for a few weeks the unfortunate Snow White was continually put

---

[26] I imagine that these were prisoners of war who were allowed to work on the land rather than be in a prisoner of war camp.

Altschlage

to bed, taken out again, put back, etc., etc. Although the doll was rather large for Inka we are pleased that we gave it to her then. Thus her last weeks in Altschlage were fully occupied in playing mother and child. For the last time in her life! The memory of that last Christmas has remained for us all like a beam of light.

## Refugees followed by the first wave of Russians

I interpose here a passage from Anthony Beevor's vivid book *Berlin: The Downfall 1945*,[27] in which he portrays the position of the millions of civilians who fled west away from the Russians. I do so because, as will shortly appear, my grandparents welcomed such a trek, and my Aunt Marianne and her family formed part of one.

---

[27] Anthony Beevor, *Berlin: The Downfall 1945* (Viking, 2002), pp. 46ff.

Beevor writes:

If those January days [1945] were disastrous for the Wehrmacht, they were far more terrible for the several million civilians who had fled their homes in East Prussia, Silesia and Pomerania. Farming families who for centuries had survived the harshest of winters now realised with horror how vulnerable they were. They faced merciless weather, with homesteads burned and homesteads looted or destroyed in the retreat. Few acknowledged however that this had recently been the fate of Polish, Russian and Ukrainian peasants at the hands of their own brothers, sons and fathers.

The 'treks' from the regions along the Baltic coast – East and West Prussia and Pomerania – headed for the Oder and Berlin. Those from further south – Silesia and the Wartheland – aimed for the Neisse, south of Berlin. The vast majority of the refugees were women and children, since almost all of the remaining men had been drafted into the Volkssturm. The variety of transport ranged from handcarts and prams for those on foot to every sort of farm cart, pony trap and even the odd landau exhumed from the stables of some schloss. There were hardly any motor vehicles because the Wehrmacht and the Nazi party had requisitioned them already, as well as all fuel. Progress was pitifully slow, and not just because of the snow and ice. Columns kept halting because carts were overloaded and axels broke. Hay carts, filled with household objects, hams, kegs and jars of food, were turned into covered wagons with a crude superstructure and carpets draped over the outside. Mattresses inside provided some relief for heavily pregnant women and nursing mothers. The undernourished horses found the icy surfaces hard work. Some carts were hauled by oxen whose unshod hooves were worn raw by the roads, leaving bloodstains in the snow. ... Fear of the enemy drove the refugees on.

At night the columns were directed into wayside villages, where they were often allowed to camp in the barns and stables of manor houses. The owners would welcome fellow aristocrats fleeing from East Prussia as if they were extra guests arriving for a shooting party ... Baron Jesko von Puttkamer slaughtered a pig to help feed hungry refugees on a trek. A 'short-legged, pot-bellied' Nazi official turned up to warn him that slaughtering an animal without permission was 'a serious offence'. The baron bellowed at him to get off his property, otherwise he would slaughter him too.

My grandmother takes up the story:

On the 4 January 1945 the first refugees came from East Prussia, then West Prussia and Pomerania. Every night different people with different sad histories. It remained like this till the Russians came. We had cleared out the dining room and my room and placed straw paliasses there. The guest rooms upstairs were also full. When the Russians arrived we had sixty people with us in the main house.

On 1 March I drove with one of our Frenchmen to buy some rations in the one horse carriage to Schievelbein. At the shop an educated Pole was employed as a salesman. He spoke fluent German and French so he could talk easily with our French prisoners. I had brought some sausage to him once or twice, since he often had to help me when I drove alone, because the moment one got out of the carriage with the reins the stallion wanted to leave. We thought up various tactics to get round the Nazis and I always treated him as a gentleman. After the Poles took over, he became mayor of Schievelbein and often helped me. He inquired after us the moment the Russians marched in. Unfortunately he was removed from his post after a few months since he was too friendly to the Germans for the Lublin regime. On the way back the Frenchman asked me to take all four Frenchmen with us if we should decide to go on a trek to the West. I asked him full of surprise: '*Mais les Russes sont donc vos alliés? Et nous les enemies?*' '*Mais Madame, un Russe est un Russe.*' I promised to do so which clearly removed a burden from him.

'When we got back, our friend Schlote rang and asked whether I had remembered that they were all coming to us on Sunday. I said, 'Yes, if the Russians aren't there.' He was amazed: he had never known me like this. After Mrs Schlote had gone, we, Schlote and the Brauns [friends of the family], used to take turns to entertain each other. The previous Sunday we had been at the Brauns' without having the faintest idea that within a week they would take their own lives when the Russians marched in. The previous Friday Thor [my grandfather] had to go to Schievelbein, and I went with him in the car. As he phoned the Labes [again, perhaps friends of the family], one could hear the noise of battle from there. Then we knew for certain. Westphal [a friend, I assume] wanted us to swear to go with him to the West. But we were not prepared to leave our people in the lurch. He kept a couple of places free for us, but then indeed escaped with his family and eighty people. When we got back to Altschlage, Thor telephoned the

Party and asked for permission to leave. They curtly said that it was quite unthinkable that the Russians should come. They were not puppets to dance to our tune, and we would receive orders in due course. Of course, we did not believe them, because exactly the same thing had happened to all the refugees. The orders always came too late. On Sunday morning Thor had already seen several cars with Golden Pheasants [officers decorated with gold braid] and their women with lots of baggage racing towards Schievelbein. Then we knew that our hour had come.

On Saturday afternoon we were sitting with Frau Blank and suddenly heard strange voices in the hall and found that half of Altschlage had gathered there. Irmgard, who had been a housemaid with us for years, clutched me. 'My lady, my lady, the Russians are at the Rega bridge.' As we heard later, she was quite right. The Party some eight days earlier had ordered that the bridge should be barricaded by a number of wagons filled with stones. The Russians laughed themselves silly, as we had done.

On 3 March they crossed the Rega and stood on the road, handed out cigarettes and sweets and played the mouth harmonica. A man from the Volkssturm shot at the Russians from a nearby roof, fortunately without hitting anyone. As a result a volley of automatic fire was directed at the house, which wrecked the roof. The Russians pushed on through Altschlage, so that this was the only fighting that we saw. Well, a bomb was also dropped on a house, but no one was hurt.

At this point we went into the coal cellar, and Thor told me that he had his pistol with him and asked me whether we should not shoot ourselves. I did not want to do that. We had just had news from Gerda. We thought Thora [another daughter] would be reasonably safe in Berlin. Beate was with Konrad with her father and Helmuth in north Italy. It did not cross my mind that he might fall there.

But there was indeed a battle in Neu-Schlage [the neighbouring village].

In the morning of Sunday 4 March I was sitting in the kitchen and, looking through the window, I saw two Russian officers come directly to the house. I told Thor and asked him to keep out of sight since I wanted to deal with the Russians myself. The Russian mayor and his adjutant arrived and told me that they would need to move in with their staff, and would I show them a room. I got all my Russian together, and it was sweet to see how the little Russian major was pleased at this. I showed him Helmuth's old room, with which he was very pleased. There were a couple of rooms downstairs which seemed suitable to him. I said that unfortunately I could not give them to him since we had sixty people in the house, and those were the rooms in which we lived. We were still naive then. The major said with a friendly smile, 'My lady, I am afraid you will have to. There are some more troops coming and they will have to live in those rooms.'

Soon afterwards, they went, and I returned to the kitchen to finish roasting two enormous chickens. One for the four Frenchmen and one for us, Gretchen and Feodosia. As I took them out of the oven, the door opened, and two Russian soldiers entered, saw the roasted chickens, each took one and ate them in no time at all. At that moment the four Frenchmen came in to say farewell. I showed them this somewhat comical situation and said that I had intended the chickens to be our lunch. I wanted to give them a couple of eggs but Vidal said I should not bother. They wanted to thank me for the five years with us. They had been interrogated by the Russians and had told them how well they had been treated by us. They had tears in their eyes and wished us well. They had to go straightaway to Schievelbein. Fortunately Gretchen had run with my permission to her parents. Feodosia remained and tried to help as much as she could. I am doubtful whether the Frenchmen were really sent home to France as had been promised to them.

Half a year later, we again had some Russians quartered on us. A 'cook' in Russian uniform was at my stove. He spoke a few words of German. When I spoke Russian to him he could not understand a word. It appeared that he had been a French prisoner, had been dragged by the Russians all round Germany and parts of Russia, had been given a Russian uniform to wear and travelled with the Russians as a 'cook'. He was delighted to be able to speak French again, showed me pictures of his wife and children and said he was driven mad by the grub the Russians made him cook for them. 'Would he ever get home?'

On 4 April we had to clear out of our bedroom because there was a telephone there, and the room was needed by the phone operator. The adjutant apologised profusely and moved us to the red guest room and made the two beds used by my parents free for us. The refugees were moved to the sofa and the floor. There were seven of us in the room, which was 5 × 6 metres. We were allowed to bring whatever we wanted from our bedroom. I had packed my jewellery, some tortoiseshell things, underwear and clothes in a small suitcase. Thor also had some things ready. I returned once to fetch some suits of Thor's and took the opportunity of secreting the splendid

Emperor's diamond tie pin in the lapel. I hid my wedding ring among calcium tablets. When I asked the sergeant whether I could take some more he replied, 'Of course. It belongs to you.' That dream soon came to an end.

On 5 April Thor wanted to go to the stables – we had been forbidden to speak to civilians [I suspect because the Russians were fearful of potential collaboration] – and I went with him, but a Russian soldier aimed a semi-automatic at us, and I took Thor back into the house on the basis of the old saying 'Der klügere gibt nach'.[28] I went straight away to the major, told him what had happened and asked him whether this was pursuant to his orders. Not at all. But I had to wait a bit. They had found Thor's decorations, papers and maps, from which it was clear that he had been a colonel, but I had said that he was a *Hauptmann* [literally, 'headman', but in the army the title given to a captain]. That must be a mistake, I said. Then it occurred to me that, in answer to questions earlier, I had said that Thor was the head man of the farmers' cooperative and had for that reason been made to join the Party in 1933. We had burned the Party membership book but not his officer's papers. A small picture of Hitler, our only one, still hung on the wall. A Jewish-looking officer who spoke excellent German tore it to pieces in my presence. He did the same with a signed picture of Hindenburg on the basis that he had simply been keeping the throne warm for Hitler. The many signed pictures of the Kaiser remained untouched, as did the picture of Field Marshal Schlieffen. The large picture of the Kaiser was still hanging on the wall when we were expelled.

---

[28] Literally 'The cleverer yields'. The best English equivalent in the present context is 'The better part of valour is discretion' (*Henry IV Part I*, iv 4).

Then the major asked me if I knew whether my husband had been at Rzhev [the site of a prolonged battle between the Germans and the Russians]. Of course; and I could even show him the dispositions where the division was stretched along 30–40 kilometres. He asked me some more questions, and since I had read Thor's daily diary I was able to answer them.

Then they wanted to speak to my husband. When I wanted to go, the major told me I should remain because this would interest me. So I stood by the oven, whereas Thor had to sit with them at the table and be asked some questions about Rzhev. He said exactly the same as I had but with some more details. I heard the major say to his adjutant that they had not believed that they were facing only one division. Then he said they should ask Thor what had happened to a Russian Major So-and-so whom the Germans had murdered. My heart practically stopped. Thor replied that he had been a gunner and had had nothing to do with prisoners. This satisfied them.

Then the major said that he had been in the opposing division and that was why he was so interested. 'Look, Colonel,' and he showed a decoration on his breast, 'I got this for my time there, and you got the German Cross in gold.' Then we were allowed back to our room. While this was going on, a young non-commissioned officer fished my father's golden Swiss watch out of Thor's waistcoat picket. He liked it. Showed it to the major, and put it in his own pocket! At the time we could not understand it and did not know that the whole of Pomerania had been declared an area where plunder was allowed and all women were fair game.

The major told me that I should ask my husband whether he had any weapons and that he had better tell the truth otherwise things would go badly for him. Thor showed him a small revolver in a sofa. The major told me that they had made the hunting guns unusable and I had better note this.

At midday the good Feodosia brought us a beautifully cooked young turkey under her apron, which sustained us for quite a while. She had baked it secretly since she had orders no longer to work for us. Perhaps that was told her later.

On Tuesday 6 March, during the morning, Thor was separated from me and taken to Thora's guest room, where there were some thirty Volkssturm soldiers. Around midday, I asked the adjutant whether I could speak to my husband. 'Yes, but not for long.' Thor asked me to bring them something to eat, since the others had not eaten for a long time. I made as many sandwiches as I could and some imitation coffee and returned to the room with a fully laden tray. At the door there was a giant Siberian soldier with a loaded rifle. I told him who I was and that I wished to bring everyone something to eat. He looked at me with huge eyes and turned his rifle towards the wall. I could get through and fed them all.

Afterwards the Russian came to me in my room and asked whether it was true that my husband was a colonel who had been at Rzhev. I said it was. Then he showed me a huge scar on his neck and arm caused by shell shrapnel and asked what he should do with my husband. I saw from his eyes that he did not have any evil intentions and answered him that he should thank my husband. This shook him. 'Why?' 'Look, my husband aimed badly, and that saved your life.' He could not stop laughing and kept on saying, 'You are a one.' He often came and visited us later.

## Rapes, suicides and terror in Altschlage, and yet some kindness

Of course, I knew that all wars over the centuries have involved horrors of various kinds, and that the Second World War certainly had its share. Each side invariably uses those perpetrated by the other side to stiffen resistance at home. As I have mentioned, I knew from my outraged grandfather that the German soldiery had raped Russian women and knew from general reading that the victorious Russians had taken their revenge in kind in Berlin.

But to have in my hands the description by my grandmother of what had happened to her made me shiver with an added immediacy.

Towards evening I had my first difficult experience. A non-commissioned officer with many decorations wanted me to show him the rooms so that he could choose the best for himself. We went upstairs. After he had looked at them all he said he wanted to have me. I was not to scream; that would be bad for my husband who was in his power. I was completely shaken since it had not occurred to me that this could still happen to me. I told him how old I was, but that did not matter to him, he did not want a young one. He took me and said he would come back in the evening. I then gave him the golden watch I had been given for my confirmation and thus bought myself free.

In the afternoon I heard a thundering noise upstairs. When I opened the door I saw two soldiers who were busy prising a chest open. I ran to the officer's quarters on the second floor. There was only a gigantic Siberian officer whom I did not know. He came down with me, but the soldiers did not hear us. The officer pulled out his revolver, pointed it at the two soldiers and said something to them. They turned round surprised and laid down the crowbar. The officer pointed silently to the stairs down which they raced. I was glad matters had ended thus because I believe he would have shot them without hesitation. I thanked him, he bowed, and each returned to his room.

Round about eight in the evening, I saw Thor and behind him the adjutant to the blond major who made various calming gestures in my direction. Thor was to go to the major for further questioning. After fifteen minutes, we heard two shots in our room. At that point I inwardly said farewell to my previously happy life. Feodosia soon arrived in tears. 'The master, the master.' She thought the same as I. Her stepson had been dreadfully beaten up by the Russians when they discovered that he had fought in Vlassov's army.[29] He must have been the person hit by the second shot.

Suddenly, about 10 p.m. we heard voices in the corridor, and Thor entered safe and sound. We were happy beyond belief because when he left I had seen farewell in his eyes. He told me that he had been brought to Kath's house, where there was a large laid table at which the blond major and various Russian officers sat. Thor was asked to join them and to eat with them, which however he declined. As the other officers pressed him, he said they should ask their major whether, if the roles had been reversed, he would have joined the table. He said, 'No.' So Thor only took the usual brandy and cigarettes. After an hour the Major asked Thor whether

---

[29] A collaborator army from the Russian standpoint.

he would like to come back to me. Naturally Thor said yes and he was returned to me.

On Wednesday 7 March we were pretty busy in our room. Soldiers came in all the time wanting to look at the German colonel. All very polite and apparently very satisfied. The soldiers largely had their fingers full of wedding rings, which they beamingly showed us. I asked our Rzhev fighter – who had visited us again – what would he do with the rings. 'Make golden teeth.' We were speechless since he had simply excellent, healthy white teeth. He explained that golden teeth were much more attractive. One cannot argue about matters of taste.

An older small Russian officer came with the others into the room. He was very disturbed and told us that he went into one house in Altschlage and there on the floor were various bodies which had been shot, among them three small children, of which one was only six months old. He could not calm down. 'Just think of it – children. You cannot picture it.' Later, I heard the following. The lame tailor had, at Frau Litzkov's request, shot her and her children, his own young wife and daughter and, at his mother's request, the youngest son of the publican Frank and finally himself. Apart from them, the Giese couple had shot themselves. Young Frau Buske had hanged herself, as had an old man from the Blank trek, and I think someone else as well, since there was talk of eleven people whom the Russians had buried in a mass grave. The school teacher was forced to write in German on a placard, 'Murdered, but not by the Russians, but because of the propaganda of Dr Göbbels.'

The Russians never did anything to the children. On the contrary. One heard later the same story from other villages.

A young soldier, who spoke a little German, continually brought us quantities of food from the Russian field kitchens, all of which we simply could not manage. At our request he did the same for the imprisoned Volkssturm men and wanted us say that he had looked after the Germans well.

In the evening – we were already in bed – the tall officer took Thor's duvet with the apologetic words that it was warm in our room but bitterly cold outside. I kept mine for the next year and a half. Then the door was pulled open, and a squad of Russians came in and asked if we had any room because a lady from the Blank trek was having her baby. Since we were already seven, they later freed Theodosia's room and the lady was delivered by a Russian doctor.

Discipline was kept in the house, and no one was raped from the trek. But the Russians pulled the women out. In the cottages nearby, however, they had a dreadful time. Gretchen alone was raped thirteen times. The same elsewhere for the women and girls in the village who did not have their men there. But I heard nothing about torture or shootings.

Thursday 8 March dawned. In the morning Thor was told that he had to put on his colonel's uniform with his boots. With it he had to wear a hunter's cap, since his own hat was missing. The tall Siberian officer came again to me bringing Thor's grey officer's coat. 'Lady, you keep this, it's good and warm.' Fortunately, later, Thor was made to put it on. After a while, Thor returned to bid me farewell. He was going to be questioned by a general because the Russians could not understand how it had come about that an officer with his qualifications had not been taken into the Volkssturm. I was frightened to death and asked the adjutant what would happen next to my husband. 'Nothing.' He looked at his watch. 'In one to two hours your husband will be back.' I waited hours, days, months. No sign of him. That is typically Russian. The adjutant often came on Wednesdays to find out if all was well with us. Furthermore, he brought a map in order to show us where the Russian and German troops now were. That was very interesting, since we had no idea how surrounded we were. But on the 8th he simply did not have the heart to tell me the truth, which he must have known. I went to the window and saw that the Volkssturm men were lined up as platoons. Thor and the stationmaster were put into a carriage, which then drove off. The Volkssturm men marched off. In my fear I ran to the blond major, who also said that my husband would return shortly. 'Now, lady, you can return to your rooms.' They, however, did not look inviting. The papers from the desk and the library shelves were all over the place. There was also all sorts of silverware which we had moved when all the refugees came. But, I believe, nothing was missing.

Feodosia and I used the next few days to take all the provisions in the room in which Feodosia now lived. But she slept in our room in Thor's bed. During these days I looked out all the papers which seemed important to me and a few things which I wished to keep. Feodosia was only interested in food. She said that I would in any event not use the other stuff. I left the wardrobes locked. Thor and the Frenchmen had put suitcases and other things including silver in the apple cellar 'for safety'. But the Volkssturm people had been imprisoned there and had helped themselves to what they wanted. According to Feodosia the Meinberg trek helped themselves generously. A

Russian had given Schneider a canteen of cutlery for a loaf of bread. Schneider gave me the canteen back. I buried it in the front garden by the morello cherry. So long as we were there, it was never found.

On Sunday, a Polish squad was quartered with us. Their leader – I think they were musicians – spoke fluent Austrian German. Always called me 'Knädigste', and all of them were polite and correct. He fetched the Polish commandant, who was quartered with the Grosskreuz, to show him the mess which had been left so that he was not blamed for it. The slim, tall Polish lieutenant – who as Pissin told me later always behaved faultlessly and had been a very educated man – said to me with a distinct smile, 'There you see Russian culture.' In order to move into their new quarters they tidied up the two lower rooms and asked for permission to bring beds from upstairs. These they returned to their place before they left. A Hungarian cook with a sparkling white apron had asked me whether I had any pepper for a Szegatine goulash. When I gave him what he wanted from the locked cupboard as well as some paprika and rice he was filled with boundless joy. Later he gave me back the remains of the rice as well as all sorts of things from his food supplies. He sent the lunch up to me on a tray covered with a white napkin via Feodosia, who spoke excellent Polish. I have never eaten such delicious goulash and what followed it – strudel. Then a glass of wine and a coffee afterwards. So far as I was concerned, they could have stayed a week!

The cook asked me down in the kitchen whether my children were crying upstairs. I told him he must have made a mistake, since everything was empty upstairs. And yet I too heard the crying, went upstairs and to my astonishment found Frau Blank with her children in Thora's large room all lying in the bed. In answer to my questions she said that, although she had left with the trek, she had turned round and wanted to stay in Alschlage. Suddenly she asked me whether I had noticed that the Russians had installed gas and how the damp rose from below and all sorts of confusing things. I noticed to my horror that she had gone completely mad. I asked her whether she had eaten, and she replied that neither she nor the children wanted to do this. They all had to die, and the sooner the better. Her husband had been taken away by the Russians. I then went down to the cook who went on to cook all sorts of things for the children and also some goulash for Frau Blank. I then returned upstairs with my treasures, and they were still there. But the two bigger boys were crying loudly from hunger. I fed them all while Frau Blank remained in bed. Then it occurred to me that I simply had to approach her differently. I told her firmly to get up, wash the children, tidy everything up and eat herself. She obediently did all of this. In the evening the cook sent up a variety of good things.

On another day the soldiers serenaded me, bade me farewell and, kissing my hand, thanked me. It all felt rather like being on manoeuvres. Frau Blank had become fairly normal and then at my bidding looked after herself and the children.

A few days later, another Russian unit came led by a young, smart and good-looking officer. In the afternoon he came to our room, spoke with me and then went away again. He said he was a Pole, spoke no German but only Russian. He behaved like a gentleman. Imagine my horror when he returned about ten totally drunk into my room and declared he wanted to sleep with me. We were already in bed fully dressed, without light, and he shone his torch in my face. I tried to discourage him with long tales which he found very amusing. But in vain. When I noticed that he had fallen asleep I crept across to the other bed. I tried to loosen my left hand which he held firmly and at this moment he woke up and called after me. I was of course faster and knew what was where in the room. Feodosia whispered in my ear that I should go right into Thora's room, where there were eight German-speaking Abyssinians. Then I heard that he bumped into Feodosia, but she kept him at bay. Later she told me that he had complained that she had not declared her presence and asked where I was. 'Probably in the old bedroom.' Feodosia took him to the empty room, and they examined everything very carefully with the torch. Of course, with no result.

Meanwhile I had got some way ahead and ran into Thora's room. To my horror I saw three Russian soldiers at table by a wretched lamp. I asked them to hide me, told them that I had been raped and that I was fifty-six. One of the Germans translated into Russian. The soldiers said they would not give me away, they knew their lieutenant. But the Abyssinian German was told to tell me that I should not lie. They had all seen me in daylight, and I was forty at most. When I disputed this, they just laughed. I overcame my disgust, since they all had dysentery, and crawled into the end of the bed. This was my last chance. The door opened, and the officer asked whether I was there. No, said the soldiers. They had not seen me and did not know where I was. Then he went away again to sleep in my bed. In the morning I went to Helmuth's room, where now Frau Blank was living. There I washed myself and smartened up. Then both of us quietly went and looked into my room. He was still fast asleep on the bed. I removed my small suitcase from under the bed and took it with me. He had broken into it, but none of the jewellery was missing. Only later, I found that my 'well-hidden' wedding ring had gone. Frau Blank came in with her little one. The door opened, and the lieutenant appeared. When he saw Frau Blank, he said, 'Oh! Sorry,' and then he saw me. Looked at me with cow eyes, bowed and withdrew. In the afternoon, I was lying on my bed, when suddenly the door opens and the totally drunk lieutenant came in again.

My cousin Ingrid found these pages in a kitchen drawer of the flat in which my grandmother died and was kind enough to send me a copy. Ingrid wrote at the bottom of this memoir: 'HERE THE MEMOIR ENDS. HER HANDWRITING REVEALS HER INTERNAL TENSIONS.'

I can well believe it.

I wondered whether I should keep this document to myself and not share it with the outside world. But it is now more than half a century later. It gives a vivid account of how wars affect perfectly ordinary people. I thought of those now fleeing wars and claiming asylum and the adverse reactions they so often encounter. I came to the conclusion that anything one can do to evoke understanding for their plight was worth doing. I recollected how my grandmother was and I think that she would approve provided this was done after her death.

## What happened to the Schwerdtfegers

After the war Marianne wrote to her brothers, describing what had happened to her when the Russians advanced.

You will all know that my family now consists of four-and-a-half-year-old Bettina and the two-year-old Andreas. Also, there is my mother-in-law and her maid, who has been with her for twenty years and has no one else in the world. We all had to leave Siegersdorf at the end of January 1945 and have been together ever since. At that time the front was always getting nearer, and orders were given to leave. Our neighbours had it in mind to trek with horses and carts and took a lot of luggage for us since we were only allowed to take what we could carry. Since the children were at that time small, I could hardly take anything.

We drove to our neighbour's daughter, who lived south of Berlin near the Körtes, and awaited the arrival of the trek, which arrived safely after a few days. So we escaped the greatest danger, but the future was pretty dark. I then took everything to Körte, who welcomed us charmingly, and there we experienced what turned out to be our last comfortable living conditions. At that time, I was still telephoning Beate very often until she left with Konrad to go to Father. The rumours that the Russians were coming increased, and on 19 April things had got so far that we, who did not want to fall into Russian hands, had to leave. Everything was in a fearful muddle, and each had to look after himself.

Thus we rejoined the trek of our neighbours and drove day and night until we reached the Elbe. We had the children in a sort of living cart, a luggage cart and some more. Altogether we were thirty-four people. At the Elbe people stood in kilometre-long queues but were not allowed to cross the bridges, since these were being kept free for the army. So there was total chaos until it finally became possible for us to cross at Torgau [some 136 kilometres from Berlin].

'We thought we had escaped danger and were very happy and relieved and rested after the enormous exhaustion of the journey. But we had lost touch with what was actually happening. The Americans and the Russians agreed to take the Mulde as the border between their zones and we were sitting between the Elbe and the Mulde. The Russians occupied the territory. We disappeared into the wood and lived there for four weeks, like gypsies, unseen by the Russians, whose behaviour in all the villages was even worse than we expected. They saw none of us and so did nothing to any of us. It was not always easy to keep all the children quiet! Also there was a food problem, since our supplies naturally ran out. However, we always secured something in time so that we had a minimum.

Then we found someone who transported people secretly over the Mulde, which is a small river but with a very strong current. So, one evening, we drugged the children and succeeded in getting ourselves and the horses and one waggon to the other side. You cannot believe our relief when we had everything on the other side and thought ourselves in safety. But unfortunately we only thought that we had achieved this. The Russians had seen us and saw what a large mouthful they had missed. Greed triumphed decisively over international law. The Russians crossed to the American side and took money, valuables and indeed practically everything that we had. At first they wanted to take us as well but they forgot us in contemplation of their booty and did nothing with us. Some of us had escaped to the next village to tell the Americans and ask for help. But they were indifferent to our fate and only said that crossing the river was forbidden and that they ought to return us but that they would not do this if we made no fuss. But they could not help. So we lost everything ...

From there we travelled westwards in haste with the Russians behind us, who then occupied Saxony and Thuringia. We successfully escaped to the British zone, where we obtained pretty primitive lodging in three rooms in three different houses. The children were able to be properly fed, at any rate better than in the town, and it is only 20 kilometres from Hildesheim, where I work.

I had to look round for work straight away, since there were five of us without any money reserves. Max's salary was not paid to him after January 1945, and whatever money I had with me had been taken by the Russians. So I earned money as an interpreter with the military government, which was tolerable work and well paid. That was in July 1945. At that time, I had a room in Hildesheim and only saw the children at weekends. At the end of August, Max came back from prisoner of war camp in good shape. He, with the exception of one year in Germany, had spent the whole War at the front but had received only grazing wounds. Once we were separated for eighteen months, but even for the rest of the time we only saw each other at most for fourteen days a year. Bettina was at that time almost permanently seriously ill because she frequently had inflammation of the middle ear until she was operated on in February 1944. But the suppuration did not stop even after that. However, the change of air, which we gave her most unwillingly, has made her well, and I think she hears well in both ears.

Max had been transferred to the General Staff in early 1943, but in early 1944 put into a lowly position because of his mother, who was born English. After the 20 July he was thrown out of the General Staff, no longer promoted or decorated. When he came out of the prisoner of war camp and heard how they handled the denazification and demilitarisation process here, he wanted to present himself to the English and explain that he had been in the General Staff, which as you know was accused at Nuremberg. We all counselled against this, but he thought that since he had been disadvantaged because of his English origins the English would do nothing to him. But that's not what happened. Three months later they collected him, imprisoned him for fourteen days and then put him in a concentration camp for three months. However, since he speaks English as well as German, he succeeded each time in extricating himself since he really did not belong there.

Finally he arrived at a prisoner of war camp and he has been there for another year. Release does not seem in prospect. The demilitarisation rules are such that Max is still being examined as to his political convictions. He is automatically put into Group II, which means long imprisonment, allegedly with his family, so that I would go into the camp with the children. Then at least we would all be together! But every soldier has the right to try to talk himself into Group III, in which case he can be released but can only be employed in routine tasks, may not leave the British zone, must report every three months, etc. I really don't know whether the camp is not the more carefree life for us, apart from serious hunger which will probably apply there.

In fact it is our aim to go to a brother of my mother-in-law as farmworkers and from there, as soon as possible, to Curt in Argentina. But I fear that someone who is in Group III [there are still Group IV (for collaborators) and Group V (for those who have been released)] will not get permission to leave the country in order to settle elsewhere.

This all sounds rather depressing, but you are getting this all at once. That we have some problems is obvious but, so far we all remain healthy and we have enough money to live on, I was thrown out of my very pleasant job at the time of Max's arrest but have, however, after a couple of months, secured another, very boring, employment which is nonetheless well paid.

So have no worries about me but do write to me since I am very lonely and cut off from everything. I have not seen Father for years and cannot visit him because I wish to save my leave for the time of Max's release, and then he will not be able to leave the British zone. Moreover I am not physically up to travelling in present conditions.

In the event Max was freed in January 1947. A few years later, he joined the new German army and was sent to the headquarters of Supreme Allied Command in Paris. His son Andreas shared his enthusiasm for the military life, was equally proficient in languages and in due course was the German defence attaché first in Athens and then Beijing. His daughter Bettina, whom I had first encountered in Siegersdorf when she was a baby, worked for much of her life for the British Council in Germany. She and her brother Dettloff naturally share the linguistic facility of the rest of the family. He is a German lawyer and kindly persuaded the German authorities in a correspondence that took the best part of a year that, notwithstanding my acquisition of British nationality, I had never lost my German one.

## My Schiemann grandparents after the war

Later that year, Thor managed to escape from imprisonment and walked some 300 kilometres back home to Altschlage. He told me that he walked across the Russian fields and, although it must have been obvious that he was a German, the peasants all treated him with kindness when he asked for food. Nonetheless he arrived in Altschlage very thin and ill.

*Hertha and Thor Schiemann in the 1950s*

There, they continued to exist in a single room in their old house. In the summer of 1946 they received the news of the death of my parents on a postcard of twenty-five words, the most that was permitted at the time.

He and Hertha wished to remain in Altschlage even though it was now under Polish suzerainty, and they asked their friends and relations in the West to send what supplies they could since they had no income and little left to sell. The Allied governments forbade the dispatch of stuff which they felt was needed in the West. Nonetheless, some things could be sent. But a large part of what could be sent never arrived. This was due to a variety of reasons: genuine loss or muddle, theft, prohibition of imports by the Polish government and so on.

In the event, in 1947, Thor and Hertha were forced by the communist Polish government to leave Altschlage. They were told that they could only take one or two pieces of luggage each. However, some of his Polish farmers drove them to the station in a farm cart and heaved the luggage on board. At first they were put into temporary accommodation in West Germany but eventually obtained what was the equivalent of a council house in a country village and, whenever I visited them, seemed happy there.

Between 1950 and the time that they died, I came over to see them several times for a week or two. As we shall see later, until 1956, there was a long dispute about my future – should I return to Germany or carry on in England? By this stage I had just become accustomed to being English, and fortunately my uncle Werner took the view that I did not need to play an active part in that dispute.

The first time I went to my grandmother, who at that stage was all but penniless, she had prepared especially for me a Baltic fish soup with fish heads swimming in it. I am afraid I found it disgusting. Nevertheless I dutifully thanked her profoundly and said with such enthusiasm as I could muster that I found it delicious. This was a mistake. The next year the same happened, and so Baltic fish soup became a dreaded tradition for my visits. When I reached my twenty-first birthday and was visiting them, my grandmother asked what she could give me as a present to mark the occasion. I plucked up my courage and said that I would let her into a secret, namely, that if she promised never again to give me Baltic fish soup I would regard that as a wonderful present. She laughed, and my relationship with the soup ceased.

Although as a teenager then living in England I used to look on the prospect of visiting my German grandparents as a duty rather than a pleasure, in fact when I got there we always had a good time together, and they were clearly fond of me, regarding me as the last surviving Schiemann.

I was struck by how contented they were with their modest lot. Once, when I asked my grandmother why she was always happy, she taught me that at different stages in your life different things make you happy and unhappy. When she was a young woman, she could be unhappy about having a less elaborate tiara than one of the others at a ball, whereas now she could not remember when she was last unhappy about jewellery. On the other hand, that morning she had been delighted to see that her radishes were growing well, but never in her early life had she found radishes a source of joy.

Another thing which they told me that their experiences had taught them was that it is often people who are at the bottom of the pile who rise up and help you at the time when you need them most.

I have passed on their wisdom to our daughter, and she is in the process of passing it on to her children. So do we outlive this earthly span.

# VI

# The End of the War and the Deaths of My Parents

## Helmuth's last letter

On 16 April 1945 my father wrote what turned out to be his last letter to my mother.

> I wonder whether this letter will still catch you in Berlin. I am very doubtful and hope that you have meanwhile been able to get to your father and have recovered from the strains which travel with the boy will have imposed on you. So I am sending this letter simultaneously to your father's address and also to Gabriele's. Let's hope that you will get this greeting somewhere or other.
>
> Last week, post from you arrived from January and February whereas in the previous week I received a letter dated 18 March. This leaves me way ahead of the others so far as

post is concerned. No one here has received such recent news. Moreover, some postal money has come which you sent off in March. This will no longer be possible in future, so please do not try even if the opportunity offers itself. Since no parcels can be sent to you and that is all would I spend it on, I have no interest in receiving any money.

I read your letters, my dear Atchen, with much joy particularly your descriptions of our boy. As I wrote last week two letters came with pictures of you and the boy which you had made in January. It is always a joy for me to see this picture. It would be so wonderful to meet again, and we must not give up hope that this will be possible.

*The last picture of my father*

We have not so far been hit by any of the events described in the army bulletins. Whether and when this will alter no one can say, and by the time you get this letter things may perhaps look different. We live here on a byway away from the action, but it is obvious that major happenings will also affect us. What can have happened to Gerda and Marianne and their children? After recent developments I have come to the view that despite everything Marianne was right to give up her property. Is anyone in touch with Max? It is damn difficult for him when he probably does not even know that Marianne has left Siegersdorf and he will have no idea where he can send his thoughts and letters. I also am not sure but I still have certain contact points and possibilities so that you dear Atchen are not wholly without news. Until now we have both had grounds to be thankful for what we could know of one another.

All the best, my dear Atchen. I kiss you and the boy in my thoughts with all my heart. Perhaps news of you is already underway which will tell me what has happened to you. All the best and many, many thanks for all that you have been for me during these long years. Greet father and Gabriele.

Helmuth

Unfortunately this letter did not reach any of the addresses to which it was sent until ten months later, in February 1946, by which time they were both already dead.

## Escape from Berlin

My mother took me out of Berlin fourteen days before the Russians arrived there in April 1945. We went after a difficult journey to her father, who had been given some rooms over a sawmill owned by Prinz zu Leiningen in Bavaria. I have a vague recollection that a train in which we travelled was stopped and that we all had to hide nearby in hedges as a plane flew overhead and machine-gunned the train. It is a tribute to my mother that I have no memory of being frightened but rather of amusement at the fact that the bullets were directed at the train after we had hidden elsewhere. In my mind it was a form of what we then called 'Cowboys and Indians'.

It must have been on this journey that we came across the advancing tanks of the American army. I have a flashback of waving a white handkerchief – whether to show I had no hostile intention or to welcome them I cannot now remember. The incident, in any event as I remember it, was not accompanied by fear on my part – probably because the Americans were giving us a friendly wave. I marvelled at the white star painted on the sides of the tanks.

In due course we joined my grandfather at the sawmill.

While we were escaping, my father fell to a sniper's bullet as he was being driven near Venice. Someone bagging their last German I suppose. A fortnight later, hostilities in the West ceased. Of course, I find this all terribly moving. Stepping back, as my father would have done, one says 'That is what happens in war.' But this background explains my eagerness to take such part as I could in the reconstruction of Europe after the war.

My mother and I remained with my grandfather until June 1945 but received no news of my father. There was a housing shortage, and residence in Berlin was controlled. My mother did not want to forfeit her right to reside in her flat. She thought that the most likely place where he would turn up was the flat in Berlin and so we set off on the return journey.

## Return to Berlin

We went first to her sister Gabriele in Munich, stayed there a while, then went onwards by bike; after various adventures we arrived in Berlin in September. I cannot remember the journey, although I have a vague recollection that it involved queueing for food and crossing the Elbe. Apart from physical difficulties, there were bureaucratic obstacles involved in moving from the French, to the British and then to the Russian zones, each of which required permission from the appropriate ruling power. I gather that the Russians in general were uncooperative, but we did manage it.

We were back in Berlin by 6 September 1945. When we arrived, our flat was still more or less intact, if cold. There was a wood stove on which I seem to remember one could toast a slice of bread if one

*The last picture of my mother, taken by her sister Gabriele*     *KS at the age of 7, taken by Gabriele*

could get hold of one. People were beginning to use furniture as fuel. There was no news of my father, who in fact had died four months earlier. However, my mother did learn of the suicide of Widmann. She made it her business to inform his sister, with whom she kept in touch until her own death a few months later.

Our flat was in the British sector, which was advantageous when, in due course, my journey to England was being planned.

I enjoyed playing for a while in the bombed-out remains of houses and flats and (if we could get hold of them) eating peanuts there with friends. The British soldiers kindly gave us children packets of things to eat and were generally friendly; perhaps the little English which I had learned from Aunt Hilda in Siegersdorf helped smooth the path to the cherished bars of chocolate.

During this time both our personal financial situation and indeed that of the whole national currency was uncertain. Each of the Allies printed their own occupation currency. The Reichsmark disappeared. and banks and insurance companies were not paying out as expected. Something of the flavour of the time can be gathered from this excerpt of a letter which grandfather Hermann wrote to my mother: 'I am sending you an unappetising gold-filled tooth from me and a little medal from mother, which you can give to Mr Hautzeneder, who needs gold for his teeth. Perhaps he will give you some food in exchange.'

**We hear of the death of my father**

In November, we learned of Helmuth's death. In the middle of that month, my mother took an overdose of sleeping pills, but her cousin Dr Walter Wolf was able to keep her alive. I, then aged eight, broke the news to my aunt Marianne:

I will give you some sad news. Mummy has become ill because we have received a telegram which says Daddy had the bad luck in the last days [of the war] to be ambushed by partisans. He was wounded on 30 April 1945 and then died in a military hospital near Padua (grave number 178). Many greetings to Bettina, Andreas and Aunt Hilda.

Marianne described it as the most pathetic announcement of death that she had ever received. It is clear that I wrote a similar letter to grandfather Hermann, to which he replied:

My dearest Konrad. How much I think of you. You dearly loved boy. You write such dear, brave and understanding letters and yet I feel and know how sad you are that your dear daddy will not come back to you. But you know that you, together with Mummy, were the greatest happiness of his life and that surely he had thoughts of you both as he lay dying and the hope that you would in the near future continue to give Mummy yet more joy, just as you have done so far and that you would in the future be a support for her throughout your whole life. You must become like your dear, dear daddy my dear Konrad. You will not find in the whole world a better example to follow. And later, those who knew your daddy will never be able to say anything better of you than: he is exactly like his daddy. You last saw him two years ago when you were only six. But you know how much he loved you, and you have pictures of him, and your dear mummy will when, soon if God wills it, she is better again always tell you of him. So you will keep your daddy in your memory and never forget that you must become what he was.

I have been told by several people that I am indeed very similar to my father, although I now have no memory of him at all. I suspect they are right. Reading through his letters, I find nothing that I could not have written myself. I think I would have reacted as he did to everything that confronted him.

For the last two months of my mother's life, she struggled to find the will to live, and her father sought by correspondence, since travel was all but impossible, to give her the strength to do so.

The difficulties of the time are well illustrated by the fact that different zones of occupation had different regulations as regards censorship. Thus the Americans required that the addresses on envelopes both of the recipient and the sender had to be in capitals with the word 'GERMAN' also visible. This was not required in the French and British zones of Berlin. The Americans simply destroyed letters which did not comply with their regulations. However, the sender did not know they had been destroyed, and the addressee did not know that they had been sent.

In a letter to her father dated First Sunday of Advent (2 December 1945), Beate wrote what in effect was her last will and added:

> I don't want to leave you without news and anyway I can't
> sleep. Today your loving letter of the 19th arrived. At that
> time I too thought that Helmuth and I would see one another
> again. I am by no means indispensable for Konrad; indeed, he
> may well be able to breathe more freely if he no longer has to
> live in the immediate presence of what must seem to a child a
> frightening, dry, serious, strange woman – a woman who for
> one day after another does not speak a word to him and yet
> who gives herself such trouble to remember him … as you see
> I work hard but I can't steel myself to meet with people. For

ten years, day and night, I was in the company of two men whom to love was life itself.

## Christmas 1945, Berlin

Christmas 1945 was described by my aunt Elisabeth Schiemann, who wrote on 11 January 1946 that:

We came to Beate, who had prepared a Christmas room for Konrad with lights and a beautiful advent wreath, a small tree, on Konrad's desk and a rich gift table which the boy rushed towards with stormy joy. She had made him a pair of pyjamas out of Helmuth's dressing gown, there were many books. A scooter from Herr Lassen was his greatest joy. My sister had produced some piano music, and I gave him some added happiness with a tennis racket and ball. We then spent the afternoon chatting over coffee and a cake which Annchen had baked and talked peacefully of future plans.

A few days before, she had received from us a good Schwechten piano, which stood almost unused by us and we then sold her old bad piano [a replacement for a Steinway which had been sent, in vain as it turned out, to Marianne in Silesia]. We spoke about how she could work as a piano teacher since she had obtained the appropriate certificate. It had to be some work which she could carry out at home or which in any event did not keep her away from home for the whole day. We drew attention to her literary talents, which she could use in the musical field. On Christmas Day itself she was with us with Konrad for lunch, to which we had invited a friend whose vivacity and joy in life and love of children would, as we hoped, do her good. We had a happy afternoon with one another in our Christmas room.

Was all this done to deceive us about her intentions? The sad deed which followed a few days later can only be understood as the consequence of the illness of her soul at this time.

## Despair of my mother

That evening, Beate ended her biographical letter to her father:

By Christmas 1945 my last two remaining friends are dead.

No child can give a fulfilling life back to me. I have personally enjoyed more luck than is given to most people. If living means fighting, I have fought as best I could. I have fought so hard that nothing is left of which I am afraid. That is the end for a woman. I can give no more to Konrad. May he develop into someone who is at peace with the thought, which we cannot master, that Germany exists no more.

On the following day she wrote another letter to her father which, however, he did not receive until after her death.

Yesterday I received your second letter [of 12 December], for which I thank you from my heart. In the night I wrote out for you whatever I could for no other reason than to show you that perhaps it is not pure egoism which makes a life only for Konrad seem impossible for me. There are two things which I believe make me different from most other women. First: the fact that Konrad was always placed miles behind Helmuth, a fact of which he, despite his youth, has known for a long time.

Second: my peculiarity that I must work. Now if one takes away from a person the basic needs of her life then she simply cannot fulfil the tasks which life has given her.

Or, to put it the other way round: I could put up with everything while Helmuth lived and so long as I could work. When I said to you in Bavaria that we three would only wait for one another I meant the same thing, namely that these two men would not want to live if there was no work for them to do. Now I am grateful for the fate which has spared him the necessity of having to make a decision of his own free will.

It has never occurred to me that my siblings would not treat Konrad as one of their own. Helmuth and I would not have hesitated a second in similar circumstances.

I have today written to Marianne. Your *dégout* [at the way Max was being treated by the British] I share vividly, but then you should look here. But that can be borne. At the end of the day nothing will happen to him, and that is most important thing.

I never see Uncle Walter [Wolf]. Konrad [Weil] sometimes comes here. Even he, the greatest optimist, thinks reconstruction is impossible. But he is above all a family man, and therefore things are easier for him to bear. [She then quotes at length from a letter from Widmann's sister Frau Krais and continues] … I had a lot of pleasure from this letter and the ones that followed it. When I can I will go to Stuttgart in order to help Frau Krais in all that she wishes.

Konrad sends you greetings. He has grown a lot since the summer and is very serious for his age. This sometimes makes me sad, and I am pleased that good old Lassen, who because of some muddle has been imprisoned again for five days, gave Konrad a scooter for Christmas. Konrad sang and played on the new Schwechten: '*Verwaiset sind nun die Kinder nicht mehr und vaterloss*' [The children are now no longer orphans without a father]. Mother would have been pleased.

Yes, Daddy, I too am sorry that these times hit you in your old age. But I don't think that our twins will bring a human disappointment. Perhaps they are not quite old enough … That which you are good enough to call my 'strength' was only the surplus of him who had so much more than I and so could give some away! I could only be hit with difficulty. But once this happened it was all the deeper. But that was always clear to me, and I do not quarrel with my fate. Perhaps it would be more human if I were not so stone-like. Konrad has far more reason to curse his fate. I had Helmuth for nearly fifteen years. Him and then Widmann. It was perhaps too much, and during these last four years I could hardly understand that so much happiness was possible. But as you say, one has to pay for everything. I have done it since the 20 July.

Heartfelt greetings to you all. In so far as I still have thoughts, they are also with you. I am amazed, as always since I have been able to think, at your gift of treating your children as persons whom one refrains from trying to influence.

All the best! Beate

On 30 December 1945 I wrote a thank-you letter to a cousin of Beate's containing a mixture of sadness and rejoicing in food which was typical of my eight-year-old self.

I thank you for the delicious macaroons. I tasted them straight-away, and Mummy asked me, 'Well, what do they taste like?' 'Good.' And then Anna, Mummy and I jointly ate the upper half, and I ate the lower half with coffee. The beautiful ribbon from the lid I cut away. If one is always eating potatoes and flour soup then it is certainly something else to have maca-roons. It was very kind of you to think of me. Then I also got books and scores. Mummy has played all the music for me, but I don't yet know with which I would like to begin. I am so sorry that you still need to be anxious about Uncle Wolfgang. I do hope that he comes back soon. Then at least you will be spared that worry. Mummy and I also were worried about Daddy for these last few months, and I know exactly how it is when one cannot see one another.

But are things better now? Many thanks once more and many greetings from your Konrad.

To this Beate added, 'Thanks from me too. Please excuse Konrad's messes. He wrote all this in my absence.'

On 4 January 1946 she wrote a postcard to her father:

It is unfortunately again too cold to write. I hope that Konrad will remain well. I give him what I can, but everything currently seems against us. The day after tomorrow Uncle Walter [Wolf], according to a telegram, wants to make it possible to visit us. In substance we are cold and hungry and I am glad that Helmuth does not need to experience all this.

The Boy greets you. All the best.

## Beate's last letter

The next day she wrote her last letter to her father.

Despite the freezing cold I want to answer your circular letter of 27 December immediately. [Post in Germany was very unreliable at the time and several copies of the same letter would be sent to different addresses each with a request to pass it to the others.] I find your care for us very moving. Please in future care for Konrad.

You need have no worries that I shall take too many drugs. I would do so gladly in order to be able to continue to survive till the spring, when with luck we can be in touch again. But I can't because by reason of lack of food every trace of medicine is so powerful that I cannot take that which I have.

I do ask you, if it's at all possible, to send something for Konrad to eat. Up to 500 grams is possible, and I have received one such parcel from Lisi. Fat is the most necessary since we only get 7 grams daily. I can't allow the boy to work any more and so I fear he has forgotten everything. He is not actually hungry since I can buy potatoes and flour but he is becoming oddly fat and limp.

One cannot find work here ... I have so far not needed to borrow money and don't need to. On top of your worries about Konrad you should not have to take responsibility for my debts. I always intended to outlive this winter with the Berliners but not at your expense. Konrad will never forget this time as well as his memories of his father and Uncle Widmann because he is too old. But it would be good if he can grow up for a few years without cares. Please let me assure you again and again that I am not particularly sad: don't worry about that. If there is any difference between the time after 20 July and the present it is only this: that I am calmed by the thought that the other two do not have to live through it.

You and I are very different, and you will find it difficult to conceive of someone to whom her private life is of secondary importance. But remember that after 20 July, so when Helmuth was still alive, I was convinced that I too would be shot and would leave our child to him. Just as I was sure that Helmuth would agree, since matters could not be altered, so I am also sure that he would have agreed with my dispositions concerning Konrad. I could not ask him because of censorship, and when he left [in January 1944] I did not know about the 20 July.

Please forgive my increasingly bad handwriting, but it is only 2 degrees in the room. Next week I will sell Helmuth's coat so that I may buy enough coal so that the boy can remain warm until March. Had I not been so weak I would have done it long ago so that he would not always need to stay in bed.

I see practically no one. Why should I, by my presence, take away from others their well-deserved pleasure in being together again?

Perhaps I worry too much, and all boys get thinner when they reach eight. Konrad never complains. He only keeps on asking me to take him with me. But I firmly believe that Werner will be very nice to him, and perhaps he will become somebody. Everyone thinks him very intelligent and, according to Schopenhauer, he must of necessity have his father's character.

[Widmann's sister] keeps on inviting me to go to her. When it becomes possible to get permission I will indeed go there, but it is seems hardly possible before March. The piano is fine, but I cannot play it because of my arms, and Konrad can't play because of the cold.

Try to realise how often I, quite apart from the July assassination attempt, because of the way I looked after Uncle Walter [Wolf, who had Jewish origins], had to reckon with being killed and leaving Konrad behind. There are situations which one simply cannot survive, and all these years I have firmly trusted that my siblings would look after Konrad as they would after their own children. I still believe it but I would like to receive a letter from Werner.

## Beate's death and what followed

My mother was expecting Dr Wolf to come and visit her on the afternoon of 6 January 1946, which indeed he did. She had taken some drugs in the morning. When he arrived she was already unconscious. He arranged for her transport to hospital, where she caught pneumonia and died on 10 January.

He wrote on 20 January of that year:

She was not oppressed by lack of money. I found a couple of thousand Marks in cash in her house. She knew that I, who was now earning again, would stand by her and Konrad at any time. We often spoke of it long before she knew of Helmuth's death. She knew the same of Konrad Weil ... It is true that I was unable, by reason of the long distance between us and the ghastly travel possibilities [because they were in different sectors of Berlin] to visit her as often as I would have wished, but I do not think that she felt herself more isolated because of this. I had written to her that I hoped to visit her on Sunday 6 January and had received a card from her that she was looking forward to this and hoped I would be able to stay some time and possibly spend the night there.

When I arrived, she had, according to someone who was in the same house, at most three hours before taken the sleeping poison (*Schlafgift*). Since I by sheer chance had the antidote with me I could immediately give her an intravenous injection. I then contacted Konrad Weil, asking him to arrange transport to the Elisabeth Hospital, where everything happened which was humanly and medically possible. I was not surprised because I had immediately taken a pessimistic view, unlike the previous time, when it did not seem harmful. When I spoke to Beate after that occasion and very solemnly reminded her of her responsibility to the boy and told her that she simply did not have the right to commit suicide, she replied that others were far better placed to look after Konrad than she was.

I think I can say ... that our Beate was not driven to this through circumstances which others could alter but rather through an intelligent and clear appreciation of the problem of living and that her final decision to leave this life only came to her when the two men died whom she rightly believed to be of particular value. And if we are totally honest, can we say she was in error?

It seems that it was generally thought that my mother had deliberately committed suicide, but, having looked at more letters than were available to any one of those who formed that opinion at that time, I have come to the view that this is indeed possible but doubtful. She certainly talked of doing so at some time in the future but wrote and acted like someone whose immediate intention was to continue living for a few months. I myself have never had the feeling that I had been deliberately abandoned.

My nursemaid Anna, of whom I was very fond, came to our flat and looked after me there for a while until arrangements were made for my aunts Elisabeth and Gertrud to receive me in their house.

# VII

# *An Orphan in Berlin*

## My introduction to administrative law

My judicial life has been concerned with overseeing the actions of the civil service. The problems are the same all over Europe and elsewhere no doubt. Behind many of the difficulties lies an understandable unwillingness to entrust important decisions to relatively lowly officials. So rules are laid down which they must follow. Inevitably things happen which were not foreseen by the rule-maker. The correct application of the rules by the civil servant can produce unreasonable results.

This happened to me aged eight, as is vividly described in a letter of 11 February 1946. The authorities would not give permission for me to move from one part of Berlin to another until those looking after me produced sworn proof from three witnesses that I, aged seven when the Nazi régime collapsed, was not then a Nazi. A family friend, Dr Konrad Weil, wrote to the *Bürgermeister* (mayor) of Wilmersdorf district of Berlin.

I write directly to you about a case where bureaucracy seems to have gone mad and feel convinced that you have an interest in taking note of these facts.

On 10 January 1946, the widow Mrs Beate Schiemann (née von Simson) died and left behind an eight-year-old boy, Konrad Schiemann, as a full orphan. I am the guardian of this unlucky boy.

His great-aunt, Frau Professor Schiemann, has declared herself ready to take him in and bring him up. She lives with her sister in your district at 11 Binger Strasse. Both these elderly ladies are in employment. Frau Professor Schiemann is a well-known botanist and university professor. She was disciplined during the Hitler regime and has now – after the reopening of the university and after thorough examination by all conceivable authorities – been restored to her professorship. They can only look after the boy if they can have the old nurse who was already employed in the parental time of the mother to join the boy.

This simple and humanly satisfactory solution to the question what is to be done with this young orphan boy has now run up against some incomprehensible difficulties raised by your housing office. We have put at the disposal of the Charlottenburg authorities the two-roomed flat of the mother and have obtained from them a transfer certificate. The fact that apparently the Charlottenburg housing office is not entitled to issue this certificate is not our fault.

One of the rooms in Professor Schiemann's house has been set aside for compulsory occupation but has not yet been occupied. This is the room intended for the boy and the nurse. Frau Professor Schiemann, who is now up to her eyes in the preparation of her university duties, has not succeeded after hours of waiting and negotiations with your housing office to secure a disposal of this matter. I can well believe that nerves of the no doubt overcharged official are stretched to the utmost and that this is responsible for the intolerable way in which he addressed this learned lady. But that she has been sent away once more because of the absence of three declarations on oath that at the conclusion of the war this seven-year-old boy was not a National Socialist is surely bureaucratic overkill. He could not even be in the children's branch of the Hitler Youth because of his age and the official should have realised that one would not get a professorship unless one had been thoroughly examined.

The parents of the boy, as I can declare in the absence of an oath, were never members of the Party. The mother, a born von Simson, was indeed discriminated against on the grounds of her racial origins, which you may know since the case of her famous great-grandfather, the first president of the German Supreme Court, was much discussed on several occasions. I can make the same declaration in respect of the nurse, who is a strong Catholic.

What is all this about? I am convinced that you too, Herr Bürgermeister, will share the view that one ought to be as helpful as possible in this unhappy situation and not to create unnecessary difficulties for a willing foster-mother.

I am conscious that in the great housing shortage it is necessary to be strict, but just because of this it should be all the easier to solve a perfectly clear case. I would be most grateful to you if you were to give the appropriate instructions to your housing department.

This did the trick, and eventually permission was given.

Before my mother's funeral I had written to my grandfather:

Dear Opa, I am crying so much and am sad because Mutti has now died and I have no parent at all. and I'm only eight and a quarter. Soon I will move to Tante Gertrud and Tante Elisabeth. They are so nice to me but Mutti remains Mutti and Vati remains Vati. Today I am still in the Eichenallee.

The burial is on 26 January. I am sorry you cannot be there. She will be buried in the family grave. I celebrated such a lovely Christmas with Mummy and the aunts. On Christmas Eve it was like this. First, I had to go out; then they called me in. I got a scooter, games and books.

Just now your butter packet arrived. I was very pleased. Many thanks once more. Your Konrad

Then came the funeral.

Dear Grandfather, I already told you about 26 January. The burial took place. I will now tell you how it was. First, Anna and I went at about 1200 to the Neu-Westend station. There we met Aunt Lise. Then we went to the Belle-Alliance Strasse. Shortly after there came the other relatives and Pastor Kurz and his wife. The ceremony started. He spoke well and told me a lot about Daddy. After the ceremony, the aunts took me to their flat, where I got a cup of chocolate. In the evening Aunt Gertrud took me back to Eichenallee, where I live with Anna. Many greetings, your Konrad

A cousin of my grandfather wrote to him:

Yesterday, I was at the funeral. The little boy stood holding the hands of his charming aunts and listened intently, fortunately without showing any emotion, to what Pastor Kurz said to him. When it was all finished, he came beaming towards me and said, 'The pastor spoke very well. I understood everything.'

When I read this recently I was reminded of my grandson saying at much the same age to the waiter at a restaurant where he had been taken out to dinner, 'My compliments to the chef. Excellently done.' Children never cease to astound.

**My grandfather copes with the death of his daughter**

Whereas children live in the moment, I find that as I get older I can step outside the moment and look at it from afar, as it were and see what is happening in a historical context. I have the impression from the letters that my von Simson grandfather was a man of faith in the sense that he took a loving God for granted. My Schiemann grandparents and both my parents, so far as I can see, lacked this dimension to their lives, but it has surfaced again in me.

After my mother's funeral my grandfather wrote to Pastor Adolf Kurz:[30]

---

[30] The pastor at the Twelve Apostles Church in Berlin. One must remember that Adolf for centuries before the rise of Hitler was a perfectly respectable name in Europe. The pastor's wife had Jewish ancestry and he behaved admirably in the face of Nazi persecution of the Jews.

In my great sorrow it was a great comfort to know that you as an old friend were able, after having given her a blessing at her confirmation and at her wedding, to give her a blessing on her way to eternal peace. I thank you, and your dear wife, from the bottom of my heart that you accompanied my dear Beate to the grave of my unforgettably dear wife. You know how close I was to this particular child, who was always ready to help and who came to the world on my birthday after four sons. In your lovely speech at Beate's confirmation which I often call to mind – a sad day because my wife could not come because she was gravely ill – you compared Beate to a rose which showed thorns before its flower opened. Thorns which one later forgets because of the beauty of the flower. You were inspired to make this comparison because of a rose named after my mother 'Beate von Simson'. So indeed did Beate develop and in those years with husband and child her whole life developed in a charming harmony as she describes in her lifetime's history written to me on Christmas Eve. Though the efforts imposed upon her by the last war years in Berlin were far above her bodily strength, she was not prepared to forego them. She was unable to face the destruction of Germany, which she had realised for years was unavoidable, after the death of her peaceful, clever and serene husband. I struggled for months personally with her here in Bavaria and in writing thereafter but increasingly realised that one could not make clear to her the mentality which we call healthy.

My great-grandfather Schwerin, whose beautiful property Schwerinburg is now also completely ruined and divided into seventy-two parts, was one of the nearest friends of Schleiermacher. I used to own – now I own nothing – a letter from him after the burial in Trinity church of his son

Nathanael (who gave rise to great expectations but died at sixteen). Schleiermacher did not start with an opening but said, so that only those who were sitting nearby could hear, 'I can no longer believe in a good God,' was then silent awhile and then gave one of his most beautiful sermons whose text I also used to possess.[31] If Schleiermacher in a moment of gravest temptation found his belief in God's goodness shaken, I do not need to be ashamed that currently I am in the same situation. I do not have his greatness and not his depth of theological knowledge. But you cannot now even ask of someone that he fights – even with himself – for his belief. The unparalleled unhappiness which surrounds us guards us from overestimating that which has been laid on our own shoulders.

Can you send to me the biblical citation which you took as your text at Beate's grave?

The pastor replied on 6 March 1946:

I found the way to Beate's grave unendingly difficult and I had to struggle with myself and somehow or other the price of victory over all within me which said 'no' was paid in blood and wounds. It was the third time in a short period for a person whom one had taken to one's heart not purely as a matter of caring for a soul who had chosen this way driven by deepest need. Since May of last year, I have had to stand by some 350 graves, and there were dear people there for whom one mourned deeply, but nowhere did I find the inner need as strongly as by Beate's grave.

---

[31] Reproduced in translation in Albert L. Blackwell, 'Schleiermacher's Sermon at Nathanael's Grave', *The Journal of Religion*, 57(1) (January 1977), pp. 64–75.

I can't get rid of the feeling that I should have bothered more with her but I simply did not know she was in Berlin. Moreover, I would never have believed this of her. She was splendidly brave throughout the ghastly time when the bombs fell. We last saw each other one and a half years ago [at the time of the assassination attempt] and I was pleased to see with what internal sense of superiority she came to terms with the challenges of the day.

Our Old West is now a heap of rubble, the Tiergarten exists no longer, church and vicarage are still standing but very damaged. Four times we put fires out in the house, on the last occasion on the day before the fall of Berlin under heavy bombardment, otherwise we would no longer be standing. The flat is half burnt out. In a word: we live. Nevertheless, the congregation has reassembled so that on average we have 200 in the congregation on Sundays.

## I learn to cope

Meanwhile my grandfather Hermann was trying to sustain my spirits and indeed largely succeeded in this it seems. I wrote to him on 18 February 1946:

> I thank you from my heart for your letter of 1 February. I was very happy that you wrote so lovingly. I will take trouble to bring joy to Mummy and Daddy ... I practise a bit of Handel practically every day. I go to the Children's Service every Sunday. Please give my greetings to Princess and Prince Leiningen, Anna and Aunt Irmgard. The aunts send you greetings, but I greet you the most.
>
> Your Konrad.

It was about that time that I wrote the following, which is undated but in childish writing:

*Gott da Du es bist der die Dinge so gewendet hast So ergebe ich mich darein und will was Du willst. Hebe mir das Glück das Du mir genommen für die Ewigkeit auf! Ich danke Dir für die schöne Vergangenheit Die Du mir geschenkt hast! Die Gegenwart will ich in deinen Gehorsam und Glauben durch kämpfen und die Zukunft vertraue ich ganz deiner ewigen Liebe an.*[32]

I suspect that I had been given this by Aunt Elisabeth to copy out. My letter written on 28 February seems more like the real me. But a child's moods can change very swiftly.

I would so like to know what Uncle Werner has written. Please write to me the main points of the letter. I will write weekly to you. It will generally be a Thursday. Aunt Marianne sent me a very nice letter and has promised to send me a parcel every Monday. The first parcel has already arrived. Aunt Gertrud and I have had two games in the snow, of which the second was the best. On Saturday we had to fetch coal because otherwise we would have frozen. We dragged the toboggan happily down the street. The snow was wonderful, but halfway there it had all melted and it became dreadfully mushy. Our feet became all wet and we were only halfway there. Finally we came home soaked through …

---

[32] God, since it is you who has turned things round, I will surrender myself to them and desire that which you desire. Keep for eternity the happiness which you have taken from me! I thank you for the wonderful past which you gave to me! I will struggle through the present in obedience and belief and entrust the future entirely to your eternal love.

Werner had written that he and Kathleen would look after me. Grandfather Hermann wrote to Werner:

It was a great joy to me to see the way each of my children offered, as a matter of course and without further thought, to take young Konrad and to replace so far as humanly possible the parents which he has lost. And here I must immediately say to dear Kathleen that your decision has moved me to my innermost soul.

The unconditional way in which you declared your willingness to treat the boy as one entitled to an equal share with your own children of what you have is for any mother a sign of greatness, the more so in one who comes from a foreign country who has hardly had time to feel her way into our family and to find her place there. Please make this clear to Kathleen. I would do it myself if I felt that my English (admittedly recently become more fluent) could do justice to my feelings in relation to a matter so close to my heart.

When I read your letter I was happy for the first time since Beate's death. Oddly enough my heart, which has been most unreliable for the last couple of months, immediately improved.

Finally permission was given for me to move. On 9 March Aunt Elisabeth wrote triumphantly to my grandfather:

We have finally got the permit for Konrad to move. It took six half days of waiting for various officials to achieve nothing. Finally, through the good offices of the dean of Berlin (Grüber, a past internee in Dachau concentration camp), who got through to the English commandant, we secured the permit in ten minutes. Now we have ration cards and all the relevant permissions and at the very last minute admission to a very good school, where he starts on Monday.

Grüber had returned from a visit to England a few days before with a search request from the Church of England. When I visited his office, I was given the search request to read and found the following: 'Konrad Schiemann 8 years. Father shot in Berlin in August. Mother suicide. It is the wish of his uncle Werner von Simson that he be brought up in England. Contact Dr Wolff Kronprinzenallee 18–20 and Dr Konrad Weil.' The letter to Dr Wolff had not yet been sent, and I was able to give the necessary information. The search request was then marked 'Fulfilled'. I wrote to Dr Wolff and saw Dr Weil yesterday.

Konrad's school, with which he is happy, is only open for two hours a day because of lack of coal, but they also arrange a play afternoon once a week. He goes to Children's Service on Sundays with great enthusiasm. The religion lesson is for him 'the best lesson' and he claims, using Beate's words, 'a great interest in religion'. He much enjoys singing which we have substituted for the missing piano lessons. We hope with love and firmness to help him fight some character weaknesses which after all every gifted person has. May God give us the insight and the right way of handling the matter.

Your letters are a great pleasure for the boy, and I hope that the converse also applies. He talks a lot about Father and Mother. They play a part in all his thoughts, and it is good that we can do so much to keep these memories alive for him.

On 12 March I wrote to Grandfather Hermann of my delight in food and music:

Today I will tell you about my first concert. I had already heard the first two pieces played by Aunt Gertrud with Herr Horvath at the piano. I heard a sonata of César Frank and some very beautiful variations by Joachim. I am now entitled to school meals. There one can sometimes get cheese, white beans with ham. Burkhard was with us on Sunday, and we played chess, Nine Mans Morris and Sheep and Wolf. Also we played Black Peter and Life and Death. I have found several beautiful songs in Mummy's songbook, for instance *'Befiel du deine Wege'*.[33] The aunts had great pleasure from your letter and greet you, but most of all there greets you your Konrad.

On 31 March I wrote:

Dear Opa! I thank you with all my heart for the wonderful parcel with butter and for your two loving letters which you sent me. I have all sorts of things to tell you.

1. We are in the midst of garden work. We started a couple of days ago. First, we levelled the earth, and then I turned over some of it. Admittedly the aunts did more than I, but nonetheless I did something useful, and that was enough for me. Then we spread some earth on top and raked it. Then the aunts sowed spinach, carrots, dill and parsley.

---

[33] *Befiehl du deine Wege,*      Entrust your ways
*Und was dein Herze kränkt*      And what grieves your heart
*Der allertreusten Pflege*      To the most faithful care of
*Des der in Himmel lenkt!*      Him who governs heaven!
*Der Wolken, Luft und Winden*      He who gives the clouds, air and winds
*Gibt Wege, Lauf und Bahn,*      Their ways, their course and path
*Der wird auch Wege finden*      Will also find ways
*Da dein Fuß gehen kann*      Where your feet can go
Bach's *Matthew Passion*

2. I now have lessons with a very nice piano teacher called Frau Wundram on Mondays and Thursdays: chords, scales, contrary movement and other practice pieces. Apart from that, the accompaniment to '*Weißt du wieviel Sternlein stehen?*'[34]

At this stage in my life I was a regular letter writer to my grandfather. A few snippets suffice to give the flavour:

On Monday we went to Mummy's grave. It was a little mound. We laid some fir branches and wild currants near the grave and we planted crocus and pansies and it looks pretty good now. By the way Frau Wundram my piano teacher wrote a beautiful poem about Mummy. I will send it to you soon. On Sunday Aunt Elisabeth was with me in the botanical gardens. There it was wonderful amidst the many flowers which exist in the world. We looked a long time for some from the Italian alps and eventually found them.

I also heard a concert by Mr Horvat; I enclose the programme.

Frau Wundram's poem moved me greatly at the time and it still seems to me well done:

*Wenn die Amsel überm Stein rut, im letzten Sonnenschein*
*hebt sie schwingend ihr Gefieder*
*Hat ihr Tageswerk vollbracht fliegt ins West zur Nacht.*
*Nun der Werktag ringsum schweigt.*
*Sich ein Engel still der Erde neigt*
*die die Mutter eng umgibt, die Du geliebt.*

---

34  A 19th-century lullaby.

*Sein Antlitz wandelt sich im Dämmerschein,*
*Kann heute Vater morgen Sohn, wohl sein.*
*Bringt Ihr den Geist der euch vereint*
*die Träne die du stillgeweint.*
*Es senkt der Engel*
*Breitend seine Flügel*
*nachts schützend über ihren Hügel.*
*Ein weicher Sommerwind bringt Stimme Ihr*
*von Ihrem Kind, Konrad, von dir.*
*Sie schläft und träumt*
*von guten Dingen*
*und hört dich singen.*[35]

On 22 May 1946 Werner wrote to Konrad Weil in Berlin:

You are worried about the future. I am not worried about you if you can hold out for another couple of years. I have no doubt that the economy of Central Europe must find its feet: that is a European necessity and therefore a European concern.

The next letter from me which I have was written in June.

I send you heartfelt thanks for your loving letter. It would be lovely if your Italian friend found something out about Daddy's grave. And if he could send a photograph that would be nice.

---

[35] When the blackbird rests in the last sunlight on the rock with her songs all sung and the day's work done, she lifts her wings and flies into the night. Now the working day is still. A silent angel quietly nears the earth which surrounds the mother whom you loved. His appearance changes in the twilight: today he seems the father, tomorrow the son. He brings her the spirit which unites you all and the tears you quietly wept. The angel sinks down spreading his wings, nightly guarding her mound. A soft summer breeze brings her the voice of her child – your voice, Konrad. She sleeps and dreams of good things and hears you singing.

I want to tell you something about my piano lessons which give me great happiness. I will describe to you the best finger practice and also about the pieces. First then the finger exercises: scales, contrary movements, triads and triplets. As regards pieces, I play an écossaise of Beethoven, the Hunters' chorus from Freischütz by Weber and a Mozart minuet.

Later that month, bearing in mind that my grandfather's birthday was the same as my mother's, I wrote:

Dear Opa, I congratulate you, while thinking also of Mummy, on your birthday and wish you a happy new year in your life with much good fortune and many blessings. I hope you can celebrate a good birthday with Aunt Irmgard. I think so often about Mummy that she can no longer celebrate her birthday with us and neither can Daddy.

On 16 June Aunt Elisabeth was able to write to Hermann about having found me a boarding school, where in the event I was happy for a few months.

I was with Konrad today in the graveyard, and we have planted fresh flowers on Beate's mound – petunias which will soon bloom and then last the summer. As for the rest, we have just removed the weeds. Please tell us whether you just had roses before. It looks rather like it. The graveyard itself does nothing.

Konrad would like to plant a rose on his mother's grave, but none can currently be obtained save perhaps in a pot, and in any event the best time is autumn and I hope to fulfil his wish then. My wish – and his also – is a cross with a short quotation. I am thinking of a simple wooden cross which would also carry Helmuth's name and dates. So please let us know your wishes and suggestions.

Konrad's thoughts about his parents are very alive – in the true sense of the word – they accompany him in some sense in all that he does. He speaks of them as if they were there, tells of his memories. Even his father, whom he last saw such a long time ago. On 1 July, Helmuth's birthday, we will go to the grave once more.

We have enrolled the boy at the Jugendheim Anna von Gierke in Finkenkrug. They are prepared to take him from 1 July for six weeks, where he will be lovingly looked after with a certain amount of teaching, in the forest with enough to eat and a strictly regulated daily routine … We were influenced in this decision by the fact that Miss Annchen is leaving us on 1 August to get married.

You ask whether Konrad writes his charming letters by himself. We can affirm this so far as content goes. He writes them in pencil without either of us in a notebook and comes from time to time with questions. But on the other hand one has to help him with the outward forms of the neat version, which is strictly supervised, just like schoolwork; in other words we insist strictly on cleanness, attention and spelling and careful writing. All of this he can do himself *if he gives himself the trouble (which he usually does for his grandfather!)*, but his clerical errors due to speed and alas negligence are quite substantial and cause him considerable unnecessary problems at school. No doubt the result of his fantasy and liveliness. This represents the greatest challenge in his upbringing – his fantasy, his gifts as an actor, together with his desire to be someone in the world, which bring him repeatedly into conflict with the truth. I hope, however, after some disappointments that this tendency can be conquered.

After the experiences of the last few years, where disappointments have played such a role in his little life, it is hardly surprising. That Konrad despite all this is a distinctly happy boy who does not find it difficult to find a useful occupation and who enjoys an appropriate fellowship with other children – that is the other side of his upbringing. He is in good health, and his earlier nervousness has left him. Now he is looking forward to Finkenkrug and his not too distant journey to England.

I suspect that his reply to my June letter has gone missing because in July I wrote:

Dear Opa,

The picture of Daddy has arrived and gave us much joy. Yesterday we went to Mummy's grave. I went to a puppet theatre where they played Hansel and Gretel but it was not anything special.

On Saturday Aunt Gertrud had a house concert where two violins, cello and piano were played. Opa from Altschlage also wrote. That was a great joy for us.

Then in August comes a letter which I suspect betrays the firmness of Aunt Elisabeth. I don't know what I had done. I imagine I had purloined something from the larder, and she, who had no experience of parenting little boys, took this rather more seriously than anyone else to whom she wrote about it.

Dear Opa,

I thank you from my heart for your loving letter of 14 July. It was a good lesson for me. I think it's a good thing that the English are a bit stricter with their children because here things are pretty sloppily managed so far as children are concerned. I really must pull myself together because I must honour not only myself but also Germany.

I wrote the following poem as a gift to Elisabeth:

*Die Bäume rauschen all, Es singt die Nachtigall,*
*Sie singt so schön, sie singt so klar, Das mir ganz froh am Herze war.*
*Die Blumen duften all so schön, Ich wünscht ich könnt sie pflücken gehn!*
*Die Sonne und der Regen Sie müssen alles pflegen.*
*Dies alles hat nun Gott gemacht Mit seinem Sinn und seiner Macht.*
*Er hat auch Dir das Leben, bis jetzt, erhalten und gegeben.*[36]

I rather like the 'bis jetzt' – until now. It seems to betray the sensibility of an old man to the passing of time and brings to mind the recent comment of my dear wife, who first met me when I was twenty-three, that I was born an old man and have grown increasingly younger.

In September one finds a report from the school.

Konrad has made himself at home here. He lives in a children's community, which he did not know as a single child and which in some respects will be very useful for him. He is a very receptive child, finds it easy to grasp things and has a good learning memory. He is making substantial progress, especially in English lessons. He is very uncertain and clumsy in anything practical, but we are trying to bring him up to the mark.

---

[36] All the trees are rustling, the nightingale is singing. She sings so beautifully, she sings so clearly, that I was happy in my heart. The flowers smell so sweet, I wish I could go and pick them. Sun and rain must look after them. God has made all this with His purpose and power. He also it is who has, until now, given and sustained your life.

I fear they failed in this endeavour.

There is a letter about me from the school to my grandfather Hermann.

He is already very much looking forward to his journey to England. It gave me particular pleasure to welcome a grandchild of yours into an Anna von Gierke home. We are building up once more the work of Anna von Gierke, which was much disturbed in 1933. We now have two homes containing forty-two children ... mostly orphaned refugees or children who lost their parents in concentration camps. We worked here illegally since 1933 and managed to bring two non-Aryan children to England and are now happy to be able to work legally again.

On 12 September 1946 Hermann wrote in a circular letter to his children:

Our dearly beloved Konrad, Beate's legacy, will, it seems, be able to go to England next month. I am so thankful to Kathleen and Werner for all that they think about and do. In particular their unconditional willingness to take the little boy.

After the news of Helmuth's death I struggled with Beate for her dear life for six weeks in vain by letter (since she could not be reached). In an attempt to dissuade her from what she had in mind I wrote to her that it was by no means certain that one of you would be in a position to take the boy. She simply could not understand this. In the midst of all the sorrow it was a source of gladness that she simply refused to believe that one of her siblings would not be prepared joyfully to take the child of one of the others in such circumstances. I also could not seriously believe that this could happen but I was very conscious of what it means nowadays for a mother of three children to bring up a fourth as her own.

He wrote to Werner:

I dearly wish that the boy comes to you. So far as his personality is concerned I can only say the following. I had him here for the whole of April with Beate and thereafter saw him for months in Munich. Beate – who at the end weighed only 68 pounds – was already then no longer the old Beate full of energy and always ready to devote herself to the boy. Notwithstanding this, the very self-sufficient boy was one of the most delightful children one could wish to have as a companion. Strong and healthy, he knew how to stand up for himself but was always very friendly, liked by his fellow pupils and teachers and with a most unusual modesty and delicacy of feeling. An occasional outburst of temper, inherited, I fear, from his maternal grandfather, could easily be set aside. Kathleen will discover respects in which he needs to catch up, but humanly he is my quite special love and not only because he is Beate's son.

According to the views of his teachers he is unusually gifted. I correspond vividly with him and am pleased to find in his very full letters a strange mixture of childishness and, for his age, depth of knowledge. He has inherited Helmuth's capacity for logic and reflection. A couple of years ago, when someone sought to explain to him the purpose of rain, he asked why, in that case, rain also fell on roofs and muttered to himself – 'Total waste!'

# VIII

# Werner von Simson: A German Who Got Out Before the War

This seems a good point at which to introduce Werner, who was waiting in England and became a much-loved father to me. There is no biography of him. The nearest one that comes is in the '*Erzählte Erfahrung*',[37] from which I have already cited a passage. He briefly sketches a blissful youth during the First World War in Switzerland under a French governess during which various artists, including Max Reinhardt and Richard Strauss, dined in the house. After the war he was sent to the Joachimsthalsches Gymnasium in Templin, where he met and befriended my father. They remained lifelong friends.

After leaving school, he went to university in Freiburg and then Berlin and graduated after six semesters. Having qualified, he lived in Berlin until 1939.

Like his grandfather August he became a *Rechtsanwalt* at the Berlin *Kammergericht* in whose main courtroom some of his friends were later sentenced to death. He then became one of the leaders of a

---

[37] See chapter 2, note 18.

syndicate of ten important industrial, trading and banking concerns who thought up an answer to the problems of foreign creditors of German debtors. The latter acknowledged their indebtedness but were forbidden by German legislation to transfer funds abroad. The partial answer lay in a scheme whereby the creditors used the frozen funds to finance new building of ships and the like in Germany which would otherwise not have taken place and in return were allowed to remove some of the profits abroad. It has never occurred to me before, and I never spoke to Werner about it, but looking at it now I wonder whether any of this money helped to finance Germany's rearmament.

*Professor Werner von Simson*

On 23 August 1938 Werner married Kathleen, the daughter of the rector of Wem[38] in Shropshire. She gave birth to their first son in England in June 1939. He was christened Godfrey Martin Eduard and was known as Godfrey until his confirmation after which he was known as Martin. As they had previously arranged, Werner moved to England to await the outbreak of war which seemed inevitable at that stage.

There he was, penniless and without employment save in his mother-in-law's garden, which he found unfulfilling.

On 27 May 1940 he was rounded up with other enemy aliens and sent to the Isle of Man. His fellow internees were in part convinced Nazis, in part Germans and Austrians who happened to be in England when war broke out, and in part people of Jewish origin who had fled Germany or Austria. Among his fellow internees were my future wife's grandfather Otto Erich Deutsch (OED),[39] the renowned Schubert scholar,[40] and his daughter Gitta. Another was Kurt Lipstein, who taught me when, in due course, I went to Cambridge. Yet another was Michael Kerr, who also became a Court of Appeal Judge and wrote an interesting autobiography.[41] Werner

---

[30] Bloody Judge Jeffreys was baron of Wem. I always thought it would be fun to become baron of Wem of the second creation and to become a legislator for a while. This, however, is one of those things that never landed in my lap.

[39] One day, an SS officer came to his door in Vienna and said: 'I am a great admirer of your work but I must warn you that if you are here next Monday you will be interned.' OED left forthwith. He was welcomed in Cambridge, and it was there that he wrote the *Schubert Thematic Catalogue* which was published first in English. Its dedication reads: 'To the Society for the Protection of Science *and* Learning (Cambridge, England) as a Token of Gratitude'. It was not translated into German until some years later. He returned to Vienna and wrote many books, chiefly on Schubert and Mozart.

[40] This expertise did not deter him from translating *The Mikado* into German to amuse his fellow detainees on the Isle of Man.

[41] Michael Kerr, *As Far As I Remember* (Hart Publishing, 2002).

*Professor Otto Erich Deutsch*

openly acknowledged that he had a much more agreeable time on the Isle of Man than his contemporaries elsewhere. Moreover, the quality of the academics there was such that one could study anything one liked with experts in the field.

One of his fellow internees was the artist Paul Feiler, who was ten years younger than Werner and after Werner's death recalled their first meeting:

By some extraordinary good fortune I happened to find myself, newly arrived, in the company of half a dozen 'grown men' in an otherwise empty room. It was at this gathering that I first encountered Werner. I was mesmerised and much cheered – given the unusual circumstances – by the light-hearted flow of conversation – the jokes, the banter, the fun conducted by this young man; and this has remained a constant throughout many meetings over the years.

His generosity of spirit and welcoming gesture made us feel that we were very special people.

Werner's wife Kathleen, who had Argentinian nationality, made various enquiries to see whether she could take him and Godfrey to Argentina, where Werner's brother Kurt was, but these proved unsuccessful.

After he had been fifteen months on the island, there was an inspection by the chief inspector of prisons, whom, as it happens, Werner had met in Berlin before the war. I gather that Werner's anti-Nazi views had then been freely expressed. He looked at Werner in astonishment:

'What on earth are you doing here?'

'I wish I knew.'

Werner was released shortly thereafter and went to Oxford, where he worked at Blackwell's, the bookshop. He told me that dons kindly extended invitations to him and he recalled sitting in front of a fireplace in one of the colleges which had been fitted with an ingenious gentle mahogany port-slide which ran from the left side of the mantelpiece to the right and thus permitted the port to circulate in its accustomed direction before beginning another round. After one such round had accompanied the latest news, one of the dons

muttered, 'If things go on like this we'll have to broach the 1896.'
Black humour is common in wartime.[42]

He had an agreeable time reading what he could. He asked
whether, as a researcher with a doctorate, he could use the
Codrington Library at All Souls College but was told that a
German doctorate would not be recognized unless it was in canon
law. He explained that he was the holder of a doctorate granted
by the medieval Freiburg University and had the formal title *doctor
juris utriusque*, which included canon as well as civil law. So he was
admitted to the Codrington, although he had not in truth ever
studied canon law.

After Oxford he went to Birmingham, where he had been
offered a job by his friend Oscar Hahn in BKL Alloys. There he was
engaged in imports and exports.

As he makes clear in 'Erzählte Erfahrung' and in a letter which
I quote below, Werner was left with an enduring feeling of guilt as a
survivor when his friends were no more, having been hanged, shot,
bombed or having simply disappeared.

On 1 February 1946, he wrote to his brothers in South America
of Beate's death:

> You, who only know the war from afar, must find [Beate's
> death] inconceivable. When I tell you that dozens of my
> nearest friends were hanged and that many, many, are daily
> exposed to the same temptation simply to make an end of
> everything, and when you consider that in addition to the
> terrible disappointment of Helmuth's death there must be
> added the lack of food, of warmth and of hope, then you

---

[42] In Moorhouse's *Berlin at War* one finds mention of Berlin equivalents at pp. 89,
349–50, 362.

can only join us in feeling the deepest sympathy for Ate,[43] who simply did not know any longer how to help herself ... Kathleen and I will take the child as a gift from her and Helmuth.

When I read this recently, I was reminded that, when Werner was on his death bed, as I thanked him for all that he had done for me, the last thing that he said to me was 'You were the best gift that anyone has ever given me.' This moved me more than I can say.

He was concerned to obtain his father's approval to bringing me up as an Englishman and wrote: 'God is the same both in England and Germany and it could be a comforting thought that the boy could do something to bring these two great peoples together.'

He took the opportunity to explain that he himself wished to take British nationality and wrote:

*You know that I turned my back on Germany at a time when, in my view it was impossible to remain there without becoming a guilty party.* That others did so, like my friends Haeften[44] and Trott,[45] has shown a greatness in them which was inconceivable to me and which I suspect was beyond my strength to carry out. People of such determination are rare ...

---

[43] A shortened form of Beate's name. Whether this encompassed a reference to the Greek goddess who induced rash and ruinous acts I do not know. It sounds unlikely, but in that classically educated family given to wordplay it is not impossible.

[44] I think this refers to Werner, who was shot on 21 July 1944, rather than to his elder brother Hans-Bernd, who was hanged on Hitler's order on 15 August 1944. It may refer to both.

[45] He was hanged 26 August 1944.

The implicit assertion by Werner in the passage which I have italicised that those who remained in Germany without giving up their lives in the fight against Hitler were somehow more guilty than he, not unnaturally made his sister Marianne furious when she was shown a copy of his letter. She wrote to her father on 15 April 1946:

> What I object to is that he considered that for him to leave at the time that he did leave prevented him from being jointly responsible. That is not right. I agree with you that those escape guilt who openly said what they thought and suffered many injuries in consequence. Undoubtedly, everyone else who lived in Germany and so knew what was happening is jointly guilty. Since Werner knew perfectly well what was happening and yet said nothing he is as jointly responsible as we are. That he spent the time of the war elsewhere and (I accept) did not kill any of our then enemies in this cause does not diminish his joint liability. That in my opinion remains a reproach which can legitimately be made against him by those who, against their will, fulfilled their duty as Germans even in a cause in which they did not believe.
>
> I do not think that you are correct when you write that Helmuth did his alleged duty. At the time when he became a soldier, matters were as follows in Germany. As a German one could only say that one's first duty was to beat the enemy (one had a good idea, as we now clearly see, what would happen to us if this did not succeed).
>
> What we would then do with Hitler was entirely a matter for us. It was this idea which made it possible for Max to endure these last few years when he knew for what he was risking his life and made it possible for him to continue, although it was

not easy for us. For us it was a matter of fighting for Germany and not for National Socialism, even though it looked like it.

It is clear that we often risked more than he did. And we put our whole way of life at risk in the attempt to prevent at least some of the evil things that went on and we stood to gain nothing from this. He also freely gave up his way of life but he did have the possibility of building it up again over there. I am afraid I can only see what he did as plain desertion. One can try to understand it and one can say that in this mad situation each must do what he thinks right. But he is not one whit better than we who remained. Don't you think that is right?

When I read this now, I have to say that I understand what she is saying and agree with her. I suspect that, notwithstanding his infelicitous phrase, Werner would also have agreed with her essential reasoning.

He wrote to his brothers:

Very nearly all my old friends from before the war have gone, most of them hanged or executed in some other ghastly way by the Nazis. Life for me is entirely different from what it was; different friends, and many gone without whom I still find it difficult to conceive my existence. It will take some time to adjust oneself, and a feeling of guilt for being alive and sheltered after all this will probably remain.

At this time he was approached by Rudi Petersen, the Mayor of Hamburg and a distant relation, to take some part in the government of Germany, whether in Hamburg or Berlin, 'because we so desperately need good people who are politically suitable'. He wrote to his father that he had decided against this because, under Allied occupation, ministers did not have any real power. Whether this added to his sense of guilt I do not know. I feel pretty sure that Kathleen would not have been at ease with a move to Germany at that stage.

Werner stayed in Birmingham till the early 1950s and moved to the Grand Duchy of Luxembourg, where he became the first advocate in private practice focused exclusively on the law of the European Coal and Steel Community. In 1954, he obtained the permission of the High Authority for the reconstitution of Mannesmann and thereafter of Hoesch. He had a very successful career as an advocate, and when I went to Luxembourg in 2004, many of my colleagues and friends had known him and all spoke of him with affection and admiration.

In the Grand Duchy we lived in rather large houses with gardens, first in Capellen and then Bertrange, both at the time small villages well separated from the capital. Werner and Kathleen entertained widely, particularly the relatives of those who had died in one way or another during the Second World War. They had four boys of their own as well as me, but they felt the lack of girls so they invited girls to stay with us for a few months at a time in order to civilise us. Three of us boys including me ended up marrying such an import.

His legal practice aside, Werner was a polymath at home, reading and speaking German, English and French, with a good memory of Greek and Latin. He played the piano and organ, and I have happy memories of listening to trios and quartets played in his house. We boys and girls sat on the steps in the hall. Some were enchanted; others let their minds wander or moved upstairs to listen to Radio Luxembourg. We had got to know Peter Carver, who was a disc jockey there and would occasionally dedicate a record to one or other of us. Years later, when he was High Sheriff of the East

Riding of Yorkshire and I a High Court judge, he and his beautiful and charming wife Jacky entertained us in great style in their house, where we had so often stayed when I did not have to sing for my supper.

Remembering his early years in Switzerland, Werner bought a chalet on the road to Beatenberg outside Interlaken in the 1950s. I remember this fondly as being always packed with people – up to twenty or so – who used it as a base for skiing, water-skiing and walking. From our drawing room one could see, when they were not hidden in mist, the snow-capped Eiger, Mönch and Jungfrau. Elisabeth, I and our daughter Juliet loved the place. At Christmas time and during other holidays we had family reunions there of the five brothers and in due course their families. I enjoyed skiing and invited my pupil John Steel to come. He was a serious skier but was prepared to overlook the deficiencies of his pupil master[46] and managed to persuade Peter Lunn,[47] whom I liked immediately, to invite us to join the Kandahar Club and even to award Elisabeth and me a silver badge, which allegedly was evidence of proficiency.

The chalet was left to us five boys in Werner's will but, although I wanted to keep it, the others were less keen, and in due course we sold it to the family who had owned it before the war. A few years ago, we returned to have a look at the place and found everything completely different. What had been a small town visited by a few quiet foreigners had been replaced by an international mass holiday

---

[46] These days renamed a pupil supervisor.

[47] I did not know that Lunn had been in the Secret Service during the war. Later I got to know Professor Engelbert Broda quite well through my mother-in-law. Broda, I have since found out, had been a Soviet spy during the war. I warmed to him also. He had been married to a lady who later married Nunn May, another spy, who had been to my school. This fact led me to one of my early infelicities when I said during a celebratory speech at school, 'King Edward's has had many famous alumni of whom none may be forgotten.' One or two people picked it up.

resort teeming with tourists who presumably enjoyed the banal music which emanated from the new loudspeakers all along the Höheweg, the main street. I was glad that we had sold the chalet and prefer to guard the memory of what it had been.

In the 1960s, Werner moved to Freiburg University, which had offered him a professorship, an unusual thing for someone who had not made his way up the academic ladder but was coming in from the outside.[48] However, he continued to practise in European law part-time.[49] In Freiburg, he taught and wrote books mostly about sovereignty, politics and the new political order which became the European Union.

Years later he came to lunch in Gray's Inn with one of the Benchers, who introduced him to Lord Denning.

'Tom, you recollect Professor von Simson. He gave a talk here last year.'

'Of course I do. I remember it well. [Pause] What was it all about?'

Now in my eighties, my sympathies are with Lord Denning.

Werner and Kathleen had their main residence from the 1960s onwards till his death in 1996 in Freiburg, although they also had a flat in South Kensington. They were very hospitable, and their homes were always filled with students, university people and musicians who enjoyed their company.

He had that reverence for the academic life which characterised his Germany, and I remember him asserting that a verse

---

[48] *Freiburger Universitäts Blätter* Heft 60 contains a speech made on his seventieth birthday by the rector.
[49] One of his clients was a Japanese firm which paid him a significant annual retainer. When he turned seventy-five, I think, he wrote to them saying that since he had done nothing for them for the past ten years they really should discontinue this generous annual payment. They, setting an excellent example which unfortunately has not been followed by any clients of mine, declined, stating that they thought it an honour to have someone of his age and eminence as an adviser.

had been left out of the account of Creation in the first chapter of Genesis. This was the verse which made clear that the German law professor was the very last thing that God had created before he saw everything that he had made and, behold, it was very good. There was an element of self-mockery in this, but only an element, I think. Nonetheless he could be biting about the self-importance of some professors, of one of whom he remarked 'he knows everything. But otherwise – nothing.' His old acquaintance F. A. Mann, who became a very distinguished academic and practitioner in England, was inclined to be intolerant of anyone who disagreed with his views. Werner told me that he used to begin conversations with Mann by saying, 'Can we, to shorten this conversation, agree on the premise that you are cleverer than I?'

He spent a lot of his time thinking about Europe, and I absorbed and shared many of his thoughts on the subject. These are set out at length in various of his books and articles. Glimpses of his thought and the tension with the mindset of some of the Schiemanns can be seen in the excerpts from letters quoted below. More than glimpses can be seen in various lectures and articles under my name.

Thinking of Werner has caused me to leap ahead chronologically, and I now return to my arrival in England.

# IX

# *I Move to England*

It was impossible for me to leave Germany without the permission of the relevant Allied authority. In my case, since I lived in the British zone of Berlin, this was the British. Werner hit on the idea of contacting his friend Peter Bielenberg's wife Christabel, now famous for, among other things, her two published autobiographies, *The Past Is Myself* and *The Road Ahead*. The first was turned into a BBC Television drama, *Christabel*, starring Elizabeth Hurley. They had all been friends of Adam von Trott and others who had been executed after the assassination attempt, and Peter had spent time in a concentration camp. Christabel was a niece of Lord Northcliffe and had succeeded in becoming a war correspondent and having a press pass, which enabled her to travel to Germany.

Werner, as an enemy alien, was not permitted to travel to Germany. Christabel agreed to try and get the permit needed for me to travel to England. Apparently she finally reached the British officer in charge of the British zone in Berlin, who said that he was willing to help but that he needed to sign the relevant papers. He said that these would almost certainly be in a certain room with a lot of others but that he simply did not have the staff to try and sort out the confusion of files in that room. Christabel offered to sort them out if she could be allowed to put the Schiemann file on top. This she did, and the officer signed and stamped the appropriate documents. I owe her a lot.

Konrad Weil wrote on 12 November:

Konrad was here yesterday to say farewell and made an excellent impression. He will do you all proud in England. His health is first class. He is going to travel on Tuesday with Mrs Bielenberg to London … There, Werner will fetch him. Naturally he finds the separation and the heap of unknown things which face him like a mountain in front of him, but I think all will be well with him.

Since in my view we shall freeze and hunger here for the next ten years, the boy can have no greater luck than to go to England.

Werner wrote to his father describing my arrival:

Early this morning in Tilbury docks I took over dear little Konrad. I arrived in good time because of a telegram by Fritz Schumacher[50] and a letter from the British Red Cross. There I saw the *Empire Halladale* and on the deck some 15–20 metres above me I at once recognised the little chap from Jella's

---

[50] E. F. Schumacher, the economist who had been a Rhodes scholar in Oxford and wrote *Small is Beautiful*. He had been a partner with Werner before the war. His sister married the physicist Werner Heisenberg. They were all friends of Werner.

picture mongst a crowd of largely Polish children. I called out 'Konrad', and he immediately knew who I was; but any conversation was impossible at this distance, and we needed to have patience for rather more than an hour till the passengers were let off the ship. I took him to where the baggage was, and he immediately sorted out his seven things amongst hundreds of cases and suitcases. He had learnt some English but was rather disturbed by the fact that the people here spoke rather fast and unclearly. He asked me anxiously whether I spoke English. I then gave him a map and showed him where we were and where we were going and the four-and-a-half-hour journey started, throughout which he told me all sorts of interesting things.

I remember this journey to this day because I was allowed to change the gears when Werner depressed the clutch pedal. This, and the accompanying revving up noises, I found great fun.

The letter continues:

My heart was heavy as I thought of our dear Beate and Helmuth. Konrad in his character is much older than Godfrey; bodily he is hardly larger. After about an hour, he said that he had now got used to me but he was a bit anxious as to whether he would like Kathleen. I dared to say softly that I was a bit anxious as to whether Kathleen would like him. At this, to my great delight he burst out laughing and said that this was indeed probably more important.

Altogether the boy gave me great joy and has many very charming characteristics and one can see great intelligence in him.

Kathleen wisely said that he should first show us his treasures before we showed him everything. This proved a good idea. He had purchased on board a tin of condensed milk for Piers! Godfrey and he immediately became great friends, although he told me later that he found the two-year-old John less sympathetic because he kept pulling at his arm and wanted to join in the game. He said that he would have to treat Godfrey with respect since in his opinion Godfrey was even wilder than he was! In the evening he became somewhat homesick. The nursemaid and Godfrey speak no word of German, and Konrad felt that he would never quite find his feet in a country where they could not speak his language. When we suggested that initially I would sleep in Martin's bed in the boys' room and Martin could sleep in my bed, he found this comforting and after he had expressed his appreciation of the warm bathwater, he slept peacefully. After this day I am convinced that he will soon be at home here and will become a great joy for us. In particular he will be good for Godfrey and vice versa.

My own perspective can in part be gleaned from a letter I wrote on 22 December 1946 to my grandfather:

Dear Opa,

I hope things are well with you. I feel reasonably happy here but am often homesick. At about 6 p.m. Uncle Werner saw me on board. He immediately shouted, 'Konrad!' and I called out 'How did you recognise me?' Further conversation proved impossible. Then we drove to Aunt Kathleen. I already have quite a good relationship with Godfrey. He too is very wild. At Easter I will go to school with him.[51] Uncle Werner is in the office practically all day. But nevertheless everyone is very friendly to me, and I will soon feel at home. I hope it's not too cold where you are [the winter of 1946–7 was particularly bitter]. Your loving Konrad.

## English schooling seventy years ago

When I arrived in England we went to 3 Carisbroke Road, Birmingham, where the Simsons lived at that time – an early twentieth-century house of no particular distinction but which was large enough for all of us and an English nurse.

Kathleen's parents lived in the Rectory, Wem, where her father, the Reverend P. R. Turner, had been rector since before the war. We usually went there during the holidays. He was a graduate of Pembroke College Cambridge, became ordained and then went to Argentina as a missionary. At the beginning of the First World War, he took a ship back to England. He then became vicar of St Paul's, West Hartlepool, and then domestic chaplain to the Marquess of Londonderry before becoming rector of Wem. In the Rectory hall there was displayed a collection of arrows in memory of one of the missionaries who had been killed by such an arrow. I was very fond of him, a quiet thoughtful man who never had a cross word for anyone. I write this under his portrait.

Very soon after my arrival in England I was sent to the George Dixon local primary school, a late Victorian building whose smelly and cold outside yard and lavatory I recall. I was simply put in a

---

[51] In fact, he was at a private preparatory school, and I went to a state primary school, which I left at eleven years old to go to King Edward's Birmingham, where he joined me two years later.

*The Rev. P. R. Turner*

class and rapidly picked up English. However, I was behind in maths and so was given some catch-up tuition in this at home.

In Birmingham at the time there was a special exam in order to secure one of the much-sought-after places at King Edward's School. I do not have a copy of the paper which I sat but I do have a copy of the paper from 1922, and I suspect the 1948 version was rather similar. Here are some of the questions:

> Give some account of our dealings with Ireland from the time of Henry II to the present day.
>
> Give a short account of either a poem you have read, or a picture you have seen, which describes any event in English history.

Write a list of five events in 1922 which you think will find their way into future history books.

Name the Parts of Speech. Give a definition of each, and also compose simple sentences to illustrate each Part of Speech.

Give an example of the use of the following constructions:

- A collective noun with a plural verb.
- A transitive verb with a double object.
- A gerund governing an object.
- An adverb modifying a preposition.
- A prepositional phrase with the form of an adverb.
- A subordinate conjunction introducing a conditional clause.

To modern eyes it looks daunting for a ten-year-old and indeed his parents. But one must remember that in those days the only distractions from work were games outside, bicycling and books. Grammar was taught as a discipline like arithmetic; there was a right and a wrong way to construct a sentence. All this is no longer the received view, which adopts Pope's dictum in his *Essay on Man* that 'Whatever is, is right.' Perhaps because I learnt English as a second language and a certain amount of Greek and Latin at a time when grammar was regarded as an essential tool for clear communication, I am very attached to what I then imbibed and so am upset at what I regard as daily grammatical infelicities in conversation, on the radio or elsewhere. When, years later, I presided over two other lord justices in the Court of Appeal, I would occasionally allow myself a cheeky comment on a draft judgement such as 'If you'll forgive this coming from a German, should this pronoun not be in the accusative?' I hope they forgave me. Intellectually I understand that usage changes over the years and sometimes I recognise an improvement. But not often. Frequently a subtlety is lost.

I have no recollection of the process of sitting the exam, but three of us from George Dixon passed it and went to King Edward's. On offer were scholarships, so-called free places and, I believe, fee-paying places. I obtained a free place, largely I suspect on promise rather than performance. Looking back on it, this was a huge stroke of luck. In due course at King Edward's they were kind enough to convert it into a scholarship.

In my early years at the school, I had not got used to all the local customs and must at times have been tiresome. I recollect getting into a fight in our classroom with a boy called Howard. He was smaller than I but pluckily took me on. He had called me a Nazi but pronounced this in what I did not then know was Churchill's pronunciation – 'Nazzi' as in 'snazzy'. I informed him that he was mistaken in thinking me a Nazi but that in any event the proper pronunciation was 'Naatsi' as in 'part see'. This naturally infuriated him further, and in attacking me he got so het up that he slipped and landed with his bottom firmly wedged in a metal waste-paper bin with his legs sticking out in one direction and his head in the other. I regret to say that I promptly thumped him while he was in this disadvantageous position. This displeased the onlookers, who told me that you did not hit a man when he was down. I replied that this was contrary to common sense; after all, what better time to hit a man than when he could not retaliate? A typically German response, I was told at the time. Now, of course, I can see that the observance of this rule helps to instil the noble qualities no doubt universally associated with the English.

I enjoyed playing rugger, Eton fives and chess and being in various choirs. I did a certain amount of acting – in *The Tempest* where I, in those days blond, was Ceres, and in *Twelfth Night* in which I played Lady Olivia. Personally I enjoyed it, but not many others did. Someone was unkind enough to say it was the worst school play in living memory. My problem was not the verse but that I lumbered about taking huge steps and could never manage walking in a way which looked even remotely feminine.

That year's report included the hurtful but justified and effective comment by the then headmaster, T. E. B. Howarth: 'If he thinks that he will ever make a living as an actor he is much mistaken. It's time to start some serious work.' I have not acted on stage since then. However, the Bar gives one plenty of opportunity for playacting and, although one's client furnishes the sought-after goal, at least one can choose one's own lines.

I was fairly consistently near the bottom of the class for my first two years. Then one had to decide whether to remain in the mainstream or do classics, which was, or so it seemed to me, what the brightest boys generally did. In any event, it was decided that I should do classics, which I did for the next three years and enjoyed, especially ancient history. But I lacked the concentration and application required in order to succeed and continued near the bottom of the class.

In those days we translated from English into Greek and vice versa and read classical Greek and New Testament Greek. Enoch Powell had been at the school, and I recollect later reading that, faced with an exam question asking for a translation of a passage into Greek, he provided two translations: one in the style of Herodotus, the other in that of Thucydides. The theologians would describe this as a work of supererogation. I fear I never even confronted this problem consciously.

One used to refer to what are now called religious studies lessons as divinity lessons. These were spent, so far as I can recollect, entirely in translating passages from the Gospels and St Paul's letters from Greek into English. Our form master was an Anglican priest who taught Greek and wished thus to kill two birds with one stone. He was justly known as 'Stuffer' because of the work habits which he sought to instil in us. One of my friends, his son Martin, generally behaved well. On one occasion, however, he aroused his father's ire and he was either slippered or caned in front of us all. Whether it was because of this or notwithstanding this I do not know, but Martin also became an Anglican priest.

I too made the acquaintance of the slipper but escaped the cane in unusual circumstances. We used to sit at individual desks each of which had a lid which, when lifted, revealed storage space below. We had a rather ineffective maths master who was teased mercilessly by us boys. Whether his ineffectiveness was one of the results of his experiences during the war did not cross our minds but has since troubled me.

One day I took a water pistol and a jar of water into class and hid them in my desk. When the master had his back to us because he was chalking an equation up on the blackboard, I filled my water pistol and squirted water at the board in order to wipe out what he had just written. Unfortunately I got him in the back of his neck, Understandably he turned round, furiously asking 'Who was that?' Silence overcame the class. However, a trail of water drops led directly to my desk – something my understanding of physics had not equipped me to foresee – and his question was answered. I was called to the front. He fetched his cane, which I had never seen him use. He ordered me to bend over by his desk, which I manfully did. However, as the cane came down, my courage failed me, and I ducked. The cane, instead of making contact with my soft backside, hit his hard desk, and the result was that his hand stung mightily. Kind man that he was, he must have felt uncertain as to whether he could control himself and, instead of proceeding to thrash the daylights out of me, sent me out of the room for the rest of the period. Shortly after-wards, he left the school and became a priest, and I imagine he was very good at meeting many of the challenges which this must have presented. For my part, I failed my maths O level and had to retake it. Arrogantly, I suspected that there had been a mix-up in the marking. In those days one did not challenge the official results.

It was during that time that I became friends with Christopher Long, who was always at the top of the class in everything, and with whom I remain friends to this day. He subsequently became our ambassador in Switzerland, Egypt and Hungary and learnt numerous languages. I remember him showing me his Linguaphone record of Schwyzertüütsch, the Swiss-German dialect which I suspect remains a mystery to most ambassadors. But he already had German, French and Italian and so learning Schwyzertüütsch seemed the obvious thing to do since his Russian and Arabic were of not much use in that posting. I gather that those who heard him were pleased that he had made the effort. I observed the same sort of thing in Luxembourg years later. Visiting ambassadors in general contented themselves with French and German and left Letzeburgesch, the Luxembourg patois, to the natives. However, when Peter Bateman was the British ambassador, he gave an excellent parting speech in Letzeburgesch to wide applause before moving on to Azerbaijan.

When I was sixteen and Martin fourteen, Werner wished to move to Luxembourg, and the question was what to do with the children. At that stage money was tight, and I do not think boarding school was discussed. I certainly wanted to stay at school in England, and so far as I know so did Martin. Werner and Kathleen found a German lady who had married an English soldier after the war. They lived in a council house in Birmingham, and her husband, as

I recall, was a postman. They agreed to take us two boys as paying lodgers and keep us fed and watered. This worked very well. We shared a room, and I do not recall much friction between us, though we did not do much together. We were too different.

At that point I left the classics side and moved across to history, where I started to do better. They made me a school prefect and head of house and secretary of the Debating Society. Round about that time, I picked up a few prizes and a lot of self-confidence. I worked seriously for the first time in my life. Indeed, I don't think that I have ever worked so hard as during my last year at school preparing for GCE Advanced and Scholarship levels and the Cambridge scholarship exam. But I enjoyed all this because, as I now see, the masters were very good at giving me faith in myself.

Before the exams, one had a lot of time for private study, and I recollect making my way to a very old-fashioned library/club, which has since closed down, in the centre of town. There, one found old leather armchairs with the stuffing frequently spilling out and a strong musty smell of books going back centuries. For a few pence one could order a cup of coffee and some biscuits, and I found it most congenial to study there and be treated like a grown-up. At the time, Martin and I were living in a bedsitting room, so there was no incentive to work there.

The ethos of the school seems odd nowadays, when the very word 'elite' is used to arouse a sneer. I recollect the chief master, the Rev. R. G. Lunt, saying at morning prayers, 'As pupils of this school you are an elite: the chosen ones. You have some duties which follow from this.' He openly mocked the suggestion that 'all must have prizes' as ridiculous and depriving the concept of a prize of any meaning. These comments would be regarded by many now as reprehensible and as unnecessarily divisive. He established the Cartland Club, which was given a special room in the school furnished with armchairs, newspapers, coffee facilities and so on. Lunt had been at Eton and had, I suppose, been inspired by the ethos he had experienced there and by reading Plato. The club was designed as something to membership of which any could aspire but whose numbers were limited. I was flattered to be invited to be a part of it. I loved it and also the Shakespeare reading parties in which members took part. In deference to the spirit of a later age, it has now been disbanded as being divisive.

Similarly, nowadays the word 'master' raises hackles in many quarters as it implies that we are not all equal. For my part it has never occurred to me that we are all equal *in all respects* and I have never had any difficulty in accepting my inferiority to others in most respects. I am comforted by the fact that the same is true of everyone else. I agree with the judgement of Justice Frankfurter that it was a wise man who said that there is no greater inequality than the equal treatment of unequals.[52] I am happy with much mediaeval usage, certainly in some contexts. Yet usage changes. At the Bar in the 1960s I regularly consulted what was then the standard volume on employment law, *The Law of Master and Servant*. At the time I felt no sense of being ill at ease with its title but I would do nowadays. However, even today, when in the Temple I am addressed as Master Schiemann, I feel no discomfort in following the tradition of centuries. On the other hand, I do confess to a consciousness of incongruity when my distinguished female colleagues are addressed as master. But there are obvious difficulties in using the feminine, so I can see a case for changing the usage of centuries. But I confess to being quietly pleased that

---

[52] *Dennis v United States* 339 US, p. 184.

no one has yet, so far as I know, sought to persuade the Inn to abandon this old custom.

My form master Charles Blount had been at Pembroke College, Cambridge, and each year suggested one person to the college as being worth looking at. He arranged an interview for me with the senior tutor W. A. Camps, whom I then went to see. I knew that Grandpapa Turner and his son Uncle James had been at Pembroke but could see no decent way in which I could casually mention this during the interview. When I mentioned this fact to Uncle James, he said that it was just as well since the last time he had seen Camps was when he had thrown him into the Cam.

Camps wrote on 26 November 1954:

If you can get three A levels next summer you can count yourself accepted for admission here in 1958. Of course, I hope and expect that you will do much better than just three plain A levels but I am not making that a condition. We shall be glad too to see you at our scholarship examination in December 1955.[53]

I strongly suspect that Blount's recommendation helped to produce the above letter. The promise in the letter gave me self-confidence and what I now see was an unfair advantage over those without such connections. I comfort myself with observing that the fact that my forebears for the past couple of centuries had received a university education has deprived me of the advantages of being able to boast that I am the first in the family in this regard.

---

[53] In those days you either passed or failed; there was no grading. One could show a certain distinction by taking an S level which was more demanding.

In the summer of 1955, I obtained the requisite A and S levels. In December I sat the scholarship exams. I remember the subject for my three-hour essay: 'True knowledge is the opposite of common sense'. After an hour during which nothing came into my head, I was left with an increasing sense of unease, not helped by the page after page which my neighbour was producing. I suddenly thought of the equation 'True knowledge equals Christianity' and then discussed the relationship between Christianity and common sense. This helped the ink to flow.

What I wrote was probably along the same lines as a remark of the bishop of Luxembourg at a dinner in Werner's house. An American lady brought up the subject of the doctrine of the Bodily Assumption of the Virgin Mary which had recently been pronounced as dogma by Pius XII. She said rather aggressively to the bishop, 'You are an intelligent man. How can you believe such nonsense?' He replied disarmingly, 'Madam, I believe so much nonsense already, why not this too?' which brought her intervention to an end. At the time I thought this an elegant way of avoiding what would have been an unprofitable and uncomfortable confrontation. Now I recognise a deeper wisdom.

Back to Cambridge. I remember an interview with a don who asked me what I had been reading lately, and I said truthfully *Thus Spake Zarathustra*. 'What do you think is the point that Nietzsche is making?' I then started talking and after five minutes uninterrupted I said (truthfully), 'I'm sorry. I'm not making sense. I really don't know.' He replied gracefully 'How disappointing! Because I don't know either.' In the event, to everyone's surprise, I was given a minor scholarship.

I later found at the Bar that if you confess your ignorance when you do not know the answer with sufficient vigour and determination you are forgiven. Years later, it used to irritate me as a judge to have to listen to an advocate talking without knowing what they were saying. I tried, but not always successfully, to be as friendly as the don in question.

# X

# *The Choice Before Me: Germany or England?*

From the correspondence which has now fallen into my hands it is apparent that a number of busy people devoted a huge amount of time corresponding for a number of years about what I should do after school. The correspondence was chiefly between Aunt Elisabeth in Berlin and Werner in Luxembourg but occasionally came in my direction. She felt that not enough was being done to enable me to carry on the Schiemann tradition, of which she was very proud. By contrast, Werner felt that my challenge was to become absorbed into English life and not to be reminded of my lost childhood.

On 2 August 1951, less than five years after I had come to England, Werner wrote to her:

A grown-up would never have recovered from the events which Konrad has had to live through, but for Konrad they have disappeared. Thanks to this the child is full of vigour for life: one cannot ask for more. At Konrad's age one is not ripe enough to live in and for the past. When he gets older, then the question of the memory of his parents will become real for him and he will want to know something about them and about how they lived and felt. But that will not succeed … It would be an illusion if we thought that we could save for him a true remembrance of his parents.

Aunt Elisabeth was not persuaded and wrote regularly both to Werner and to me. On 2 June 1954, her sister Gertrud wrote congratulating me on my confirmation. She was gentler and less rigid than Elisabeth but took the same general approach:

If I come back as an old friend to you after many years of silence it is because I know that the coming years will necessitate decisions about your future which Daddy cannot take away from you. It is natural, and we fully understand that you grew up in English surroundings and while a child you did not want to separate yourself from your friends in either speech or thought. The position is different as regards the adult life on which you are now embarking. The question will become: are you an Englishman or a German, and do your strengths and capabilities belong to the land in which you have been brought up or to the land to which your mother attached herself with all her strength in her thinking and doing until her death? A land which she, of course, served in total opposition to the regime established by force which brought ruin on our native land. There is an English saying 'my country right or wrong'. Don't you think that this is as true of you and Germany as it is of an Englishman? Your history is filled with deep fissures.

Your father, despite his clear rejection of the Hitler regime and of the war, of course fulfilled his duty as a German. This shows, just as does your mother's fight in the resistance, how *dearly* they loved their Fatherland.

I interpose to say that this is the only reference I have found anywhere to my mother's 'fight in the resistance' and I do not know what to make of it. It may just be a loose expression or it may show that Gertrud knew more than is now apparent from other sources.

As you know, I was very close to your mother in those last difficult months and so I know that she expressly wished that you should spend a part of your school and university time in Germany so that you would not lose the connection to the relatives who lived here and that you should keep alive the feeling of belonging to the land of your fathers. If you decide already now to pursue legal studies, then you are going against the wishes of your mother. Legal studies prepare you for a career which can only be followed in the country in which you have taken your exams.[54] So by this step you would lose the connection with Germany. However, if you study anything else then you will be at liberty to practise also in Germany. It was your mother's wish that you should take this decision as to your nationality only when you had reached your majority.

Apart from this primary consideration there is another one which you must think through: family tradition. You are the last in the family to carry the Schiemann name. A name which was widely recognised and respected through

---

[54] This is, of course, no longer true of the European Union.

the work which your great-grandfather, our father, Theodor Schiemann obtained as a fighter for the Protestant German Baltic. Guided by this truly German idealistic world view, he left everything behind in order to keep his children free from Russian lack of freedom and let them grow up as Germans. Your father loved and honoured him and copied his diaries in order to be able to absorb his thinking as his own. He was conscious of the duty which fell on him as the sole bearer of the name to keep up the tradition and to preserve the good name of his grandfather.

Now it is for you, my dear Konrad, to carry on this tradition. You must not worry that this will harm in any sense your faith in Europe and love of England and your relations there. The wider your perspective, the better you will be able to serve your fatherland. Germans who have been brought up abroad often became the truest representatives of the German spirit. Your great-uncle Paul Schiemann has a well-known and respected name as a defender of German minorities in international relations. We Baltic Germans do not know a narrow nationalism but we have been the defenders for 700 years of *Deutschtum* (the German character and civilisation) in the East.

Think about these things. Germany needs clear-thinking people with a wide outlook in this difficult hour. Do try to get to know the land of your fathers.

This, which arrived in the middle of my exams, prompted a letter from me to Werner, dated 9 June 1954:

I have just received a letter from Aunt Gertrud which seems to contain something which, so far as I can make out, is fairly important – to her at any rate. All this business about Duty to the Fatherland and what not perplexes me. Could you please read the letter and then tell me if I am, through my bad German, barking up the wrong tree or, if not, what I am to do about it.

On 15 June 1954, my grandmother Hertha wrote to Werner explaining that her views were very different from those of Elisabeth and Gertrud.

I told Thor that I thought that we had absolutely no right to get involved in this matter since you have all the care of looking after Konrad and since I have gathered from many talks with him how completely happy he feels with you and in England. In his youth he had to undergo terribly difficult times which I have only recently fully understood ... you once wrote that the most important thing for Konrad was that he forgot the whole thing, and I agree that it would be a most dangerous experiment to rip him now out of his new life and to replant him in totally different surroundings where we have no idea whether he will be at home or how all this will affect the peace of his soul. I think I knew Beate far too well to believe that she would have wished him to spend his school time in Germany willy-nilly. The main consideration is that he should feel innerly happy and at peace. Moreover, I consider that his relationship with us is far more important than whether he is English or German. I think Kathleen has done a huge amount for Konrad's soul, if indeed she wished him to grow up as an Englishman.

In January 1955 Werner replied to repeated letters from the aunts:

I think we differ chiefly in the fact that you see being German and being English as being in opposition to one another, whereas I feel that we can no longer let these differences remain a matter of importance. Otherwise both countries will perish. When we talk of youngsters like Konraḍ we must not lose sight of the fact that by the year 2000 he will be sixty-two, at the height of his powers and capabilities. That year is one we can hardly imagine and understand just as we find it impossible to put ourselves in antiquity.

But what is becoming clear is that it will be impossible at that time to see Germany as a political entity totally different from other European countries. The same goes for France and England. Yet this is the basis of your conviction that England's gain is Germany's loss. The days of nation states in Western Europe have gone. If the nation states take a different view then the same will happen to Western Europe as happened to Greece. The time for national states in Western Europe has passed. That does not mean that Germany as a special concept should or will disappear. Germany has given the world an enormous amount and will give it yet more. Some German concepts are now part of a world view – but not in the political field in the way that it was for the ancient Romans or the Anglo-Saxons.

In this regard England is the leading power and will continue to be. That country has partially achieved to a greater degree than any other country the task of reconciling human conscience with political aims and action to such a degree that the tension which has existed since the Reformation between the individual and the state now appears to be capable of being bridged. You talk of commercial interests, power politics, etc. All that exists. But it is only one side of the picture. What is hugely important is that, in the long run, this country does not act against its conscience. Others no doubt would like to achieve this but simply don't know how to do it. England has oppressed India and Ireland. But it has also given them freedom.

Correspondence went back and forth, and I only offer a few examples, which betray the thinking of the time. On 24 March 1955 Werner wrote to Thor:

Konrad has inherited the concentration and devotion to work of his father … The School is encouraging him to have a go at the university entrance exams, and you can imagine that he is now filled with ambition and wants to demonstrate what he can do. In his particular case this is not without its problems. The more he achieves, the more he will find it fun to do whatever is open to him as a result of that achievement. If, which admittedly we regard as highly unlikely [I had written as much to Werner], he had the serious success of getting a scholarship to Cambridge then let someone try to make clear to him that he should give this up and instead go to a German university!

This shows the difficulty of the situation: I do not wish to discourage someone who seeks to achieve the highest of what is open to him and yet, on the other hand, every success in this regard drives him closer and closer to the result which in principle he should not choose at this stage before he has examined other possibilities.

On 22 April Werner wrote to Thor:

... between ourselves the difficulty arises from the fact that Konrad loves the established and clearly delineated and does not have much time for the adventurous and new ... What the aunts say is something which is simply not meaningful to this boy's experiences, and our times require the development of a national viewpoint into a European one. I have never sought to put this before Konrad but it is my firm conviction. I am quite certain that Germany will never be in a position to reunify unless it embraces this outlook – and yet unless it is reunified it is not Germany.

Germany at the time desperately lacked young leaders because of the vast numbers who had perished in the war. I was thought to be a potential leader, and my grandfather and his sisters felt that my talents such as they were should be employed in the service of Germany. Their whole political outlook was firmly based on the concept of nationhood and on the idea that the citizens of that nation had a duty to serve it. This echoed the view of their father, the professor. Starting from that premise they felt that, as a German citizen, I had a duty to serve the fatherland.

Werner took a wider view, as do I, and felt that the best way of articulating this to my grandfather was by playing to the desire to reunify Germany. For reunification to be achieved in the face of French and British hostility he thought the existence of a European Community of States was a political prerequisite. As life turned out,

I stayed in England and I think probably did do a little to diminish that hostility by explaining the peculiarities of each to the other. At least I hope so.

The question arose as to whether I should move to Germany when I had finished schooling. A further complicating factor was that at the time I was considering becoming ordained. Werner wrote to me on 11 October 1955:

> I suggested to your grandparents that it might be best if you went to a German university straight after school. It would give you a chance of testing your plan to become a priest, that is of seeing the whole question of a spiritual vocation, from outside the English orbit. I am very keen for this to happen since I abhor the idea of a national church and think it alien to the New Testament. To look at this from Germany might give you a truer picture than you could otherwise obtain on which to base such a tremendous decision. Furthermore, you would lose a bit of that conventional or rather conformist, slightly uncritical attitude of mind of which I think you are in danger. Never forget that doubt is the father of all progress and that doubt is also the thing with which you would be concerned if you became a clergyman. You must learn to understand doubt; you would do that in Germany more than you would in England.

He suggested that a year or two at a German university might be a good idea and asked for my views. He added in a letter of 19 October 1955:

> All I want is that you should take every opportunity to learn where the dividing line is to be drawn between the teaching

of Christ and the forms in which we try to apply this teaching, and which might be in danger of taking over the substance if we do not constantly watch what we and others are doing. If your conception of faith passes the test of what you will be asked to question and to answer in terms of German theological thought, then all is well, but you should consider it an advantage to be able to apply this test.

I showed Werner's letters to the chief master and another master whom Werner knew and asked for their views. They had suggested that I might leave school at the end of the winter term and go to a German university for the next few months. This in effect is what I agreed to do. I wrote to Werner:

I do genuinely feel that it is my vocation to be a priest; and that means for me to be a priest in the Church of England. If one believes that no one church has the monopoly of truth, and that is my position at the moment, it does not greatly matter what church one joins. All my attachments are to Anglicanism, and I can see nothing to be gained by leaving this church for another which is equally fallible. This will not – I hope – sound pompous or unjustifiably sanguine; I do see many faults in the Church of England and am consequently in a position to do something about them.

On 12 November 1955 Werner replied to me in a long letter in which he refers to my desire to belong. He wrote:

I feel that this feeling of wanting to belong, of conforming with what the others do, is a very good thing, especially in your case, where life has denied you the companionship and support of your parents at such an early age. But I cannot help feeling that it is in danger of becoming a weakness, or narrowness in your spiritual make-up which it would be well to guard against. I would very much like you to 'feel out of place' for a while and to see how you fare without that strong backing which you are able to get from the English way of life.

He went on to urge me genuinely to give Germany a proper try for two years. I showed this letter to my chief master Ronald Lunt, who on 21 November 1955 wrote a long letter to Werner about it.

I do agree with you that at some stage in life one wants a boy who is going to be a strong character, to stand on his own feet, to make his own way, to feel out of it. But I do rather doubt whether eighteen is the right age for the cold douche. It is a time when personality in a favourable environment comes to flower. To transplant a boy like Konrad at just that age seems to me a very great risk. What I mean is, not that he will come to any very great harm, but that he might become a meagre person instead of a big one. I have known so many boys, whose training has been deliberately a mixed one, who have come to the end of it not really knowing whether they are on their head or their heels – half-baked in fact, and not at home in either of the environments … Konrad's position is an extremely difficult one. He looks like being on the way to success in England. The position is much less clear in Germany.

Werner replied:

I agree … that his chances of becoming all that is in him to be are much greater in England, where he has been educated, than they could be in Germany. It is chiefly because of his choice of profession that I have my doubts. I believe he is probably very much impressed by what he sees in you, and that he immensely underrates the questions which a man must have found and answered in himself before he can undertake to become a priest.

He may have the ability, if properly developed, to become an important chap in life, but I should be horrified if he thought of becoming a priest with this ideal in mind. He does not, I think, realise that importance in life, such as he sees in his chief master, is in some sense a duty, but not, for a priest, a purpose to achieve.

We all discussed the matter over Christmas, and it was decided that I should go to Freiburg for the next few months and that one could decide in the summer whether or not to embark on English military service. This implied leaving Martin, whom I regarded as a brother, behind in Birmingham on his own during term time to finish his schooling. I don't recall feeling that this parting was painful for either of us at the time. We corresponded regularly whilst I was in Freiburg and in the army.

Now, looking back on my life, I see that Werner was right to say that I was inclined to fit in with what was going on around me. I have never had any strong personal ambition, and all the interesting things which have happened to me in my life, with the exception of my marriage, have been because someone else suggested that I might do this or that.

I do not claim this as an admirable trait, but it is one which has contributed a lot to my continuing happiness and thankfulness for my lot. The advantage of not setting oneself any great aims is that one is not haunted by a failure to achieve them.

## Freiburg University

In January 1956, Werner took me to his old university. On its main building there was inscribed the phrase from St John's Gospel: 'The Truth Shall Make You Free'. Werner pointed out that the Nazis had caused this text to be removed but that it had been restored after the war. He found a large furnished room for me with a huge tiled stove. But that was the limit of what was provided. It was no hardship, but if I wished to have a bath I had to go to the public baths. I could cook bacon and bananas in the room on an electric ring or eat herring salad or go and eat at the university canteen, called the Mensa Academica, which served food on plates divided into three parts, for potatoes, another vegetable and stew of some sort. Fortunately, my gastronomic standards were not too exacting.

Werner introduced me to a *Verbindung* (a student fraternity), the Albingia-Schwarzwald-Zähringia, which was the result of a fusion of my father's old *Verbindung* and Werner's. It was a fraternity of about twenty people which had a house in Freiburg and a hut in the Black Forest.

These fraternities had been an important part of student life since the nineteenth century and had campaigned for the creation of what became the Second Reich in the 1870s. In many of them a very formalised form of duelling with swords was practised so as to encourage fearlessness. Werner said to me that one of the few sensible things Hitler had done was to make duelling illegal. After the war it nevertheless went on but became increasingly unfashionable. I recollect being at High Mass in Heidelberg when students from a duelling

*KS in Freiburg in 1956*

fraternity clad in their distinctive uniforms processed to the altar with their flags. At the time of the elevation of the Host they unsheathed their swords with a flourish. It was all rather strange to me.

The Albingia had been a duelling fraternity, but the Zähringia had never duelled. The fused fraternity did not duel, was very welcoming and invited me to various meals and celebrations. As an outsider I was a guest, and each of the members in turn proposed a welcome toast to me. This led me to drink what I discovered on retiring to bed was too much beer. Fortunately I behaved myself and was regularly invited again. Students before 1968 addressed one another as *Sie* until, over a drink, they agreed to call one another the more familiar *Du*, an honour which was extended to me by a few. The proceedings were altogether pretty formal, a good preparation for an officers' mess and life at the Bar in the 1960s.

One day, I received out of the blue an invitation to a fancy-dress ball from a lady whose name was completely unknown to me. I wondered what on earth this could mean and made discreet inquiries. It turned out that one of the functions of the *Verbindung* was to teach its members how to behave with ladies and that there was a sister *Verbindung* with corresponding aims. Each sought to help the other. I was hopelessly out of my depth, having grown up with four younger brothers and no sisters and with no girls at school. I put on a mask with a black face which, since I had blond hair, I thought was amusing. Not a good idea. Not because of any fear of causing offence, which did not occur to me, but because it was made of rubber. As a result, I sweated profusely, in part because of unease with girls and lack of dancing skills and in part because of the rubber and being in a crowded room. The evening was not a success, for me at any rate.

## Further encounters with administrators

At the time when I was required to prove that I had not been a Nazi at the end of the war I was too young even to know about this. However, the old spirit was still well entrenched in the bureaucracy when I first arrived in Freiburg. I was told that I had to register with the police. This I attempted to do and, after waiting a long time in a queue, was handed a lengthy form in triplicate to fill in. I was told to go home and return when I had done so. So I filled it in and stated (truthfully) that I had both German and British nationality. In the spirit of the German bureaucracy of the time the following conversation took place.

'That's impossible.'

'It is possible. I am a living example of a dual national.'

'No, it's impossible.'

'Very well. You can see that I am British. We'll leave it at that. Here is my British passport.'

'But why did you say you were German?'

'Because I am and I wished to tell the truth.'

At this point I was irritated and bored and proceeded to cross out the reference to my German nationality on the form.

'Problem solved.'

'No. That is not allowed. You must fill in a new form.'

I was handed a new blank form in triplicate and, very cross, went back to my room and filled it in. I placed carbon paper between the sheets and duly filled in the top copy, signed it, returned to the police station, waited in the queue and fortunately landed in front of a different officer. I duly presented my handiwork which he diligently read. After what I thought a promising start he found a flaw in the copies:

'You have used carbon paper.'

'Yes. Is that wrong?'

'No, not in principle. But your signature must be the original and not a carbon copy.'

I leant forward and signed the two carbon copies.

'That's not allowed. You cannot have two signatures over one another,' he said as he handed me yet another blank form in triplicate. I left but this time did not return. No one ever chased me for non-registration.

I ran into similar problems when trying to register as a *Gasthörer* or guest auditor at the university but I had lost heart. No one kept me from attending whatever lectures I wanted. But such limited enthusiasm as I then had for returning permanently to the land of my fathers was not fanned into life by this experience.

At the university I went to a lecture by Martin Heidegger, whom I knew to be a famous philosopher. However, I fear that he did not carry me with him. I failed to understand what the question was which he was trying to answer, let alone what he thought the answer was. I asked my neighbour who had been there during November and December to help, but he said he had no idea either.

'So why do you continue to go to the course?'

'Well, he is a very famous man, and one has to hear him.'

True, no doubt, but Heidegger's words required more intellectual concentration than I was prepared to give them, and so I left his lectures. I learnt later from Werner, who had been at Freiburg whilst Heidegger was rector of the University, that the rector had been an enthusiastic Nazi and had marched the professors up and down the streets. I doubt whether this justified my lack of effort but it left me less regretful of my idleness.

In the Easter vac my erstwhile chief master came over with half a dozen prefects to go on a walking tour in the Black Forest which he had asked me to arrange. We had a very good time, and I have happy memories of picnics with a bottle of wine which had cooled in a fast-flowing stream. We slept in youth hostels.

Apart from Heidegger I went to lectures on musical composition, history, art appreciation, mediaeval manuscripts and a variety of odd subjects. That was the joy of not having to pass an exam at the end of term. It was then the custom to require students to obtain from each of their lecturers a certificate that they had duly attended the lecture. I was excused this. Werner told me that when he was there and asked his professor for such a certificate he was met with the following words:

'But I have no recollection of ever seeing you at one of my lectures.'

'Really? You must be thinking of my twin brother.'

'Oh, I am so sorry.'

The certificate was duly signed. Werner told me that he had indeed skipped the lot because he preferred to accompany a girl who was studying medicine to her lectures.

I left Freiburg in the summer with many happy memories both of the town and of the Black Forest. I have returned there many times since and observed that it is one of the select towns which look better than they did in the 1950s.

# XI

# *The British Army*

## Training

By the summer of 1956 I had come to the conclusion that it would be best if I did my national service straightaway with the British army and so sent in my name. I got back a letter explaining that since I had dual nationality I could put off doing this until I reached my majority at twenty-one, when I could choose between the British and the German armies. I replied that I wanted to serve straightaway with the British army. Back came: 'We have received a letter purporting to come from you stating that you <u>want</u> to do national service. Please confirm.' I did and a month later made my way to the King's Shropshire Light Infantry Copthorne Barracks in Shrewsbury.

Wishing to make a good impression, I went first to a hairdresser in order to present myself with short hair. This was a mistake. When I entered the barracks, they immediately put me in a queue for the regimental barber, who gave me a second haircut of regulation length. I was then put in another queue at the end of which was a sergeant who wished me to sign various documents including one which stated that I had no intention of contravening the Official Secrets Act. I said that I was sorry but I had never read this Act and so could not conscientiously sign until I had. The sergeant used various expletives of whose very existence I had until then been unaware, and an officer was fetched. He appeared with the Act, which seemed to me (wrongly as I now know) easy to understand and which I had not the slightest intention of contravening. So I duly signed and was then put at the back of the barber's queue and had my hair shorn for a third time, to teach me a lesson perhaps. A bad start.

The next task was to learn the names and ways to address various officers who were in charge at the barracks. Our company was headed by Simon Raven, who became well known for his picaresque novels and himself led a colourful life.[55] We were lined up in front of a sergeant:

'What is the name of the company commander?'

'Major Raven, sergeant,' I replied full of confidence.

'Any decorations?'

'No, sergeant.'

'Yes he has. MA.'

I was learning fast and kept any riposte about the distinction between an MC and an MA to myself.

In the first fortnight potential officers were weeded out – quite how was not clear to me, but I suspected it was just by looking at their bearing, listening to their accents, and how they put sentences together. But there was a form to fill in. One had to be able to write one's name, and a kindly sergeant who looked over my shoulder thought that I had not done myself justice.

---

[55] It was widely reported later that when asked by his wife for money he had replied by telegram, 'Sorry, no money. Suggest eat baby.'

'Have you looked this through?'

'Yes, sergeant.'

'Your name?'

'Yes.'

'Two *ns*? Are you sure?'

'Yes, sergeant.'

In any event I was sent to Strensall Camp in Yorkshire for people preparing for the War Office Selection Board, known by its acronym WOSB, which determined who should be sent for further officer training.

On the first day there, a sergeant asked whether anyone played the piano, and I had sufficient self-confidence to put my hand up.

'Good. I want you to clean the toilets every day.'

Humorous in its way I suppose. There were those who said that in the army one should never volunteer.

After three months all the rest of my squad were sent off to spend a couple of days at WOSB. It was the Board's task to discover potential officer material. I, however, was detailed to remain behind on washing-up duties. I recall putting 600 plates covered with the remains of eggs and bacon through the washing-up tunnel, where they were subjected to boiling hot water. In principle an excellent system but I, fulfilling what had been said of me as an eight-year-old, put all the plates in the wrong way up with the result that egg and bacon were baked onto each plate and I spent the next three hours hacking them off with a knife. I gather that I have inherited my incompetence, which persists to this day, from my father.

I asked why I was not being sent to WOSB and was told that my papers had gone astray. I wrote sadly to my erstwhile chief master describing the situation. He, a wartime MC, had friends in the War Office and contacted them. They explained that they were trying to find out what on earth this German was trying to do getting into the British army. He gave them my background, assured them that I was sound, my papers were found, and I too was sent off to WOSB.

This consisted of a couple of days of questionings and exercises. I recollect being asked to talk for two minutes on matches. I suspected that football matches were meant but, never having been to one, I talked with some fluency about the joys attendant upon lighting a cigarette. I was then told to get six of my colleagues across a stream and informed that I could use anything which was lying around for the purpose of cantilevering and so on – a barrel, a plank, ropes and various other bits and pieces. This was just the sort of thing which had the potential to exhibit my innate incompetence. I looked at the stream and asked the others to leap across, thus avoiding using any of the equipment. They leapt and landed safely. Rather anxiously I asked the officer in charge whether that would do. To my relief he replied in the affirmative and explained to us all that we should never make a task more complicated than it needed to be. On this slender evidence of military ability I was sent to Eaton Hall in Cheshire as an officer cadet.

I then spent three months there under the watchful eye of three regimental sergeant majors from Guards regiments with the disturbing names of Blood, Leach and Lynch, who were enormous both in appearance and sound and each of whom wielded an impressive pace stick. I think it was one of them who told us on our first day: 'You call me Sir, and I call you Sir. The difference is you mean it.'[56]

At one stage we were sent off for three days and nights on an exercise near Trawsfynydd in Wales, at the end of which we had to march back to camp. For the last mile we were accompanied by

---

[56] I read an obituary of one of them which recounted that he had addressed King Hussein of Jordan on parade with the reprimand, 'You are an idle king, Sir'.

a military band. We were completely exhausted but discovered, as so many soldiers had discovered before, how the sound of a band cheers one up.

One evening an officer cadet in my barrack room had drunk too much and was becoming a nuisance. An Enniskillen Fusilier gave him a straight punch to the jaw, which knocked him out. Then he carefully picked him up and laid him on his bed saying, 'It's much the best thing to do. He'll be fine tomorrow.' Indeed he was.

From time to time, we were put on to patrolling round the outside wire of the camp so as to give warning of any IRA activities, of which at the time, so far as I knew, there had been no sign. I fear that I tended to disappear to the chapel, which was warm and where one could read. Fortunately, this misdemeanour was never discovered.

On one occasion we were sent into the hills on a wet and windy day on a map-reading exercise which consisted of going to various reference points and recording what one could see from there. A friend and I decided that it would be more agreeable to go instead to a pub and look at the map and work out what we would be able to see and report that. This we did, apparently successfully. We suddenly saw a subaltern who had come in for a pint. He gave no signs of recognising us, and so all appeared well. The day before we were commissioned he mentioned to me that he had indeed noticed us there but thought that we were displaying drive and initiative and did nothing about it save to check the competence of our reporting – I suppose by looking at the map and the reports of other, more conscientious, cadets. Fortunately, the matter never officially came to light.

So it was that I, wearing Ronald Lunt's Sam Browne belt, emerged a subaltern and was thus more fortunate than a young friend of mine who on the night before his commissioning slipped off to London, was caught and was denied his commission.

I had been asked whether I had any special knowledge which might be of use to the army and told them that I spoke German. But it was apparently thought that I was not the right person to be sent to Germany, and to my delight I was sent to Cyprus. I travelled on a troopship which was pretty agreeable, at any event for the British soldiers. My only duty was to start each day by inspecting 300 feet to see whether any of them were infected. So far as I could see they were not.

## Cyprus

I recollect being welcomed to Cyprus in the officers' mess of the Lancashire Fusiliers by being wrapped inside a very dusty carpet and stood up against a wall. I thought I was dying and have been claustrophobic ever since.

We lived in tents when in camp. Officers had one each, and they were fairly basic, hot in summer and cold in winter. Peter Simor, a subaltern in the Intelligence Corps who was stationed with us, showed that he had not been put in that corps by accident. He built sandbag walls for the lower part of his tent. He installed a large pottery jar of water of which the ancient Athenians would have been proud. It even had a tap. There was a carpet on the floor and, I rather think, a couple of icons on a shelf. He was free of regimental discipline and led, it seemed to me, a charmed life mixing with the Cypriots. He even had a boat at his disposal onto which he invited me once to go on patrol. While standing on the shore clad in uniform and a pistol at my belt, I placed a foot on his boat and transferred my weight. The boat shot off into the distance. I, legs akimbo, fell into the water with much loss of face and dignity. It was not his fault, and he and his wife became friends for life. I have never been able to match his sense of originality, style and ability to get things done.

Cyprus at the time was a British colony in the midst of strife between the Greek and Turkish communities. Following Peter's example, I accepted a few invitations by villagers to have a meal with them, which I much enjoyed. My smattering of ancient Greek impressed them more than it had impressed my schoolmasters.

I now realise that accepting such invitations was not wise and contrary to orders, particularly since I was wearing a pistol. Fortunately, nothing untoward happened. Nevertheless, on one occasion my host's aged and toothless father, after a few glasses of brandy, raised one to me and toasted 'Zeto EOKA' (Long live EOKA, an organisation regarded as being responsible for the deaths of several officers). The rest of the family hushed him, and I pretended not to have noticed, and we parted amicably.

We spent much time on the hills looking out for things suspicious and sleeping in very small bivouac tents. One night I suddenly woke up to find someone licking my face. I had no idea that I had aroused such emotions and kept my eyes shut while I pondered on how to react to an amorous soldier. There had been no mention of this possible challenge during training. Then the licking stopped. There was some movement against my sleeping bag, which then stopped. I slowly opened my eyes to see a goat leaving the tent. Never have I been so relieved.

Those Greek-speaking Cypriots who favoured independence had a habit of writing slogans in Greek such as 'English go home' on the walls, and it was official policy that we should force the villagers to wipe these slogans out so as to discourage the painting of further slogans. One of the villagers, with a sense of humour and a knowledge of the linguistic barrenness of the average British army officer, painted 'Drink our coffee' outside his shop. As he had foreseen, an officer unwisely forced the villagers out of bed at gunpoint to wipe out this evidence of Greek sedition. The next day the local wireless and press was full of people poking fun at the British. I was fool enough to say in the mess that really officers ought to acquire at least the rudiments of the language of a country in which they were stationed. I got my reward. For the next few months I was regularly woken up to decipher and check slogans for signs of sedition.

Some Greek Cypriot men, when they were not writing slogans, used to gather in the squares with women and children carefully placed in front of them and throw stones at soldiers. We drew the line at charging the women and children and sought to disperse the crowd by throwing gas bombs. This was reasonably effective but could not be done unless one was wearing a mask, which was fearfully hot in summer.

A platoon was regularly sent to a tin mine which needed explosives in order to carry out its mining. The function of the army was to protect the mine against an attack by terrorists wishing to remove the explosives. The orders stated that the platoon commander was to be present at every distribution of the explosives to the miners. This distribution took place every six hours, day and night. We were there for a fortnight at a time and I, following what I believed was common practice, took turns with my sergeant to be present at the distribution, which was carried out by the police.

One day the senior policeman told me that sixty sticks of dynamite had gone missing. I had been fast asleep at the last distribution, which had been attended by my sergeant. There had been no raid. Neither the policeman nor my sergeant knew how the dynamite had gone. I said I had to report this to my colonel. The policeman's reaction was full of foresight.

'For heaven's sake, don't. There will be the most frightful fuss.'

However, I did, and there was. I was summoned to the colonel, who gave me a fearful dressing down, confined me to my tent, told me to hand over my sword and said he would seek the brigadier's consent to my court martial. I had not been conscious of any wrongdoing and felt very sorry for myself. The kindly adjutant dropped in on the way to the brigadier and told me not to worry. He did not think that I would be court-martialled. In the event I was not but was given extra duties instead.

It was, I suppose, quite a useful discipline for a future judge to experience, if only for a day, the loss of liberty and what it feels like if you consider yourself unjustly imprisoned.

As a judge I was always aware of the fact that, by reason of the errors committed in all human endeavour, a proportion of prisoners, small one hopes, had in all probability been convicted of offences which they had not in fact committed. I became particularly conscious of this when on the Parole Board, whose function it was to decide which prisoners were suitable for early release. We were helped by guidelines, one of which stated that people convicted of sex offences were not to be given parole unless they had been through a sex re-education programme. One prisoner claimed that he, a teacher I think, had been wrongly convicted in that he had not had any sexual contact whatsoever with the complainant boy, who must have acted out of spite or for psychological reasons of his own. The prisoner wrote that he could accept being wrongly convicted but he was not prepared to have his psyche interfered with in order to sort out sex problems which he did not have. I, and others I suppose, tried to get the guidelines changed. The genuine problem is that clearly the Parole Board should not attempt to criticise the trial process. That was the Court of Appeal's function. However, the guidance has, I believe, now been made less rigid.

Because I was vice chairman of the Parole Board I was sent by the Home Office some draft guidance for comment. The guidance stated, 'The Parole Board shall carry out its duties with no discrimination.' I wrote back that I had always done the contrary by trying to discriminate between those who should be granted parole and those who should not. I supposed that they intended us not to discriminate on some grounds. If so, could they identify these. I cannot recollect the reply. So far as I know, the Parole Board is still instructed to decide cases without discrimination but, I believe, on various listed grounds.

I return to the army and the dynamite. I met the policeman a couple of months later, and he asked me what had happened. I told him.

'I am so sorry! The fact is we miscounted and there was no dynamite missing. I should have told you.'

I mentioned this in the mess to the colonel, and he pointed out that the presence of the dynamite was immaterial: I had not been charged with losing dynamite but with disobeying instructions to be there every time it was handed out. A fair point, I suppose.

One of the tasks I had to do in Cyprus was to take my platoon to keep order in a camp where people who were suspected of being terrorists were kept. Again, I suppose some were terrorists as seen by us and others were not. Some were quite distinguished academics. It was very hot. The detainees were ill-tempered and, as happened in Northern Ireland later, there were dirty protests which involved smearing faecal matter all over the windows. We were supposed to get the prisoners to clean the place up. There I observed how perfectly decent people can start holding others in contempt and disgust. I remember talking to my soldiers of the concentration camps and what this could lead to. I wrote of this to Werner, who replied:

The stories or reported stories about the treatment of EOKA people are grave, because nothing is so bad for people's characters as when they're given a free hand to ill-treat others: it is the beginning of the disregard for human dignity which leads to concentration camps. No behaviour of the EOKA can justify it, if only for the reason that it is the <u>doer</u> of a brutal act who suffers, often irretrievably: he learns to forgive himself things which a decent man does not forgive himself. Whenever you have any say in such matters I would strongly advise you to think of the fact that you will remember in later life everything you have done, and that you would be wise to see to it that many are pleasant memories and not shameful ones.

The adoption of this mindset led to my reaction to a phrase which was doing the rounds at that time. The leader of the rebels on the island was a Colonel Grivas, and one heard it said that he was to be shot while escaping. I ventured in the mess that I thought that this was what Nuremberg had been about. I must have been an irritating companion. I seem to remember that one of my reports shown to me to countersign said 'This officer is too intense,' or some such adjective.

I tried to give a snapshot of army life in Cyprus in 1958 in a letter to Kathleen:

In the last four days my platoon has had about eighteen hours' sleep and has spent the rest of the time patrolling or sitting on trucks or in some gutter. Sooner or later – and I say this in deadly seriousness – one of them will go berserk and fire off a burst of machine-gun fire. Already when the

Greeks spit at us I can feel the tension rising. The men are really splendid – they grumble like hell and use the most vile language, but good humour keeps making itself felt. They still have enough energy to whistle at the pretty girls and to enjoy chasing a car and playing – in effect – a form of Cowboys and Indians. I am afraid that many a civilian gets the shock of his life to find one roaring past him at 50 mph – which if you are driving on a goat track is quite something – and screeching to a halt in front of him and taking his car to pieces in the hope of finding a weapon.

Yesterday we came across a particularly hideous murder of a Greek farmer and his wife who were aged about seventy. They had been told by their neighbours to move or else. They packed all their house and home on to a donkey. 50 yards away from their home they all but had their heads removed. This is a frightful life. It is as though the island were peopled only by murderers and assassins.

Yet at the same time this sort of thing can happen. Two nights ago I spent two hours talking to the 'Turkish Home Guard' in Ormophita village. While he brought me coffee, we discussed his fears and hopes in the most friendly fashion. He – who may well have done someone to death – was a charming fellow. Yet he told me – quite *en passant* – that of course he was always pleased when the Greeks murdered an Englishman because that meant that we would sooner or later shoot some Greeks. This is typical of the ruthless emotional thinking that goes on here. Things have now got to such a stage that a Greek will kill another Greek whom he does not know so that the Turks will get into trouble.

In another letter to her I wrote:

> ... my sergeant's mother is dying and he has been sent on compas-
> sionate leave to England, leaving his wife and child behind him.
> I have been looking after her, and it really is amazing how
> these people confide in one. She very much wishes to return
> to England in order to show her child to its grandmother. This
> raised umpteen difficulties which one tried to sort out.
>
> The other case is more complicated. A soldier suddenly
> drank too much and went into Nicosia, which was out of
> bounds, and into what is politely called a house of ill fame. He
> has been apprehended, and I now find myself explaining the
> situation to his wife, who is out here.
>
> Another fusilier has got his girlfriend in the family way
> in England and now wishes to get on and marry her. This is a
> recognised way of getting back home for a leave – which will
> give you an insight into the rather strange moral values which
> these men have. All this sort of thing changes one rather.

As must by now be obvious, I was not cut out for military life.
One day, however, my moment arrived. It was thought that Grivas
had hidden in an area of the Troodos Mountains, and a huge operation was mounted to catch him. The aim was to surround the whole
area with a ring of soldiers, many of whom were dropped by heli-
copter. The rest came on foot and by vehicle. The plan was to get an
outer ring in place in broad daylight so that Grivas and his compan-
ions would find escape impossible. The ring was indeed put in place,
and my platoon was part of it. On this occasion we were operating
on a no-challenge basis, which meant that you were supposed to
shoot on sight.

A few ambush parties, one of which consisted of me and ten of my men, had been told to move towards the centre of the encircled area, form part of an inner ring and find a place to settle down. It was accepted that Grivas would realise this was going on and probably stay still. The plan did not stop there, however. Each commander of an ambush party had been instructed that at about 02.00 he was to send the majority of his party back to the outer ring while remaining behind with a couple of others. The theory was that Grivas would hear people going back, think that this was the lot, and that he could move around freely. The plan was that, when he did, those who had been left behind would have a chance of shooting or capturing him. Strict wireless silence was to be observed.

At about 22.00 I told those who were going to be sent back later that they should keep their eyes open and that we remainers would have some shuteye until they woke us at 02.00. This we did, and in due course a hand was gently laid on my shoulder. I was sleeping on my automatic and opened my eyes. There were two eyes staring at me – obviously Grivas. I immediately started shooting. A startled rabbit limped away. At this point the whole forest echoed with automatics firing. Everyone thought they saw a terrorist in the shadows cast by the moon. Any element of surprise had been totally lost. With some embarrassment I broke wireless silence and contacted headquarters and explained what had happened. I was told to report for debriefing. I vainly tried to say that this was pointless. The brigadier was terse, and it was obvious that decorations for gallantry were not coming my way. I had to comfort myself with a General Service Medal, which even the incompetent could receive.

The colonel was forgiving enough to suggest that I might apply for a permanent commission in the army, but I realised my limitations and returned to the Rectory in Wem. I described my arrival there in an article I wrote for *Wooster Sauce*, a magazine for enthusiasts of P. G. Wodehouse.

Before I turn to life at Cambridge in the 1950s, I should describe my erstwhile chief master, who had been corresponding with me throughout my time in the army.

# XII

# *Two Mentors*

## The Rev. R. G. Lunt,
## Chief Master of King Edward's School

Ronald Lunt, who had written to Werner about my future, joined
us in Interlaken for Easter 1956 with his wife Veslemöy, and they
became friends of the family. Ronald and I became increasingly
close to one another as he guided me through various intellectual
and spiritual conundrums. I have many of the letters which he wrote
to me at the time, and a few extracts will give an impression of the
time, energy and affection he was prepared to give to his ex charges.
I will cite a few to give the flavour, as it were, of our friendship and
of the problems on which I sought his advice.

On 25 April 1956 he wrote a letter which echoed very closely the
thought processes of those on the German side during the war such
as my aunt Marianne.

I wonder about personal responsibility; of course we cannot plead as was pleaded after the War the excuse of Higher Orders for our crimes. But I cannot think that the soldier who kills a man he does not know in the course of his soldiering is responsible before God for a breach of the Sixth Commandment. As with everything else the decision and the responsibility lie further back. I joined the army because it was my duty as a member of the people it pleased God to make me a member of. I cannot contract out of that. I am sent about a beastly task – it might have been another but it happens to be I. If not I then another, equally innocent and unbloodthirsty, must do it for me, for my protection. It happens to be I in the course of my duty. The concept of a just war seems to me to be relevant. We undertake bloodshed to save others for whom we are responsible from having their blood shed. There is something worse than war, and that we have learned is slavery. The soldier who pulls the trigger or the airman who releases the bomb is no more and no less responsible for murder than the man who made the aircraft or the man who paid his income tax to see that the war was successfully carried on.

As with every other social situation we are all in this together. We are responsible for the personal witness that each of us shows but the situation in which we show it is always a sinful one, so that perfectionism is an illusion. For me to abstain from killing because I must love my brother but leave it to my neighbour to do the dirty work seems to me moral cowardice. When I say 'I' I mean not I as a priest but I as a chap who has to settle this appallingly difficult moral decision in his own life. For the true pacifist I have a high regard but I think he must go the whole hog. For the man who says, 'It is not to my taste to kill,' but otherwise accepts membership of the community and draws his rations and so on – well, for his logic I have scant respect. I think he is shirking the real issue and casting the load onto his brother's shoulders.

All of us bear a share of the responsibility; to come right down to brass tacks, even I for the death of your father. And that I cannot escape, though in my job I did not, save on one occasion, bear arms in the conflict. At the same time your father had his share of the responsibility for the gassing of the Jews and the horrors of the concentration camps. The sin of Hitlerism was worked out in untold misery throughout the community he infected, in Europe and America and other parts of the world too. Yet he alone was not totally responsible for it: we too did our bit to bring about a situation in which such sins could run riot – not I think by what we did but by what we smugly failed to do.

And now I have come so close and deep to these terrible and frightening choices, let me send to you herewith one of the treasures from my Commonplace Book that lifts one right up from beastliness. A letter from an English airman to the mother of a young German whom he had shot down over the British lines. 'I know you can't forgive me, for I killed him. But I want you to know he didn't suffer. The end came very quickly. He had your photograph in his pocket. I am sending it back, though I should like to keep it. I suppose I am his enemy, though I do not feel so at all. I'd give my life to have him back. I did not think of him or you when I shot at his machine. He was an enemy spying on our men. I could not let him get back to tell the news. It would have meant death to our men.

'I know you must have loved him. My mother died when I was quite a little boy; but I know what she would have felt if

I had been killed. War is not fair to women. God! How I wish it were over. I feel if I just touched your boy he would wake and we would be friends. I know his body must be dear to you. I will take care of him and mark his grave. After the war you may want to take him home.

'My heart is very heavy. I felt it was my duty.'

And here is the German mother's reply:

There is nothing to forgive. I see you as you are in your troubled goodness. I feel you coming to me like a little boy astounded at having done ill when you meant well. I am glad your hand cares for my boy. I had rather you than any other touched his earthly body and laid him to rest. He was my youngest. I think you realised his fineness.

I know the tortures of your heart since you have slain him. To women brotherhood is a reality, for all men are our sons. That makes war a monster, that brother may slay brother. Yet perhaps women more than men have been to blame for this world war. We did not think of the world's children as our children. The baby hands that clutched our breasts were so sweet, we forgot the hundred other baby hands that stretched out to us. And now my heart aches with repentance.

When this war is over come to me. I am waiting for you.

On 18 October 1956 Ronald wrote:

Yesterday I came across two things that I wanted to send to you. They bring to you my love. The George Eliot one describing what you have done for me and what I have found to be true from time to glorious time in my life ever since I first went up to Oxford. It was Oxford, much, much more than school, that gave me experience of friendship … and then messes and slit trenches and voyages and situations of war – and all have served to fill out what George Eliot puts so tellingly and straight and simply. And the Clive Bell passage is [a] good point, a bit savage perhaps, but an effective warning.

'Oh, the comfort, the inexpressible comfort of feeling safe with a person; having neither to weigh thoughts nor to measure words, but to pour them all out, just as they are, chaff and grain together, knowing that a faithful hand will take and sift them, keep what is worth keeping, and then, with the breath of kindness, blow the rest away.' George Eliot.

'Never to the overbearing and underbred are we tempted to betray our dearest secrets. That is why the cad, the bounder, the bully, the mistrustful wiseacre and the self-assertive super-man shove or slink through life without tasting it; all the contacts are one-sided: a man with hooks at the end of his arms can sometimes catch you by the ankle and bring you down, but he can never have the thrill of taking the pressure of a handshake.' Clive Bell, *Essay on Civilisation*.

On 29 August 1957 he wrote:

Ingrid [his daughter who was about ten at the time and became a very successful academic and remains a friend] was lamenting that you are so far distant, as we did the washing up together today, and was saying how she wished you could come every weekend, adding with some maturity and perception 'He is so much more than one of your boys, he is one of your best friends.'.

And on 8 November 1957:

Thank you so much for your letter and your counsel. Life is a bit difficult, as I said; and the trouble is that I am tempted to lose heart. Satan has it all ways: if he fails in tempting you to shirk and be lazy, then he lays off until the moment when you are physically worn down and at that moment delivers some dispiriting blow and tempts you to lose heart ... But I suppose that as always the fundamental thing is one's own state of spiritual health, and the knowledge that one has been a fool does not alas make one wise.

On 5 January 1958:

This Christmas I read Sir John Kennedy's book and in it came upon the enclosed quotation from Ruskin which I send you for your Commonplace Book. It certainly does not answer your problem but it puts it in a different light. I think we have got to keep very clear in all our thinking the distinction between evil and suffering. When we say that God is good we are too ready to introduce a wholly anthropomorphic calculus, and to equate good with felicific. Pain and suffering appear to have a value of their own in that they arouse sympathy, one of the finest of human feelings, they challenge courage, they teach us how to meet them and how to beat them. This sounds smug and so it would be if I suggested that it was the whole story: it is not.

About cancer – I wonder whether we have the right to call it 'an evil in life which is not due to man'. Only after centuries did they discover that typhus was not a visitation from God but a necessary sequel to wrong ways of living. I have often pondered upon the why of a mother's travail pains – horrible to witness; why must it be that this high price has to be paid for the renewal of life? Pain and suffering are the spin to humanity to be more human, and that is what I conceive progress to be. God showed in Christ (a) that it is <u>His</u> world (b) that he <u>does</u> care and that suffering is not a block upon His will, that in fact it is often His way and His will. Men – you and I – were designed to be made fit here for eternal companionship with Him thereafter.

I wonder whether we have a right to speak of 'the fantastic amount of suffering'; suffering has its great purgative effect. Even the hardest treated of us does not, I suppose, have true suffering for more than a tenth of his time on this planet. We may not actually be happy for the other nine-tenths but that is because of our self-pity, our envy, our failure to adapt ourselves to our lot. God must feel like a mother who is prepared to suffer agony 'for joy that a man is born into the world' and to slave for him, in his infant needs and through his period of growing away from her, and to find her ultimate purpose and happiness in just that.

Illness <u>is</u> a problem: much of it like economic crisis and poverty is ultimately not a person's fault but the fault of society of which he is a member. We are not judged for our own individual sins: remember Christ's words about the tower of Siloam. You must indeed think these things through and go through doubt if you are to be of any use as a Christian spokes-man. I do not at any rate in my more courageous moments envy the RC his retreat into someone else's assurance. I don't think it works unless you are prepared to hand over the liberty of judgement.

Ruskin writes in the *Crown of Wild Olives*:

'We talk of peace and learning, of peace and plenty, and of peace and civilisation; but I found that those were not the words which the Muse of History coupled together: that on her lips, the words were – peace and sensuality, peace and selfishness, peace and corruption, peace and death. I found, in brief, that all great nations learned their truth of word, and strength of thought, in war, that they were nourished in war, and wasted by peace; taught by war, and deceived by peace; trained by war, and betrayed by peace; in a word, that they were born in war, and expired in peace.'

When Ronald died in 1994, Veslemöy asked me to speak of him at his memorial service in Birmingham Cathedral. This I did gladly and in gratitude for the way he had given me the feeling that I was worth taking trouble over. Here is part of what I said:

His significance to the boys at King Edward's, of whom I was one, was that he treated them as persons with the capacity to choose between right and wrong, between working and being idle, between trying to think things through and repeating, parrot fashion, the current orthodoxy. In short you were treated as an adult. If you responded you were rewarded by a totally extraordinary degree of attention and affection. Equally if he knew of a boy who had been harshly treated by life or was in personal difficulties of one sort or another he would be prodigal with his time and care.

After leaving school, whilst in the army, I received a letter from him once a fortnight for months on end. School gossip, local and national politics, the problem of evil, the problem of pain, books to read, advice on how to deal with corporals and generals, various points of dogmatic theology, pacifism, quotations from his Commonplace Book and advice on all manner of matters. It is astonishing that he found time to write these sorts of letters to his pupils – I was not the only recipient. I know from the following years that he had a huge circle of friends to all of whom he wrote with care … What is astonishing is the degree to which this deliberately impressive man was prepared to reveal to one so much younger the vulnerable side of his personality which he kept from the world. It is the sharing of such confidences which gave strength and self-confidence to the younger man.

He wrote in one letter dated 20 April 1958: 'I agree with you very much in the feeling of acute discomfort when one tries to sort one's life with one's Christian profession: one does not do enough, one ought to be something different from what one is, in brief one ought to be better and holier – yes one ought. And then that feeling of ought is as painful as a toothache, and one seeks aspirin to be rid of it. One finds the anodyne in comparing oneself to other conveniently chosen people and giving oneself a pass mark. Or one says I ought but I know I cannot, therefore I will give up trying. Or one says – I know I do – if I fill the day to the brim, then I shall have done as much as I can and thus I can put thinking and introspection away; how many a priest falls into the trap of being busy just to keep his conscience, his longing for perfection asleep. Yet in the Bible it is usually the devil – in Job and the Parables, and the Epistle of Peter – who is represented as the busy one.

'I think that Protestantism has – to my mind wrongly – rather too much stressed the matter of feeling. I have at moments of crisis, searched, hoped and prayed for an inner conviction that I was acting as God would have me do, but no mystic experience has been mine, my search has been largely in vain – I see that I have wanted a special advantage, an aid not given to others, and therefore I have rightly not been given it. Yet I know that it is my job to respond to the highest when I see it … We say and say too glibly, but I think it is true, that of two ways open to one the way that is marked with a Cross – if either is – is more likely to be the Christian way, but before that one must have arrived, and I can only do this by quite cold and deliberate decision, at the certainty that one really wants to follow Christ. I do even though always it is jolly difficult to know how; just at the moment I'm always coming up against the little decisions over matters of my time … Am I right to spend a long time on writing to you, or ought I to be doing next year's timetable because my colleagues will soon be wanting details of it?'

As one on whom he spent what I fear was an undue proportion of his time, I can only say that I am hugely grateful. There must be many others in my position. At the time, as a self-centred adolescent, I took it for granted and never considered what was being sacrificed so that he could devote this amount of time and energy to us.

**The Rev. Meredith Dewey,
dean of Pembroke College, Cambridge**

With a sense of some excitement I made my way to Cambridge in October 1958. By this time, although still a regular churchgoer, I felt that I should not train for ordination, at any event not straightaway.

I had adopted the view, propounded to me by Werner, that I should not become a cleric unless all alternatives were inconceivable to my conscience. I felt that a whole world of choices lay before me and had an open mind as to which I should investigate further. At that time the idea that a Cambridge graduate who had held a commission would have difficulty in securing interesting and challenging employment simply never crossed the mind of any one whom I met, so far as I know.

Further, I had realised that, while I thought that taking services and preaching were things I might learn to do well, I simply did not love my fellow human beings sufficiently to feel that immersing myself in their problems would be fulfilling. Neither the dean nor the chaplain of the college, nor indeed Ronald Lunt, ever encouraged me to persist with my earlier desire for ordination. There were several potential ordinands in the college, some of whom were and have remained my friends. They too did not seek to impress on me that in any sense this was my duty. At the time I did not specifically notice this. Looking back on it now, it seems to me that they were wise and recognised my limitations. In any event I never subsequently seriously returned to the idea, although I remain a pretty regular churchgoer and read quite a number of theological books and articles.

As well as Ronald Lunt, another quiet influence on my life has been the Rev. Meredith Dewey, who was dean of Pembroke during my time there. The flavour of the man can be captured from the following extracts from a circular letter which he sent for Easter 1976 after his retirement.

Now that I go to hall less frequently I am more appreciative of all this luxury of dining in elegance and congenial company. On a highly polished medieval table decked with ancient plate, surrounded by portraits of college worthies gazing down at us across the centuries, is presented a sensible meal graciously served. When a silver ewer and basin has been passed round for ablutions, the company adjourns to the parlour for coffee and wine by candlelight, and agreeable conversation continues; moral issues of the day are discussed with levity and women and wine with gravity, both with urbanity and neither with acrimony ... Now each time I say to myself, 'Revel in this, it may not go on for ever.' What the war failed to destroy may well fail to survive the age of equality. Living on the edge of things, one is made conscious of all one's blessings and thankful for *la douceur de vivre* that remains. It is encouraging that there develops in the young a yearning to retain what is left and a regret for what is lost. I find their company agreeable and labours in the garden helpful, and all this adds to felicity ...

In the past decade waning religious practice coincided with waxing zeal for moral issues. Wrongs to be righted and abuses to be rectified prompted boycotts of S. African oranges, Greek colonels, and Barclays Bank among other evils ... At the moment a minority agitates for liberal guest hours – a genteel expression for sexual licence. The present generation is not all that more dissolute than its predecessors, but it is not helped by clever sillies who mistake indifference for tolerance and identify charity with acquiescence. Because the principle of one in a bed at a time cannot be enforced by penalty, it is assumed that the ideal of self-discipline and chastity is better abandoned. A delusion. Whatever their past performance or present practice there are still very few who do not revere the

Ideal, and respect those who stand by it, for demanding at least that homage of shame which keeps alight a spark of honour in disreputable habit and makes recovery possible. That old Victorian rectitude in these things is closer to humanity, closer to sanity then the false prophets, who deride it, allow. One can be aware of the relative validity of all such convictions yet still stand by them steadfastly and so save society from slipping into sluttery and thence by a short slither to a brutality.

I would go to his rooms, I think, nearly every week. I thought him a holy and good man, but in public he hid this under a sardonic way of talking designed to puncture the self-satisfied and the received truths of the *bien pensants*.

Anyhow, I and many others, including convinced atheists like my friend Hugh Mellor, whom I shall mention later, were very fond of him and shared some of his prejudices. As one who also has spent his adult life in a world in which I felt at ease and which treated me well I share his feeling that changing social habits have not necessarily made the world a better place or the individuals in it more fulfilled. However, I recognise that making me feel at ease can hardly be an organising principle for the world.

# XIII

# Cambridge

## Reading law

When the college accepted me, it had been thought that I would read either theology or history. By 1958 I had decided against immediate ordination, although I remained interested in both theology and history. I don't really know why I decided on law. In Germany, which had constituted my sole university experience, if you did not know what to study you read law, which was regarded as a useful discipline in a number of occupations. I rather suspect this was behind my choice. Werner neither encouraged or discouraged me. I am not sure even whether I asked him. He very much believed in letting the young plough their own furrow.

I remember in my first week being asked by my tutor Henry de Waal,[57] 'Do you want to go to any lectures? I never did. I thought

---

[57] In due course he became First Parliamentary Counsel. When I became a judge, he wrote to me: 'It is a melancholy reflection that, whereas I used to criticise your essays, now you will criticise my Acts.' A delightful man.

that those who had something to say would have put it in a book which one could read at leisure.' But he suggested some lectures outside the exam topics, and they were indeed most interesting. The lectures on the exam topics tended to be rather boring, I thought. One of the problems of doing law was that one had to learn the ABC of the subject because it had not been taught at school, and there was a lot of translation from Latin texts, mediaeval law and procedure and learning by rote of definitions, etc.

Another of my tutors was James Campbell, who was a great figure in the college because he concerned himself with the under-graduates – watching the rowing and rugby and playing bridge with them – rather than engaging in his own studies. He did not strike me as academic and, although he was always polite and friendly with me, I suspect that he thought I was a dull stick. Indeed, I must have irritated him. I recollect saying that I had had some difficulty with a passage in Gaius which he had asked us to translate. When I ventured a translation, he said it was fine. 'What is the problem?' I said I had seen half a dozen translations in the books and it seemed that there were some subtle distinctions between them and I was puzzled as to which was correct. He made it clear to me that this sort of detail was not for him and should not have been for me.

## A friend: Hugh Mellor

One of those with whom I became friends was Hugh Mellor. Hugh had one of the best undergraduate sets in college, E1, on the top floor in the oldest court. When I last looked it had been converted into two sets, but at the time it consisted of a large sitting-room/study with a high wooden ceiling, a small bedroom, and an ante-room in which one could do some primitive cooking. The sitting room was furnished with one or two bits of quite good Victorian furniture, and I was keen to take it over from him. Rooms were allocated by reference to a list in which those who had scholarships had priority. I was number six or so on that list, but Hugh discouraged those higher on the list by emphasising that the set suffered from various disadvantages. In any event, I secured it and lived happily there for two years.

The bedmaker who had been assigned to me to try and keep my rooms tidy was a lady with considerable dedication to her job. One day I returned after a morning lecture to find that all the books I had left out on the large gate-leg table had been placed on the floor in the same relationship to each other whilst she dusted the table. I was very touched and told her so. She told me that my job was reading and writing and hers was dusting, which involved placing things back as she had found them. She was a perfectionist.

I only once saw her perturbed. This was when she came into my sitting room at 8.25 in the morning to find a girl there while I was in my bedroom. On registering this, she disappeared. I nonchalantly mentioned to her afterwards that the girl in question had told me on the previous day that she wanted to meet a friend of mine. I had told the girl that he was breakfasting with me the next day and had suggested to her that she could come round to my room in the morning and join us. My bedmaker happily was prepared to believe, as was the case, that I was telling the truth.

Hugh studied chemical engineering at Cambridge, but his interests, which I shared, were the theatre and debating. He later became a professor at Cambridge and a distinguished philosopher. The flavour of the man can be gained from a talk he gave on BBC Radio 3.

Here is an extract from his talk on logic, which catches his conversational style:

When logic, that is, the validity of an argument, really is in question, laymen are apt to find logic as much of an irritant as a virtue. Often our pet assumptions lead logically to conclusions we don't like at all; and then we are apt to complain of the fact, rather as one might resent having either to pay for, or to return, one's favourite purchases.

Suppose I admit, for example, that 'justice' means treating people as they deserve, and that 'mercy' means treating them better than that. I still don't like the obvious conclusion that no one can be at once both just and merciful, since if people get just what they deserve they cannot also get more than that.

I take justice and mercy both to be virtues and, like Portia in the *Merchant of Venice*, would prefer to be able to combine them. When logic says I can't, the natural reaction is to disparage logic. That doesn't help, of course, any more than being rude to the rent collector lets one off the rent, though no doubt it relieves one's feelings.

But the rent still has to be paid; and I still have to face the real, hard, question, since mercy and justice are incompatible as I conceive them, whether it's better to be unjustly merciful or to be mercilessly just. Some will say that God at least is both just and merciful, being above mere human logic; but that's not a good move for a believer, since all it does is to provide premises for a valid argument that there is no God.

Anyway it wouldn't help the rest of us; and so we shuffle, we fudge, we extoll the virtues of illogicality, and generally decry the habit of pushing principles to their 'logical extremes'.

What laymen don't realise is that logic doesn't <u>produce</u> undesirable extremes, it only <u>uncovers</u> them. Every conclusion of a valid argument is already there in its premises; and whoever doesn't like such a conclusion still has to take it unless there is a premise he is prepared to give up. It's no use blaming logic for the fact that cakes can't be both eaten and still had.

A few years ago a contemporary of mine recalled a conversation one evening in my room in which someone said to me, 'The trouble with you, Konrad, is that you always think you are right,' and I had replied, 'Of course. If I thought I was wrong I would change my mind.' This betrays the influence of Hugh. Unfortunately it made my contemporary so cross that he crushed the wine glass which he had in his hand which then needed to be stitched up. It was not until later that it was borne in upon me that there are often more than two perspectives of reality and at times two apparently inconsistent propositions may both be true. Whether I am someone with what I believe Keats termed a negative capability or have simply been too idle to try and pin down thoughts is a judgement I leave to others.

## Undergraduate life

Financially I was in the fortunate position that I not only had a state and a college scholarship but also a German orphan's pension. None of these amounts was huge but added together they left me without financial worries and no indebtedness of any significance. Looking back on it, I clearly had reason to be grateful to the taxpayers of both countries. At the time it just seemed a given in life. It did, however, give me another chance to encounter bureaucracy.

Every year I was sent two forms by the German Ministry of Pensions, which I was supposed to get signed by my tutor. One of them certified that I was studying diligently, the other that I was still

alive. I obtained these but sent a covering letter stating that my innocent tutor had asked why two forms were necessary. He thought that a
certificate that I was studying diligently must have proceeded on the
premise that I was alive. I got a polite letter back patiently explaining
that under German law the Pensions Authority was responsible for
ensuring that pensions were only paid to the living. Moreover, his
Authority was not entitled to pay pensions to anyone at university
unless the Education Authority certified that it was satisfied that the
pensioner was studying diligently. The writer was minded to send
one of my two certificates to the Education Authority. He added
with some humour that if I wished myself to prepare two envelopes
and the appropriate covering letters to the two Authorities he would
happily send the certificates back to me. I thanked him, apologized
and begged him to stick to his original plan.

The British authorities posed a different problem. I had to
certify whether I had any other sources of income apart from the
scholarships. I replied that I had none apart from a small German
orphan's pension. This sufficed for three years, but in my fourth year
the file obviously went across the desk of someone in the fast stream
who asked me exactly *how* small the small pension was. When I told
him, he promptly reduced the state scholarship but still left me better
off than I would have been without it. Fortunately, he did not try and
recover any overpayment made in the three previous years.

So I was able to afford wine and wine glasses and ate my butter
with a butter knife – a fact remarked on as extraordinary by my daughter when she, a quarter of a century later, went up to Cambridge.
I think in my time it was unusual but by no means unique. I gave
it no thought.

One year I was invited by Christopher Long to go to a Commem
Ball at Balliol and of course accepted. He also sent a couple of ornate

stiff invitations to the Trinity Commem. In the bottom left-hand corner there was printed 'Bring Bird and Bottle'. Later I learned that the invitation was a joke by Balliol. Perhaps I should have guessed. The girl who went with me and I had a good time initially and indeed went to Trinity for half an hour without being stopped. There came a time in the early hours when both my companion and I felt that we had had enough, yet tradition demanded that we stay awake and go punting to a breakfast place.

This we duly did. Breakfast was enlivened for Christopher because, clad in white tie and tails and closely watched by a photographer from a television network, he fell into the river. He splashed across the Oxford screens during the following week. In due course I made my way back to Cambridge to see the exam results, which in those days were posted by the Senate House. On the way back to my rooms I met a Pembroke don who pointed out that I looked a bit glum and I explained that I had been up all night and had just looked at the exam results. When he said that at the Bar what class you had got was really of no importance, I countered by saying no doubt but that my self-esteem had suffered. 'Your self-esteem can take it,' he replied with a smile. In any event I have survived the absence of a first-class degree.

One of the side effects of becoming a lord justice thirty years later was that Pembroke made me an honorary fellow notwithstanding this academic *lacuna*. The fellowship, apart from a couple of talks, involves for me nothing more onerous than meeting other fellows and dining with them a couple of times a year, a duty I seek to fulfil conscientiously. I heard that on my appointment to the ECJ someone put up a sign by the Porters' Lodge announcing this fact. At the time I was pleased and, perhaps naively, assumed this was a gesture of approval rather than obloquy. After my appointment, however, I came across many people in England who felt a degree of hatred for the European Union which I found totally inexplicable. There were those who felt about my departure to Luxembourg in much the same way as my aunts had felt about my remaining in England, probably for much the same reasons.

Whilst at Cambridge I had already been astonished to find that among the undergraduates there was much more interest in what was happening in various parts of the Commonwealth, which they had never seen, than in what was happening on the mainland of Europe, which many had seen or foresaw visiting. I, already inspired by the idea of building a new Europe, tried to encourage others in the same direction and met with some initial, but not always an enduring, success.

I stayed on for a further degree – then known as an LLB (Bachelor of Laws) and now as the LLM (Master of Laws)[58] – and here the course was much more interesting and had a more international aspect. We discussed legal philosophy, administrative law and private international law. I enjoyed these subjects enormously. Legal philosophy was taught by Bryan King, who had studied in Vienna before the war and introduced us to Hohfeld and his fundamental legal conceptions. I enjoyed his teaching greatly, although others found it too abstract for their taste.

Private international law was taught by Kurt Lipstein, who had come over to Cambridge before 1939 and had spent part of the war interned on the Isle of Man. He told me that in the spring of 1940 he was cycling in Cambridge and that he was stopped by a fellow don who informed him that the police had orders to arrest him because

---

[58] Some years later the university wrote to me offering to 'upgrade' my LLB to an LLM for, I think, £10 but I declined the offer. I had no academic ambitions and no one else was interested.

the government had ordained that all enemy aliens were to be interned. Kurt said that he had agreed to take his wife out to lunch, whereupon the don explained that the policeman had said that he should present himself at the police station before 4 p.m. It seemed to follow that he could go and have lunch first. So Kurt did both those things and then joined my uncle Werner and my future wife's grandfather, O. E. Deutsch, and many others on the Isle of Man.

In those days it was fashionable to suppose that the English had no such thing as administrative law, which was not all that far from the truth in as much as the courts were rarely concerned with testing the legality of government and local government decisions. But my German background had given me some interest in the relationship between government and the governed, and I decided to take a course in French administrative law given by Professor P. J. Hamson. He was a great admirer of the Conseil d'État and of French administrative law. I too became one.

## The choice before me: the Bar or the European Working Group

While still at the university I helped found the Cambridge University European Group, membership of which was open to those interested in the European Community. The group brought out a magazine called the *Egg* and organised two Cambridge European Seminars, each of which lasted a week.

We got together about seventy students, half of whom came from the United Kingdom and half from various universities in continental Europe. We had lectures and discussions about where we thought Europe should be heading. I remember writing to ask various distinguished people whether they would be prepared to attend and noticed that, contrary to what I expected, the most important and busy people, including Edward Heath and Shirley Williams, replied enthusiastically and personally whereas less-well-known people often replied via their secretaries. I also did a certain amount of simultaneous translation and learned how difficult this was.

I have remained in touch all my life with several of the people who came to this seminar. One of these was a Dutchman, Bas de Gaay Fortman. He turned up unexpectedly in my Pembroke rooms in the summer of 1962 and asked whether I would be interested in coming to a castle in Kaub on the Rhine, where a number of young Europeans were being assembled on the initiative of Princess Beatrix of the Netherlands to see whether there was any enthusiasm for the foundation of an umbrella group for young volunteers from various different European countries wishing to work together on a common enterprise. I had helped earlier that year to organise a trip to the Council of Europe in Strasbourg. Apparently someone there had mentioned my name as a possible enthusiast. He asked whether I might be prepared to lead a British part of this group. I told him that at that point I was committed to going to the Bar but that I would happily give the group my summer holidays to help it get off the ground. I suggested that another member of the Cambridge University European Group might be prepared to play a part. This in the event he duly did.

# XIV

# The European Working
# Group 1962-8: An Attempt
# at a European Peace Corps

The nature of this new group and its rise and eventual dissolution
in 1968 are well documented in a book by Peter Bak.[59] For present
purposes what is significant is that the meeting at Kaub in 1962 gave
rise to enduring friendships and gave me an introduction to the
funding difficulties of charities.

In due course a committee was formed with Princess Beatrix
as president and a Dutchman, Frans von Geusau, as chairman. I
was chairman of the British branch, and Karl Sanne chairman
of the Norwegian Branch. We all became friends and remain so
to this day, meeting in one another's houses and talking of old
and new times.

---

[59] *Young, Inspired and Committed: The Chronicle of a European Venture 1962–1968* (UCL
Dutch Studies, 2008).

My most useful contribution was to interview various candidates for various positions. One of these, David Mitchnik, was chosen to lead what was eventually a successful rebuilding project after an earthquake in Iran. He had been an Israeli goatherd. I found him at the London School of Economics, where he had gone after parting from the goats. He seemed to me a chap who could get things organised and done.

I asked him how he would find competent and honest workmen. He said he would go to a big local employer, tell him about the project, drop the Princess' name, and say that he needed his help but not his money. He would ask the employer to identify the workmen and to tell them that if they swindled the Group then they would never work for that employer again. The employer would see that, at no expense to himself, he would get kudos in the local community for being associated with the project. I was persuaded. In due course David was appointed and successfully put this plan into action. After the Group was dissolved, David worked for Oxfam and the World Bank in the so-called Democratic Republic of Congo and elsewhere.

Another interview was successful for a different reason. The candidate's application papers seemed to promise so much by way of achievement that I became suspicious. I noticed that he claimed to speak fluent German. When I started asking him questions in German, he was unable to carry on the simplest conversation. He was so shaken by this unexpected turn of events that even speaking English he was hesitant. He seemed a pleasant young man, but I told him then and there that he would not be accepted. I made clear that German was not needed for the task in Iran but honesty was vital, and that this seemed to be absent. I explained that many of his alleged skills which we did need I could not evaluate but this one I could, and he did not have it.

I hope that he succeeded later in life without such deception, but we have not attempted to keep in touch.

# XV

# *A New Family*

After a couple of months in Amsterdam in 1962 helping to set up the European Working Group, I moved to London, first to a room at the edge of Regent's Park and then to one in South Kensington. In 1963 I found a flat up four flights of stone stairs of a block of flats called Argyll Mansions in the King's Road, Chelsea. This was large enough for me to share with a number of friends. The sitting tenant wished to be paid £600 to assign the tail-end of the lease. Kathleen and Werner kindly provided this, and so I was able to take the tenancy in my name. We had six rooms plus bathroom, lavatory and kitchen. The rent was £460 per year, which even in those days was regarded as very cheap. We divided it between us.

The King's Road in the early 1960s still had bakers, butchers, greengrocers, bookshops and such like but was starting to swing. We took turns at cooking and entertaining. Usually some of us were in and others were elsewhere. Not far from us was a flat shared by four or five girls, and quite often one of them joined one or more of us for an evening. In due course I introduced one of them, Linette Hoogewerf,

*Chilham Castle*

to her future husband Karl Sanne from the European Working Group. She and some of the others remain friends to this day.

As for me, I looked up Elisabeth Holroyd-Reece, whom I had met in Luxembourg at Werner's house. Her parents were living in the keep of Chilham Castle in Kent. Chilham Castle had been built in 1616 by Sir Dudley Digges, who later became Master of the Rolls. In its beautiful grounds designed by Capability Brown stands a hexagonal keep whose origins date back to the twelfth century, perhaps earlier. Although the keep was a massive building, it only had two bedrooms, and so Elisabeth had a flat in the castle.

In 1960 Elisabeth's mother, Gitta Deutsch, had married John Holroyd-Reece. I thought John a most interesting and mysterious man. He had worked for a previous inhabitant of the castle and had founded the Albatross Press, which was the inspiration behind Penguin Books.[60] In return for restoring the keep he was granted a

---

[60] See Michelle K. Troy, *Strange Bird: The Albatross Press and the Third Reich* (Yale University Press, 2017).

life tenancy and lived there in considerable style. Werner knew both him and Gitta, and thus it had come about that Elisabeth spent a few months in Luxembourg to help civilise us boys.

In 1964 I started courting her in the keep and its wonderful surrounds, with which my flat in Argyll Mansions could not even remotely compete. Nevertheless, she agreed to marry me in December 1965, and my friends moved out to leave us in married bliss.

I thought that it would be a good idea to book a photographer for the wedding and was given the name of a well-known one. He, however, found a better engagement and suggested that we use Patrick Litchfield, who was just starting his career.

*Engagement photograph taken by Patrick Litchfield*

He lived close to me in London, was charming, took some engagement and wedding photographs and subsequently became internationally famous photographing royal weddings.

The wedding took place in St Mary's Church, Chilham and in my case was preceded by lunch with Werner at the White Horse next door on the old square. We went across to the church only to find that most of my family and ushers had not arrived. Two minutes before the service was due to start, Werner said to me, 'I don't know what has happened. Are you happy to go on without ushers before they arrive?'

'Yes, if Elisabeth is here.'

Her mother was furious, but in fact they all arrived thirty seconds later, having been held up in traffic. The service was conducted by my Pembroke friend William Hallidie-Smith. The young assistant organist at Canterbury Cathedral kindly played Bach and Buxtehude for us. We walked across to the keep and there had a small party for the twenty or so family and guests in very elegant surroundings. In those days I had not come across the disc-jockey-dominated weddings which are now so popular. Not that I would have been tempted. To me getting married was entering on an awesome lifetime undertaking requiring solemnity.

A year later, Juliet was born. This had as a consequence that Elisabeth had to struggle up four flights of stone stairs clutching daughter, shopping and push chair. It must have been exhausting, but she never mentioned it.

Fortunately we were able to escape the confines of the Chelsea flat by going to the keep, to the Old Rectory in Wem, to Bertrange in Luxembourg, or to Interlaken in Switzerland. Each of these was set in spectacular countryside, particularly that of Kent and that of the Bernese Oberland.

*A wedding photograph taken in the White Room of the Keep by Patrick Litchfield*

Unfortunately the keep ceased to be open to us following John Holroyd-Reece's death in 1967, his life interest having expired. The owner, Lord Masserene and Ferrard, was eager to secure vacant possession as soon as possible and gave my mother-in-law notice within days of John's death. My father-in-law had been something of an eccentric. When approached by local tradesmen who mentioned that his Lordship had failed to pay some bills, he told me that he paid them himself and deducted the relevant amount from his rent, sending a covering letter explaining what he had done. One suspects that Masserene was irritated. In any event, he made clear that he did not wish to have me as a tenant.

As Juliet grew older, we had to find a school for her and found one on the Phillimore Estate in Campden Hill, Kensington.

We then looked round to see whether we could afford to live near the school and in 1971 were adventurous enough to buy the last twenty-one years of a lease of 25 Campden Hill Road, a pleasant nineteenth-century four-storey house and garden. The consensus view at the time was that this was a financially unwise purchase since the value of the term would decline every year, and we would be left at the end of twenty-one years with nothing. I saw the wisdom of this but hoped that by then our children would have grown up and I would have saved sufficient to enable me to buy or lease something else. As it turned out, some years later, a Leasehold Reform Act was passed which enabled me to buy the freehold at a discounted price. I thought the Act was very unfair on the landlord who owned all that area. Nonetheless, I fear that I took advantage of it all the same and bought the reversion. A few years later, I met the current Lord Phillimore socially and apologised. He kindly said that there was nothing to forgive.

In about 1979, a number of us in chambers jointly set up a French company to buy La Mandragore, a house and garden set on a hillside in Tourettes-sur-Loup between Vence and Grasse in the Alpes Maritimes in which we could holiday.

We took it in turns to go there for a few weeks each year and invite our friends or families to join us. We have many happy memories of holidays there until eventually in about 2009 we sold the property and wound up the company. We discovered that French bureaucracy could be as tiresome as its German equivalent.

When we returned from Luxembourg in 2012, we sold the Campden Hill House and divided the proceeds between ourselves and Juliet. There was enough for two houses in Kent, and we felt very blessed. Possibly because of my unsettled youth, as always I was sad to leave a house in which we lived.

*KS and Juliet*

# XVI

# *Music for a While*

Music had been of significance in the life of my Simson ancestors, and my own family has followed this tradition. Indeed, Juliet and her husband Ben have made it their profession. He too comes from a musical family. He is the fifteenth child of Roger and Cecilia Bevan.[61] Many of their children and grandchildren[62] are professional musicians.

I grew up with my mother playing and teaching me to play the piano and I seem to have been reasonably competent at the age of eight both at listening and playing. Since then, my attempts to be the first pianist who could play competently without serious daily practice have failed miserably.

However, I have greatly enjoyed playing a minor part in various musical endeavours as a listener, as a singer, as a pianist in family

---

[61] Roger Bevan, *A Quiverfull; Memoirs of a Family Man* (Greenbank Press, 1955). Cecilia Bevan, *Against All Advice* (Parsonage Press, 1984).
[62] Who include David Bevan, the organist for many years at the Church of the Holy Redeemer in Chelsea, and his daughters Sophie and Mary, who have built up very successful singing careers.

chamber music and as part of the governance of the Academy of Ancient Music, St John's Smith Square, London, the Temple Music Foundation and the Temple Church.

Music was very much part of Werner's life. Indeed, as a young man he wanted to become a composer but came to the conclusion that he had nothing original to contribute. He made up for it in other ways. In Luxembourg, Interlaken and Freiburg he regularly played the organ and the piano and arranged and took part in chamber music at home, to which I listened with pleasure. He listened to a vast number of records, and I often sat with him in the drawing room as he drew my attention to various things which I should notice. I particularly remember regularly listening with him to performances of the Bach *Passions* on Good Fridays and have continued that practice. Indeed, on one Good Friday following his death I was doing so alone when to my surprise I suddenly burst out sobbing because he was not there.

His tastes were essentially Germanic, and he was as didactic about the failings of those composers of whom he thought little as about most other things. I recollect him saying after hearing some Vaughan Williams, 'I already did not like it when Elgar wrote it.' He would play German and French seventeenth- and eighteenth-century organ music and listen, with a bottle of Riesling at his side, to German and Austrian operas and orchestral and chamber music and English Tudor music and Purcell.[63] He had no time for Verdi save for his *Requiem* and *Otello* and no time generally for nineteenth- and twentieth-century Italian opera. In principle he engaged with non-Italian twentieth-century composers, but I cannot say that I often heard him listening to them.

---

[63] I think it was I who introduced him to Tudor music via a record I gave him in the 1950s, with which he professed himself much pleased.

I have always spent quite a lot of time singing and attending concerts. I recollect vividly a midsummer performance while I was in Cambridge of Verdi's *Requiem* in King's College Chapel. This was in the days before electric lighting was installed. Initially the sun shone in through the stained-glass windows. During the terrifying 'Dies Irae' it set, the bass sang, or rather whispered, 'Mors stupebit'. Darkness descended leaving only the light of the candles on the music stands. It was magical.

With me at Pembroke was Christopher Hogwood, who became a friend and later founded the Academy of Ancient Music. At a musical evening in the dean's rooms I sang the part of the Statue of the Commendatore inviting Don Giovanni to dinner. Years later, Christopher announced at an evening for Pembroke alumni held in St John's Smith Square that I had thus introduced him to Mozart opera. I count that as possibly my most useful contribution to the musical scene. By contrast, totally useless was my attempt one bibulous evening to sing the bassoon part in a wind trio. I comfort myself with the thought that probably no one could do this satisfactorily.

Christopher in due course asked me to be a director of the Academy of Ancient Music (AAM) when he incorporated it in 2001. Although I resigned when I moved to Luxembourg three years later, I have been closely associated with it ever since and am still on the council. Christopher himself died in 2014. He had been an honorary fellow of Pembroke along with me, and the college held a memorial service for him in the Wren chapel at which members of the AAM played exquisite music, all of which had been discovered or edited by him. I was touched that when I entered the chapel someone came up to me and said, 'Why don't you sit in the place in which you used to sit when you sang in the choir?' and so I did just that.

Elisabeth and Juliet got as much pleasure as I did in surrounding themselves with music but they were more serious about their practising.

Once a week Philip Thorby, who later became a professor at Trinity College of Music London, used to come round to teach Elisabeth the various recorders from descant to bass. She and I spent many happy evenings playing seventeenth- and eighteenth-century recorder, flute and keyboard music, and Juliet grew up happily listening to this as she lay in bed upstairs. She recently told me that 'when

*Juliet and Elisabeth. Photograph taken by Mayotte Magnus*

my favourite Bach one started, I climbed out of bed and lay on the floor with my ear to the floor to hear better'.

In the 1970s, I had a long planning case, and we all lived at the Priory Hotel Bath, where Juliet practised her viola da gamba which we had bought her and on which Philip had given her lessons. Elisabeth and Juliet both joined the Early Music Centre and played there. Elisabeth learnt the transverse flute. They both loyally continued to make music with me at home. Initially we all enjoyed playing together, even though they were as conscious of my shortcomings as I was. Gradually, however, they understandably made more and more music away from home with other, more competent musicians.

However, my singing has continued, partly with church choirs and partly with the delightful 250-year-old Noblemen and Gentlemen's Catch and Glee Club. This meets four times a year when we eat together and, after dinner, sight-read and sing catches and glees from scores in the Club's library.

In 1990, I became a trustee of Saint John's Smith Square, London, which functions primarily as a concert hall, and learnt something of the economic imperatives of the music business. It was, however, difficult to function effectively as a trustee during my first few years, since I spent so much of the year on circuit as a judge out of London.

During one of my absences, the trustees decided to order a new organ from the German organ-makers Klais Orgelbau. Klais quoted in Deutschmarks and insisted on payment being made in Deutschmarks. I had written a typical lawyer's letter to my fellow trustees warning of the dangers inherent in agreeing to this course unless one made suitable arrangements to deal with the possibility of the pound devaluing. However, they decided not to do this since the cost of hedging was substantial. The reason for it being substantial became clear when in the event the pound did devalue. Because of this and various other unforeseen factors we had to raise significantly more than we had budgeted for, which put us in a position of considerable embarrassment. Fortunately, one of the Sainsbury charities came to our rescue and financed the shortfall.

I was chairman of St John's between 1994 and 2004, years which I greatly enjoyed. This is equally true of my years between 1995 and 2001 as a governor of the English National Ballet (ENB), where again I saw the precarious nature of the financing of bodies dependent upon charitable donations.

The difficulty in essence is that, in order to function effectively, before one can employ people, lease premises and so on, one needs to enter into contracts for a few years. Both the UK government and the Commission of the European Union, in the light of inevitable future uncertainties and for reasons of internal budgeting, were reluctant to commit themselves for years ahead. Moreover, they wished to check on how well money was being spent before committing themselves to further financing.

St John's was independent of government finance, so that was not a problem there. However, the ENB obtained a significant proportion of its funds from the Treasury. In my time as chairman of the Busoga Trust, which I shall describe later, the European Commission and the predecessor of the Department for International Development were persuaded to donate generously to the Trust. However, the funding was intermittent and never a reliable source over a period of time. Similarly, the ENB, although we knew that enough money would never be raised through ticket sales to make the books balance, was nevertheless in a position where it had to enter into forward contracts to employ dancers and musicians and to hire premises for practice and performance for a number of years ahead. This it did, fortunately without misadventure, during the time that I was on the board.

While I was busy with St John's, Elisabeth was much occupied with the Philharmonia Orchestra, of whose Friends she was chairman for many years until we moved to Luxembourg. We each took the other to concerts organised by our separate musical charities and tried not to be in competition in raising funds for them from the same sources. Elisabeth was also chairman of the Migraine Trust and in that capacity was also seeking funds. The difficulty was that we were both milking the same few milch cows. Fortunately they continued to give generously.

The Philharmonia Friends had a private bar at the Festival Hall when the orchestra was giving a concert where we met other friends. One evening, I saw someone trying to enter this bar whom the staff did not recognise.

'Are you a friend?'

'I am a friend of everybody,' came the reply in a pronounced Russian accent, which left the staff perplexed as to what to do next with a man not easily diverted. Fortunately, I recognised him as the Russian Ambassador, and the staff let him in.

I had met him a few weeks before when he had invited me to his residence to meet the new Russian Chief Prosecutor. That occasion remains in my memory because the Prosecutor – a bull of a man – had explained to me that Russia's chief problem was corruption but that he was going to sort it out. He seemed very determined. When I next met the Ambassador I asked him how his friend the Chief Prosecutor was getting on. 'He is in prison,' came the laconic reply and, although it was not clear to me whether this was the result of his doing the job well or doing it badly, I thought it best not to pursue the point.

Stour Music is a music festival held in Kent which was founded by Alfred Deller. John Holroyd-Reece, Gitta and Elisabeth were founder members, and Elisabeth and I are still staunch supporters. It was there that in 1966 we met Maurice Bevan when he was singing the monster Polypheme in Handel's *Acis and Galatea*. It stays in our memory because it was during that performance that our daughter Juliet gave her first foetal kick. This is in itself unremarkable, but she went on to marry Maurice's nephew Ben. Stour Music has, since Alfred died, until recently been run by his son Mark, who was at Cambridge with me. Alfred and Mark's vast circle of eminent musical friends, including Juliet and Ben, regularly performed there and have given us much joy.

In the Temple itself my only significant musical contributions were to encourage both Inns to commission Sir John Taverner to compose *The Veil of the Temple*[64] and to help establish the Temple Music Foundation, which puts on world-class concerts in the Inns. Sir John, spurred on by Robin Griffith-Jones, the Master of the Temple, and Stephen Layton, then director of music at the Temple Church, composed *The Veil of the Temple*, and it was performed in the church in June 2003 and thereafter round the world. It is an all-night vigil and is a combination of orthodox and other texts, some sung, some spoken. Accompanying the singers were some Indian and Tibetan instruments and gongs and a European brass section. There were well over 100 singers, including the boys of the Temple Church choir who disappeared to the then Bishop of London's house after the opening hour or two to sleep and returned triumphantly in the early morning to welcome the risen Jesus. Elisabeth and I heard it twice within a week and also heard the condensed version once. It

---

[64] http://www.stephenlayton.com/sites/default/files/server_files/user/vottbooklet.pdf, which explains the scheme of this vast work.

transported one into another world. Now we listen to the recording in wonder and dream of paradise.

A few years later, we were persuaded by one of our Luxembourg friends, Douce Loutsch, to visit the Schubertiade in Schwarzenberg, Austria. This is a music festival with eminent musicians in the Vorarlberg where during a fortnight one can combine concert-going with walking in the green hills. A magical experience.

Juliet and Ben sing in operas, oratorios and concerts, and of course we have been to quite a number of those. One which remains vividly in my mind is her singing *Shepherd on the Rock* in the Temple in 1996. Her piano accompanist was the then Chief Justice, Lord Taylor, who had also accompanied Elisabeth when I was on circuit. The concert went well. As we drove home, we heard on the radio news that Peter had been diagnosed with terminal brain cancer, and Elisabeth pulled to the side of the road to absorb this dreadful news. He had earlier handed in his resignation but had asked for no announcement to be made until after what would be his last concert. I gather that he did not tell Juliet and the clarinetist because he realised that the knowledge would adversely affect their playing.

# XVII

# A German at the Bar

I was called to the Bar in May 1962 by Sir Donald Finnemore, an Old Edwardian to whom I had been introduced by Ronald Lunt. He was extremely kind to me and even invited me to sleep in his flat in the Temple on the night of my call, which saved me a tiring journey back to Cambridge.

I found next to me on Call Night Helmuth Caspar von Moltke. Like my mother, his father Helmuth James had worked under Admiral Gladisch in 1941 and 1942. I knew the name and was pleased to find his son at my side. Helmuth James had himself been called to the Bar by the Inner Temple in 1938. Sixty years later, I persuaded the Temple Church to have a service in his memory. I shall return to this later.

I started at the Bar at a time when the United Kingdom was trying to enter the European Economic Community. I thought that I might be able to use my background to build a career as a young European lawyer. This, however, was premature. In 1963, as I was finishing my pupillage, General de Gaulle vetoed the entry of the United Kingdom into the Community. So I had to look for a different field of practice. Life at the Bar is full of such unexpected developments.

By sheer chance I developed a practice in the English law of Town and Country Planning, which in due course extended somewhat into other fields. I have just looked at my accounts approved by the Revenue for tax purposes and see that in each of my first five years at the Bar I received less than £5,000,[65] from which about a third could be deducted as expenses for tax purposes. We lived pretty frugally, but my overdraft at the Wem branch of Barclays Bank regularly increased without protest by the manager. For the next five years I kept it steady and for the following five I gradually paid it off. Since then, I have been lucky enough to receive more than I need and to live in comfort.

This is not a detailed account of my life as a barrister or as an English judge. That period of my life was very similar to that of Michael Kerr and three judges of my generation who have written about theirs: David Keene, Simon Brown and John Dyson.[66] Indeed, I shared a room in chambers with David Keene, and our practices were similar, save that I made occasional excursions to Luxembourg, Strasbourg, Gibraltar, Hong Kong and Singapore, and he elsewhere. In due course we served together in the Court of Appeal.

Simon Brown and I were both appointed junior counsel to the Crown in 1978. He then became first junior treasury counsel (Common Law), always called the Treasury Devil, a job which I would happily have accepted had it been offered to me. It was not,

---

[65] In 2019, the purchasing power of the £5,000 was £20,000.
[66] Michael Kerr, *As Far as I Remember* (Hart Publishing, 2002); David Keene *Leaving the Arena* (I. B. Tauris, 2020); Simon Brown, *Playing off the Roof and Other Stories* (Marble Hill, 2020); John Dyson, *A Judge's Journey* (Hart, 2019).

and so I took silk in the following year. We both became High Court judges and then lord justices and served together. Then our paths diverged again. I was appointed to be a judge at the European Court of Justice in 2003. He became a member of the Judicial Committee of the House of Lords in the following year. Then he became a visitor to Pembroke College, and our paths met again at college dinners.

John Dyson shares with me a Baltic heritage on his father's side and shares my taste in music. We also overlapped as High Court judges and lord justices. He in 2010 joined the Supreme Court and became Master of the Rolls in 2012.

This tale was originally intended just for my family. If I burden other bookshelves with yet another judicial memoir it is because I am German as well as British and I have served as a judge of the Court of Justice of the European Union. This is not true of anyone else, and so that is what forms the centre of this book.

During my twenty-two years at the Bar, my German origins were, I think, of no interest to anyone. I certainly did not feel myself disadvantaged save on two occasions.

The first was when, as a very inexperienced young barrister, I appeared before Ewen Montagu QC, then chairman of Middlesex Quarter Sessions, who had become famous during the war when he had successfully masterminded Operation Mincemeat – a major deception. My case was of no importance save to my client – a boy who was accused of having stolen a ring from a younger boy. He maintained it had been a gift freely given. This account of what had happened had not convinced the magistrates and did not convince the learned chairman. As I was seeking to explain that my client maintained that the ring was a gift, he stopped me and said, 'I see, Mr Schiemann [he emphasised my name in a strong German accent and paused, I thought ominously]. A bit like the invasion of

Czechoslovakia. No element of aggression. The younger boy *wanted* to be deprived of that which was his. I understand.'

I had a rush of blood to the head but said nothing, and shortly afterwards the appeal was dismissed. Then he reserved sentence and remarked: 'I shall wait to see if there is a complaint about the decision before I sentence.'

I lacked the experience and courage to say anything and retired to the robing room in confusion only to be met, to my total surprise, by the very friendly judge who said, 'Your chap seems a pleasant enough lad. I would not have thought there is any need to send him inside. Well, we'll see.'

I was nonplussed. In the event we did not start any further proceedings, for which the only possible ground would have been the judge's misbehaviour. In due course the defendant was put on probation, I think. I learnt later that this judge was renowned for his unusual behaviour.

Shortly afterwards, the second incident occurred which made me conscious of possible disadvantages arising from my German name. Bronsden,[67] my clerk, came into my room and told me that he had just lost me a solicitor.

'What? I've only got two.'

He told me that the solicitor wanted to brief someone else who was not available and that he had spent some energy in apparently successfully persuading him to give me the brief when he was asked to spell my name. When he had done so, the solicitor stated, 'I'm sorry. We never employ Jews,' to which Bronsden had replied, 'Then you need never come to these chambers again.' He told me that he knew

---

[67] In those days barristers referred to their clerks by surname only. The nice social significance of using surnames, with or without a preceding 'Mr', then prevailing, disappeared into history the moment I got on top of it.

that neither I nor any of the other of the barristers in chambers were Jews but that he had thought this the right thing to do. I congratulated him on what was quite a brave act for a clerk in 1964 and said I was glad he had done it. It was not until I attended his funeral and was faced with a service in Hebrew and thus in a book which had to be read back to front that I discovered that he was a Jew himself. I did not discover my own Jewish ancestry till years later.

Bronsden also pointed out that I fell between two stools: some anti-Semitic solicitors would assume that any German name showed Jewish origins whereas most Jewish solicitors would know that Schiemann was not a Jewish name, and some of them would hesitate before employing a German. This was before the Race Relations Act 1965, and overt anti-Semitism and anti-German feeling was no rarer in this country than anti-European feeling was during the Brexit debate. He suggested that if I changed my name to something inoffensive like Lawson I might prosper more. But I declined because I felt that it would be disloyal to abjure my family name. Aunt Gertrud would have been proud of me, but I never told her.

Incidentally, I mentioned this experience to a solicitor friend of mine, expecting him to say he was shocked. He was not and explained his position like this (one must remember this was in the early 1960s):

The vast majority of judges appear to have no anti-Semitic prejudices. However, the occasional one seems to have and might conceivably be influenced by them. By contrast, I know of no Jewish judge who displays anti-gentile prejudices. It is my job to minimise the risks inherent in litigation for my client. If I brief only gentile barristers then I avoid one possible, if remote, risk. That seems sensible.

I did not regard either of these occasions as being of great significance or consider my German origins as adversely affecting my progress at the Bar. At the time this seemed perfectly natural to me. Now I am grateful at the generosity of spirit of those whose families must have lost so much because of the activities of Germans.

In some ways my German was actually helpful in as much as I could read through bundles of correspondence in German without there being any need to pay for the translation of all of them in order to find out the half dozen documents which might be of relevance.

Nonetheless it was difficult, at any event for me, to make any sort of a living in those early years. This problem was exacerbated by the fact that many solicitors were extremely slow to pay what they owed. For years about half of what I had already earned was sitting in the bank accounts of my solicitors or their clients. I suppose that at one time most barristers were unlike me in that they had a private income. To harry solicitors for money was felt by many both to diminish the likelihood of being briefed by those solicitors again and also to reveal that you needed the cash and weren't quite a gentleman.

My German origins once more came to my mind at the end of my career at the Bar. While I was doing a long planning case in Newcastle in January 1986, I received a letter from the private secretary to the Lord Chancellor inquiring whether I could come and see Lord Hailsham in the near future at a time convenient to me. I pondered on my misdemeanours, thought none had been sufficiently serious to warrant the Lord Chancellor's immediate attention, and telephoned my clerk to tell him to suggest that he fix the appointment for a date after my return from Newcastle.

Later that day I received a call from him saying that he had been informed in no uncertain terms that this was too leisurely a reply to an invitation to see the Lord Chancellor and that he had arranged for me to present myself the following Wednesday at 9.30 a.m. I left my junior, John Steel, in charge of the case making some excuse about a medical appointment – an excuse he later told me few believed. I never was a good liar.

When I saw the Lord Chancellor, he asked me whether I was agreeable to my name being put forward to the Queen as a High Court judge. My chambers had never before produced a High Court judge. I was younger than all the serving judges, so I was not expecting such an offer, although the thought had crossed my mind as a remote possibility for the future. I said I felt honoured and that, unless my wife vetoed the idea, which I did not think she would, I would accept with pleasure. I was told not to tell anyone else save my clerk.

I was then sent to speak to the permanent secretary to the Lord Chancellor's office, who very kindly explained a variety of practical matters and then pointed out that one of the problems of being a judge was that anything scandalous in my past would inevitably be discovered by the press sooner or later. He said that if I were to reveal such things to him before the press thought it had discovered something of that nature, then he could prepare a suitable reply in advance. Being asked without warning to make a whole life confession somewhat threw me. I said rather hesitantly, 'You do know that I am German?'

He gave the impression that this was new to him. I asked whether that was a problem.

'Not as such, but there might be difficulties with the pension.'

'I am British as well. Does that help?'

It did, and there was fortunately no further examination of my past life. It still seems odd to me that my German nationality was apparently not known. I had certainly never concealed what my name manifestly suggested. Happily, at the time I did not know that the *Times* obituarist had described my great grandfather Schiemann as a spy for the Kaiser. While I think this inaccurate, it is fortunate that no columnist has ever referred to it.

In due course, a date in April was fixed as the date for the beginning of my appointment. I endeavoured to carry on my normal practice at the Bar for four months. I had been briefed to defend the legality of the action of Liverpool Council in issuing redundancy notices to all their teachers. The plan, I seem to remember, was to save on the cost of their salaries during the holidays. This would enable the budget to be balanced as required by law. It was intended to re-employ the teachers in the following term. The redundancy notices, delivered by taxi, gave rise to widespread protest and an application for Judicial Review. I rose to my feet but before I could open my mouth was met by a barrage of questions by Lord Justice Watkins, who had been awarded a VC in some outstandingly brave action against a German machine-gun emplacement, and who I imagine knew of my impending but unannounced appointment. He made clear that he thought my case was hopeless. The questions succeeded one another like machine-gun bullets but left no time in between for an answer. So I remained standing but silent while looking with raised eyebrows at his neighbour on the bench, Mr Justice Woolf, who I thought might share my view that this bullying was unseemly. The barrage stopped. My silence continued. A minute passed, followed by a 'Yes?'

'Does your Lordship now wish to hear my clients' case?'

Pause.

'Of course.'

So I did my best but to no one's surprise lost the case. My first task after I was appointed a judge was to report to Lord Justice Watkins, who was the Deputy Lord Chief Justice. He apologised and could not have been more charming.

# XVIII

# *High Court Judge*

On 9 April 1986, I was sworn in by the Lord Chancellor in his residence. He had kindly invited my wife, daughter and Werner von Simson. I was in ceremonial scarlet robes, full-bottomed wig, court shoes, breeches and holding white gloves and a black cap. The last was to be worn when pronouncing the death sentence, which was a theoretical possibility throughout the time that I was a High Court judge. Although I was opposed to the imposition of the death penalty, I rightly did not think that I would ever be required actually to pass a death sentence. So I lost no sleep over the matter.

Twenty minutes had been set aside on quite a chilly day for official photographs in one of the inner courtyards of the Palace of Westminster. I had been warned that the photographs would be available for the press and that, if I smiled, then in years to come the picture would be shown next to a report of a tragic trial. So I tried to look solemn.

This was not helped by my dear wife muttering into my ear that she was thinking of me without my pyjama trousers. Then we went upstairs to the Lord Chancellor's residence. In total silence I took the oath of allegiance to the Queen and the judicial oath 'to do right to all manner of people after the laws and usages of this realm without fear or favour, affection or ill will'. The old fashioned language and robes helped to impress on me that I was stepping into the tradition of centuries.

Then I introduced Elisabeth, Juliet and Werner and my clerk to Lord Hailsham, who, in an endeavour to put everyone at their ease, said, 'The thing we have always liked about Konrad is that he has never changed his name.' To this Werner gently replied in a mild German accent, 'But, Lord Chancellor, would that not have been rather presumptuous? After all, he is not a member of the royal

*Arrival of KS as a High Court Judge at the court in Norwich*

family.' Hailsham rocked backwards as if he had just got an electric shock. I felt that my career had got off to a tricky start. I was disappointed to hear that the only thing for which I was liked was my not changing my name; I had rather hoped that some other likeable qualities might have been turned up in the prolonged process of choosing a judge. Still, there it was.

The only other thing I remember about the occasion is Hailsham saying, 'The best judge is the one of whom no one has ever heard.' Well, I could take a hint and have by and large been able to resist the well-known judicial temptation intentionally to publicise one's views to the world while sitting in the judgement seat in the presence of reporters. Perhaps I have inherited the appropriate quality from my Schiemann great-grandfather which had impressed the Kaiser.

On 2 July 1986, I was due to be knighted, as High Court judges routinely are, by Her Majesty at Buckingham Palace and had been told to report alone at 12.40. As Elisabeth was kindly driving me there, we ran into a most fearful traffic jam in Knightsbridge. I eventually decided to get out of the car and to run down to the Palace in morning coat. I arrived with one minute to spare. The German President Weizsäcker, to whom I had been introduced at the time of the celebrations in honour of my von Simson great-great-grandfather, was paying a state visit to the Queen on the same day, and I suppose this contributed to the traffic jam.

I had asked my Bar clerk Leslie Page, who had built up my practice at the Bar and who had been a steadying hand when I was under pressure, whether he by any chance wanted to become a judge's clerk. He confirmed that he did not: it would have been financially highly disadvantageous to him and in any event he did not want to be parted from wife and family while I was out on circuit. So our professional relationship ceased, but we remain friends to this day.

By a stroke of luck, I was assigned as a judicial clerk Ian Wilson, a former chief petty officer (writer) in the Royal Navy. Ian was a grammar school boy whose education was such that he nearly always managed to complete the *Times* cryptic crossword puzzle by breakfast time. I gather that a number of judges used to phone him for help in this task. He painted and was a skilled draftsman who used to prepare illustrated menus for us when we had a dinner party.

He was a quiet, thoughtful, physically and mentally impressive individual, bearded, well built and six foot tall but capable of very rapid reaction times. I recollect going with him to Birmingham Art Gallery to look at some David Cox watercolours which he wanted to show me when I was accosted by a local with 'Have you got the time, squire?'

Before I had finished looking at my watch, I heard him say in his clear, deep voice, 'I am the squire. He is the knight. It is 3.30 p.m.' The Brummie, somewhat taken aback, retreated, giving thanks.

One example of Ian's thoughtfulness, which I never noticed at the time, he only told me of when he had retired. Before sentencing someone, I pondered, like any other judge. But even after announcing my sentence I used to retire to my room to come to terms with what I had done for a few minutes before putting it out of my mind and getting on with the next case. I don't think anyone had ever suggested to me that I should do this but perhaps it is in part because of this practice that I have been lucky enough not to fret afterwards about the effect of my decisions on others. Ian told me that, from early on in our relationship, he had made a point of leaving me alone during those few minutes. He also left me alone when I went for morning walks before breakfast in lodgings; he had something wrong with his ankle, and walking was not his favourite occupation. He preferred to get on with the crossword.

My personal experience of life persuaded me to volunteer for what was not a popular judicial job. In Germany, the idea of a judge volunteering to do a particular set of cases would be unconstitutional; people have memories of the Nazis fixing the composition of courts so as to procure a particular result. However, in England a more relaxed approach, relying on judges' sense of propriety, has proved adequate.

During my term as a High Court judge the number of cases involving immigrants was increasing rapidly. These cases frequently involved checking how immigration appeals or asylum applications had been handled by Home Office officials and ministers. The officials had had a very difficult time trying to establish, through the medium of interviews with persons who could not speak English, whether the applicant's account of what had happened in a distant country where different customs prevailed was true.

The typical case concerned a woman of Pakistani origin who was perfectly lawfully settled in England and might indeed have been born here. She then went to Pakistan and married a Pakistani man, who was not permitted to immigrate into the United Kingdom as a bachelor without a visa. However, he was, under the rules as they then stood, entitled to enter if married to a UK wife. The issue under the immigration rules was whether the marriage had been genuine or merely a device to help with immigration.

Some people, who had been perfectly normally married according to the wishes of their relatives in accordance with local custom, thought it advisable to gild the lily with untruths in order to produce an account which they thought would be more believable than the truth to someone who had been brought up with romantic marriages in the modern English context. This was often a mistake on their part and in fact caused them to be disbelieved.

I thought of the many marriages which had been entered into by royalty and the aristocracy for reasons which had little to do with romantic love but had nonetheless been regarded as genuine and indeed often produced children and mutual affection. I recollected one of my relatives in the so-called German Democratic Republic explaining how he had found a French girl who, in order to enable him to leave communist rule, was prepared to marry him in form only. I reflected that Jews in Hitler's Germany such as Sybille Bedford had engaged in similar moves.

It was desperately difficult for everyone concerned to come to a reliable decision as to the genuineness of these marriages. These cases were a strain also for counsel. I recall a young barrister who knew nothing about me saying in court that it was no doubt difficult for a judge who had grown up in the heart of the English establishment to imagine what it could be like for a teenager in a new country speaking a new language having come from a situation of utter destitution. I said I would do my best. The next day, having spoken to his opponent who knew something of my background, he gracefully apologised for having wrongly assumed things he did not know to be true.

The number of cases kept on increasing, and it was decided to try to diminish the case backlog. Because of my background I thought I should offer to spend a term doing this work. I had some experience of acting as an interpreter and of pleading and presiding in cases where evidence had been given in a foreign language. In some cases this was of some use in spotting where something might have gone wrong in the immigration process.

I once asked the late Tim Renton, who had become a Home Office minister, whether he had found it irritating to have a judge controlling how his people had done some job. I was delighted when he said that far from being irritated he had been very pleased that someone could be found with the time to go slowly with the aid of argument on each side through a complicated file of which he had had to dispose in less than an hour. I fear that this relaxed approach has not commended itself to some of his successors who lambast judges who upset decisions reached by the Home Office.

# XIX

# *The Conseil d'État*

I went over to the French Conseil d'État with some other judges and gave a talk on Human Rights in the Common Law. This was before the passing of the Human Rights Act 1998. I remember being asked how on earth the British managed without a Declaration of the Rights of Man and of the Citizen which the French had enacted in 1789. I replied that in some circles in England the Declaration had indeed initially been much admired but that after the Terror in 1793 the British had not in general been impressed by the usefulness of such declarations. On seeing that this comment was regarded as impolite, I mentioned that I would love to spend some time at the Conseil to learn how the French used the Declaration in practice. This, a couple of years later, I did.

The gastronomic highlight of our visit was a splendid three-hour lunch given to us by the President of the Senate in the lovely Palais du Luxembourg. They did these things in great style in Paris. At the end of the meal the President, although he spoke English, made a very gracious speech in French in which he paid tribute to the contribution of the British to the liberation of France. Rightly thinking that some of us might need help with our French, he was accompanied by a charming lady who then, without notes, repeated the speech in English. Lord Bridge, who was the senior English judge there, saw that a reply was required from him. He began in English by thanking the President and Madame for their kind speeches. As he congratulated them on the different ways in which they had broached the topic, it became clear to all that, whether by reason of lack of concentration induced by the excellent wine or because of forgotten French, he had not taken on board that Madame had been translating rather than making an original contribution. The President buried his face in his napkin, as did some of us.

A couple of years later, the Chief Justice, Peter Taylor, said he had received a letter from the President of the Conseil asking whether I could be released if I still wanted to spend a month there. Peter asked me whether I would like to go. On my replying in the affirmative he told me he had no objection provided that I did it in my vacation. This I did, and Elisabeth and I spent a happy month in Paris, and I was permitted to attend all the *délibérés*. We lived in a flat which the Simors kindly lent us for the duration.

We had driven to Paris and parked the car in a garage. When I mentioned the huge daily rate to someone, the Conseil then did me the honour, now no longer granted to anyone, of permitting me to park in front of the Palais Royal. It more than made up for the lack of a Légion d'honneur, the button of which most others seemed to be wearing. When I turned up at the garage to collect the car, the attendant looked at me and said 'Five days costs 1,500 francs.' I pointed to a notice which said 'If you lose your ticket there is a maximum fine of 250 francs'.

'But you have not lost your ticket.'

'I could easily have pretended to have lost it but thought this dishonest. You are not going to punish me for being honest, surely.'

He smiled, moved his arm along the table causing my parking ticket to fall off.

'Where is your ticket?'

'I don't know exactly where it is.'

'250 francs please.'

A man with a sense of humour.

When I moved to Luxembourg some knowledge of the Conseil, whose practices had heavily influenced the ECJ, turned out to be very useful.

# XX

# *Uganda*

## The Busoga Trust

My visit to the Conseil is just one of a series of unusual experiences which have enriched my life both as an individual and as a judge. Another is my contact with Uganda. In 1989, out of the blue I received from John Steel QC a letter asking how I would react to a suggestion that I become chairman of the Busoga Trust, of which I had never heard. He explained that the Trust had been incorporated in 1983. Its mission was to help in the provision and maintenance of clean water sources and sanitation facilities in Uganda. It had got off to a slow start because of a series of civil wars in Uganda until General Museveni assumed control in 1986 of what was then a chaotic country. By 1989 the Trust had some forty functioning water sources, and its first chairman had indicated that he felt that it was time to resign.

I felt I could not decently refuse. I replied to John's suggestion that I knew little about development aid, water or Uganda but that I would be happy to try to set up an appropriate organisational structure which complied with all legal and accounting requirements.

I approached the then Bishop of London, Graham Leonard, to ask whether he had any ideas as to where we might establish an office for the Trust. He immediately suggested one of the lesser-used London churches, and in due course we opened an office in St Margaret Pattens and remained there for more than two decades.

My own experiences of Uganda divide into those connected with the provision of water and those connected with the Church. Both were unusual. Relying heavily on Elisabeth's diary, I will try and paint a picture of what we saw and did.

### In the villages

Beyond the few main tarmac roads which were to be found in Uganda in 1989, red murram tracks wound down through banana trees to mud-hut settlements. The little round huts of wattle and poles with heavily fringed roofs of banana leaves were the traditional rural habitat. Gradually they were being replaced by brick-built shacks with corrugated tin roofs. Beside the mud huts there was often a smaller hut woven with reeds and standing on stilts. This was the grain store. The huts were normally grouped around a central clearing, and here the red dust had been carefully swept and was often covered by huge white circles of beans or grain drying in the sun. Goats and chickens scuffed the dust, children played, often naked, and the women, bent down from the waist like hairpins, prepared food.

Each of these communities is dependent on a water source. I remember visiting one village where everyone moved slowly and without energy. When we saw the water source it was muddy and stagnant. No European would dream of drinking the water.

It occurred to me that it was no wonder that the villagers seemed lethargic and to lack any drive. They were often suffering from diarrhoea and other ailments. We helped in the construction of a well there, and when I visited again a few years later, the water was clear and the villagers were full of energy. Our aim was to provide a source of water not more than two miles from each community. We found that once there is water and basic sanitation then people want to go there, and the church, the medical centre, the school and indeed the whole community tend to flourish.

Typically, before we arrived to visit a project area, the whole village had been involved in the preparations. The women had been up since dawn collecting water and preparing the feast which ended the visit. The boys had prepared their instruments: drums, rattles, one-string 'violins', and the xylophone/marimba, which was constructed anew each time it was used, with fresh banana stems that formed the base and twigs to hold the bone-shaped wooden bars in place. The primary school children had rehearsed their song of welcome, the women danced, and the boys and girls brushed up on their poem or play; an old sofa and chairs with stuffing and springs bursting out had been set up under the acacia tree for the guests, and tables in front draped with white crocheted cloths.

These created a rather Victorian bourgeois atmosphere, which to us seemed incongruous in an African village. Beyond them, in a semi-circle, were ranged all the school desks with their benches. All the best pupils from the senior school had been diligently copying 'The Programme' onto pages from a lined school exercise book in a careful childish hand. In some ways I was reminded of European primary schools in the 1940s. Just as, when I visited Gibraltar in the 1970s to do a case as a barrister, I had been struck by how much the atmosphere there resembled an English county town in the 1950s.

In Busoga every moment of our day was controlled by 'The Programme'. On arrival at any village or project, we were greeted by the leader, who handed us each a page of handwritten details of every minute of our visit.

Despite these meticulous timings nothing ever ran according to plan. In general, time was qualified (by us) as either 'Ugandan' time or 'Muzungu' time (Muzungu is the Lusogan word for foreigners). The only true guide to time was that the sun rises and sets every day, suddenly, at much the same times all the year round.

We would be greeted by a welcome song sung by 100 primary school children all dressed in blue. They stood in straight lines and with great earnestness sang out under the watchful eye of their teacher: 'You are wellacome, you are wellacome, you are wellacome to Uganda!' Later, children as young as five sang songs or played a scene about avoiding Aids or about the benefits of clean water and sanitation.

Life for a child in rural Uganda was a very serious business. He might very well have lost half his siblings during his young life, and probably a parent or uncle. If an uncle or aunt had died, then his father might well have had an extra ten children to care for, which might deprive the child of a chance to go to school at all. The way all members of the extended families looked after each other was most impressive. All schooling was paid for by the parents, so school places were very precious. In many respects we Europeans could see much to emulate.

We would be led to our place under the acacia tree and seated there in strict hierarchical order. Hierarchy seemed supremely important, possibly a hangover from colonial days, and everyone from the lowliest well-digger to the bishop had his title and position in the scheme of things. The guests were seated in order of precedence facing the villagers. At the sides the elders of the village were at desks brought out from the school, the smallest children sat on the ground, behind them, the taller children and youths would stand at the side of the women. All waited patiently and quietly throughout the whole ceremony, which might last several hours.

Many of them would be in the full sun, as even the largest tree could not shade them all.

After singing and dancing and much ululation from the women, there would be hand-washing followed by tea. The washing ritual began and ended every meal. A woman arrived with a bowl containing soap in one hand and a jug of water in the other, a towel over her arm. She would sink to her knees. All girls and women did this whenever they addressed a man or distinguished guest, even if female. We were touched to see a young American woman who was a member of the American peace corps with exquisite grace do exactly the same as the local women. Yet an equally young American boy found this culture so strange that he was utterly miserable.

A little water was poured over the hands for washing and for rinsing, but there was nothing like the twenty-second careful wash under running water which has become common in Europe since the arrival of Covid-19. This done, the meal began. Food would be carried by the women from some distance away, where it had been prepared over open fires. Mid-morning or afternoon tea for a visit like ours would consist of samosas, pieces of meat, boiled eggs, peanuts, small cakes, and the ubiquitous 'soda', a fizzy, artificially sweetened, warm 'pop' of various colours, bottled in Kenya. Alternatively, we got chai, a mixture of tea, milk and sugar all boiled together for a long time, which reminded me of the army. We needed to drink and accepted gratefully. The villagers got nothing while we were there.

The business of the day usually began with a visit to the well or borehole. We might watch the actual digging of the well or visit a long-established one displayed by the well technicians and villagers. The well technicians, well caretaker and well committee were all trained Ugandans who had learnt to take over the responsibility and care of their well. They had been taught basic maintenance and learned about cleanliness and sanitation. This local organisation was vitally important as it allowed the one British water engineer to get on with the next well that was needed, while leaving the finished one in capable hands.

There were three basic systems for obtaining clean water in use. The most popular was known as the Chicago Method. Shallow wells were dug by the villagers using hands, spade and a bucket. As the well deepened, the mud was hauled out with bucket and pulley. Finally, the men who had dug the hole were also brought up in the bucket which had carried them down. Planks had been sunk down the sides to prevent the earth from caving in, and metal rings held the planks firm. Much more expensive was a borehole, which required drilling equipment and was used where the water was below rocks. The simplest was the source protection scheme. The source welled up in a muddy pool, where water collected. To obtain clean water, a pipe was run directly from the eye of the source.

The trough leading from the collecting area around the pump frequently led to a tree nursery, so as to make use of all the overflow water. The little trees might be sold to villagers to generate income for the maintenance of the well.

The clinic would not be far from the water source. It was often a brick construction with bare concrete floors and walls. There were usually no doors or windows. The waiting area might have rush mats on the floor, and the treatment room a table and a chair for the nurse to write notes and give immunisations. The plastic syringes, clearly marked 'disposable, use once only', were, we were told, nevertheless used for as long as they could still be sharpened and cleaned. They were boiled for twenty minutes until they became opaque. We sometimes saw a patient lying on a mat on the floor.

Once we saw a mother who had just given birth, lying bewildered on a bare table. In one village, we saw the old and new clinics side by side. The old mud hut was cool and comfortable, whereas the new clinic under a corrugated metal roof was hot and stuffy. But the locals were infinitely proud of the new clinic – which had the advantage of not having snakes dropping from a thatched roof – and carefully noted all the treatments and immunisations in a lined exercise book.

The school was often a long, low, brick building with concrete walls and floor. At one end of the room the concrete wall was rubbed very smooth and on this area the lessons were written in chalk. For the lucky few there might be benches and desks. But many lessons were taken outside under a tree where a few children would unroll their own mats or use a traditional bamboo seat shaped like a funnel on a tripod. The hole in the seat no doubt keeps the sitter cool. The school 'bell' was an old hub cap which hung in a tree and was beaten with a stick.

The church was often a similar building to the school, but larger. The sofa and armchairs from the 1950s were for guests. The table, benches, and desks and any other chairs were shared between school, church and village tree. They were moved during the course of the day from one place to another by dozens of willing and enthusiastic helpers.

After visiting the project area, the serious business of 'speeches' began. There were many: from the bishop, me, the project leader, the project coordinator, the pastor, the headmaster. Although they were usually keen to read the speech in English, the Basoga (those Ugandans who live in Busoga and speak Lusoga) were encouraged to speak in Lusoga for the benefit of the villagers.[68] We were given a copy of each speech written out for us by hand in English. Each phrase was nevertheless translated into English for our benefit and to show off the skill of the interpreter. As for me, to my shame, apart from the odd word or two, I spoke in English. For light relief the speeches were interspersed with dancing, drums and music, singing, reciting of poems and plays, and enlivened by a great deal of joyful ululation.

An exchange of gifts might follow. Gifts to us included a goat and a chicken, both alive and kicking, a drum, a six-foot-long xylophone, wooden plates, various rush mats, a bark picture made by the Mothers' Union, a long-handled gourd drinking cup, two giraffes (wooden), two *busutis* and a *gomasi* (local dresses and tunics). The gifts we brought comprised bibles, coloured pens and paper, needle cases, footballs and second-hand clothes. It was quite impossible for either side to refuse the gifts brought by the other. Fortunately the bishop took care of the animals, for whom transportation back to England would have posed an even greater problem than was presented by the xylophone.

It was expected that we should sign the many guest books: for the school, the church, the clinic. Wherever we went, the guest books appeared (usually an exercise book with diligently ruled columns), and our signatures were (and perhaps sometimes still are) to be found in villages, towns, churches, law courts and government departments all over Busoga. So for a short period we shared the life of royalty.

---

[68] Lusoga is the only language of which I have had personal experience in which inflections are to be found at the beginning and not the end of the word's stem.

Finally, the feasting began. A procession of women now arrived bearing brightly coloured plastic picnic plates of food. There might be five to ten different dishes: matoke, rice, chunks of meat (unrecognised by us, probably goat), a watery meat juice, yams, sweet potatoes, possibly another vegetable (unrecognised), peanut paste, sesame paste and once, as a very special treat for honoured guests only, white ants. These were cooked and looked rather like caviar. The locals sometimes eat *live* white termites from a cone of paper and pour them wriggling into their mouths. The process finishes with what to our eyes seemed a genuine smile of satisfaction. Elisabeth, when offered a full cone, smiled and said she was very grateful but that she thought the offerer deserved it more than she. He fortunately did not demur.

Meanwhile the villagers retreated to the shade of the walls of nearby buildings. They had been standing, many in the sun, for up to four hours, and still they had not eaten or drunk anything. We tried desperately to look enthusiastic about the food; it would have caused great offence not to eat. However, we were told by the bishop that every morsel that we left would be devoured by grateful villagers after we had gone and so we touched very little. At one particularly grand feast, each of the more senior villagers who were sitting in rows behind us was given a polythene bag of rice, which they ate with their fingers.

A visit to the community by a respected guest was such an important event that the celebrations were normally planned to last all day. However, ours was a tightly packed schedule and we often fitted two such visits in a day. The long, bumpy journey through the bush might take two hours or more, and this was a good time for discussions and decisions. A 'two-visit' day could take from sun-up to sun-down.

We had the opportunity of visiting various ministers, the Chief Justice and other judges and the High Commissioner. Two things in particular remain in my memory. In a ministry we handed in our bags in at the cloakroom and were given a ticket which had written on it, not a number but 'The Lord is my shepherd'. When we came to collect the bags the cry went up: 'The Lord is my shepherd', and the bags were found and produced. We were told this use of biblical texts was a teaching method. The other picture in my memory is of prisoners in a semi-subterranean prison looking hopelessly out of the barred open windows at the sun awaiting their turn before a bewigged judge. I thought of the prisoners in *Fidelio* and how incongruous my presence was.

We made a third visit in 1997 and a final one in 1999. Uganda was gradually becoming richer, but the villagers did not share much of this wealth, and in many ways these later visits resembled earlier ones.

In the rural areas several religions survive together: Christian (both Anglican and Roman Catholic), Muslim and 'traditional' (witch doctors). They cohabit quite peacefully, and in one village I was warmly embraced by a very old, prickly, bearded Muslim and movingly thanked for bringing water to his people as well as to the Christians.

We went to various church services – routine Sunday services, but also a confirmation with just under 200 confirmands followed by prolonged communal feasting. The bishop said that he had half a dozen such services each year. The churches were packed, and the singing was vigorous. It was common to invite any visiting white man to preach. On one occasion in the cathedral a bird which had flown in through a broken window relieved himself above me, thus staining my head and jacket as I was in full flow. Its defecation was immediately met with loud applause by the congregation. When I later expressed my surprise at this to the bishop, he said with a straight face that no doubt they thought it was the Holy Spirit in the form of a dove. His formulation implied that he did not share this view.

What has remained with me ever since my time in Uganda is the preciousness of water, each litre of which had to be fetched from what was a clean source. We were both much moved by the willingness of large poor families to take over a whole family of children after the death of their parents from Aids and by the way the ill and ancient were looked after by their own families.

## Tensions in the diocese

My experience as counsel, arbitrator and judge was called upon in unforeseen circumstances.

Pretty well the whole time we visited Busoga there was strife within the diocese. I cannot give a reliable account of what caused this. I was not there all the time, and politeness evidently required that I should only be told what the speaker thought I ought to know. However, since I played a minor part in trying to resolve the strife – which at times involved weapons – I can give a glimpse of matters as seen from my perspective.

Two of the major actors were the bishop and his cousin James Zikusoka, the dean of the cathedral. Each had been at Busoga College Mwiri which the bishop described to me as the Eton of Uganda. They were both likeable, impressive and determined men who had achieved a lot in their lives. The bishop had become ordained as a result of pressure from Archbishop Luwum, whose statue is among the twentieth-century martyrs at the west entrance to Westminster Abbey alongside that of Dietrich Bonhoeffer, whom I have mentioned earlier in this memoir.

Cyprian Bamwoze was consecrated in 1972 as first bishop of the new Busoga diocese. He supported Archbishop Luwum in writing to President Amin a letter of protest at the way Uganda was governed by him and signed it along with other bishops. This infuriated Amin and resulted in several deaths, including that of the archbishop. Bamwoze was spared and set about trying to revive the economic life of his diocese and founded what was called the Multi Sectoral Rural Development Programme for which he secured help from various sources in various countries.

Zikusoka was known locally as the Reverend Engineer. He was indeed an engineer, had risen to be permanent secretary of the Ministry of Works, then Minister of Works under Amin, who later sacked him, whereupon he fled the country. He told me that some youths armed to the teeth had broken into his house and that, very frightened, he had heard himself saying 'If you shoot me, I will never speak to you again.' They laughed and left. In 1979, under a new regime, he was appointed High Commissioner to the United Kingdom.

The bishop, rather like a Victorian headmaster and indeed my own, was a man accustomed to command brusquely and speak frankly. I recollect being with him in a village church when the lesson was read by a local layman who, when I asked him whether he had ever considered becoming ordained, replied, 'If God wills.' 'Not while I'm bishop,' was the audible episcopal comment. This brusqueness made the bishop some enemies, I fear.

The dean, who was also accustomed to being in charge, wanted to run his own cathedral in his own way and was not an unqualified admirer of the way his cousin the bishop ran the diocese. He was ordained in 1988 aged sixty-two and appointed dean of Bugembe Cathedral in 1991. He resigned as dean four years later because he and Bishop Bamwoze did not see eye to eye on a number of matters.

There came into existence a group of those who were dissatisfied with Bamwoze as bishop and attempted to secure the consecration of another cleric as a bishop of the Church of Uganda. I was told of all this in August 1993 when Ezekiel, a local priest whom I had got to know, contacted me. I replied:

It is with a heavy heart that I keep hearing of the disarray of the Church in Busoga. Canon Eng. James has sent me a copy of his resignation letter to the bishop, which filled me with sadness. I see some force in the criticism which I gather is made about the centralisation of all power in the bishop and the difficulties which would arise if he were to die tomorrow. Indeed, I have made the same point to him myself from time to time. He is, and I suspect always will be, a source of both of inspiration and of exasperation.

My experience over decades has been that those who inspire frequently also exasperate and those who never exasperate also seldom inspire. This seems to be a fact of human nature.

It is sad that Canon Eng. James, for whom I formed a great respect and affection when I stayed with him, felt that he had to resign and it is sad that, as I gather, there is some disaffection amongst some of the clergy. But such matters are not unprecedented and the Church can survive such tempo-rary setbacks. What have perturbed me rather more are the reports that some sort of civil war broke out in the diocese between supporters and opponents of the bishop and that this war is being waged in public in the columns of the newspapers and by locking the door of the cathedral to the bishop and the manhandling of the archbishop.

Surely, when one is dealing with a mortal man of about sixty who, whatever his failings, is not killing people, it is not worth running the risk of another conflagration in Uganda. A tumble-down cathedral and a diocese badly administered in part are things worth trying to put right as best one can. But there seems to me to be a risk that in the course of righting what is perceived to be a wrong much greater wrongs will result.

I suppose that judges are more inclined than others to have a particular horror of open breaches of the law – whether canon law or civil law. I am prepared to accept that, in the most exceptional circumstances such as the regimes of Hitler, Stalin or Amin, there may be good reason to break the law rather than allow a tyrant to reign who is indulging in mass slaughter. But those circumstances are exceptional and do not currently, thank God, apply in Busoga. But I am afraid that in the sensitive situation in Busoga if one sows the wind one will reap the whirlwind.

As seen from here, the Church is a force for stability in Uganda. Of course there is room for improvement in the way the bishop does things. There always is in any diocese. But one must be careful not to let the ideal become the enemy of the good. I am firmly of the view that one should do all one can to discourage such breaches of the law even by people of the utmost goodwill who only have good in mind. I pray that Busoga does not drift by accident or human passions into the situation of lethal chaos with which it is alas so familiar and that you will play your part in helping everyone to keep a sense of proportion.

I was reminded of this when I found myself sitting with my old friend Bernard Rix in the High Court judging a case where a dispute had broken out between a parish priest and his bishop. The parish was split down the middle, people lost their tempers and sense of proportion, and this resulted in procedural irregularities. I said to Bernard, a practising Jew, that I was sad as an Anglican to be washing our dirty linen in public with him at my side. 'Don't worry. It's just the same with us in some synagogues.' I am not clear whether this made it better or worse.

In Busoga litigation was started in 1994 to prevent the consecration of the would-be rival bishop. Both Bishop Cyprian and the dean asked me to see whether the Archbishop of Canterbury would help. I believe that they each thought that their supporters had got out of hand. I did indeed contact Dr Carey, who was sympathetic but pointed out that he had no jurisdiction to intervene formally to prevent this consecration. However, he did act informally to contact the Archbishop of Uganda, and in the event the civil action was put on hold and no rival bishop was consecrated.

When I returned in 1997 matters had still not been resolved, and I invited the leaders of the rebels to lunch and did my best to act as peacemaker. The atmosphere was superficially friendly, but I had the feeling that people were playacting. However, in due course Bishop Bamwoze went on sabbatical leave, and in 1999 there was a service of reconciliation in Bugembe cathedral, during which he relinquished episcopal jurisdiction over the diocese, returning it to the Archbishop of Uganda.

Elisabeth and I were invited to this service, which was attended by I think all of the bishops in Uganda, who processed round the cathedral and then took their places inside, where we had been given very prominent seats near the altar. The service started, and

*Bugembe Cathedral: the service of Reconciliation*

after ten minutes or so someone passed us a service sheet. I leafed ahead and saw an entry 'Welcome and introductions' followed by 'Greetings from one of our visitors'. I turned to Elisabeth and muttered, 'I fear this may mean me.' The introductions made clear that I was indeed meant and moreover that I bore a message from the Archbishop of Canterbury. Neither I nor the archbishop had been warned of this. I felt I had no choice but to improvise a message which I did to the best of my ability, all of which was duly reported in the local press.

As it happens, the Lord Mayor of London had invited both the senior clergy and the senior judiciary to a grand dinner in the Guildhall during the following week. I took the archbishop aside and apologised for having improvised a message from him and the Church of England without clearly explaining that he had not actually composed it. He smiled and said something on the lines of 'These things happen. I am glad the problem has been resolved.'

By 1999, there were some 550 functioning wells, and I decided that I, with no management experience, had given what I had to give. Twenty years later, there are more than 2,500 functioning wells, boreholes and rainwater-harvesting tanks; the Trust has expanded its activities to embrace the teaching of sanitation and hygiene and has set up some micro-finance projects. Although it was named after one of the dioceses in Uganda, it has meanwhile spread to others.

In general I feel that one should not stay too long in a post because it can result in staleness and lack of drive. This one may not perceive oneself. Others, for various reasons, may decide not to point it out. So I decided that, after ten years, it was time for me to resign as chairman of the Trust.

# XXI

# Deaths in the Family

Meanwhile life continued agreeably for me as a judge. In early 1995 the appointment to the Court of Appeal of a judge junior to me was announced. It seemed obvious to me that I had not been thought to have the appropriate qualities, and I came to terms with this experience, which is, of course, a common one. I overlooked the fact that appointments are conditioned in no small part by the demands for a particular skill set at a particular time. As it turned out I was appointed to the Court of Appeal a few months later, something which pleased me and Werner. He came to my swearing-in, and, I think round about then, I arranged a party for him in the Inner Temple Hall, which he and everyone else who was there clearly enjoyed.

## Werner

But he was visibly ageing. In his mid-eighties, he had written a book which was very well received but which marked in some way what he felt was the end of his productive life. I remember him turning to me and saying, 'I do not have another book in me.' On another occasion he said, 'I have not done all that a man can do. But I think I have done all that it was in me to do.' As I reach a similar age I feel the same. He reflected, as he told me, that there comes a time when a man *can* die rather than *must* die. He became reluctant to rise from his chair and ate less. It was clear that he wished to move out of the strain of doing into the peace of the done.

He and Kathleen moved back to Freiburg, where he was surrounded by his former pupils, now themselves professors, who came and talked to him and read him poetry. He took to his bed and did not get up. At night, law students took turns to act as his nurse. He lay still – unless that is, one of his female admirers was announced, in which case he sparkled for half an hour, told her that that was enough and relapsed into somnolence.

Letters of condolence came in from all over the world and made clear to me that I was not the only one who thought him remarkable and that I was very lucky to have been brought up under his influence.

But the tributes he would most have enjoyed came from his former pupils, one of whom wrote to Kathleen:

One of the most remarkable persons I have ever met: an all-round genius, a great teacher, a profoundly humane and delightfully witty man, a philosopher. I particularly remember many lunch invitations at your hospitable house during which I was not only offered free food (quite a treat for a student) but more importantly plenty of intellectual and artistic nutrition. At these moments Werner set standards that I always admired and always wanted to achieve.

He was always a friend, a good-natured and inspiring father rather than an old-fashioned law professor. Even while teaching law (not in a dry manner but as the most integral and lively centre of human society), he made us feel as if he had personally known the great thinkers of the past with whom he had – over a good glass of wine – discussed their ideas.

There is not a day in my life in which I have not tried to emulate (ever so clumsily) his amazing ability to combine extreme professionalism (his conceptually amazing book on sovereignty; his tightly argued cases at the European Court) with seemingly limitless curiosity, love of life, love of arts, and humour, his organ playing and his hilarious Victor Hugo pastiches.

And what a great teacher he was. For example, he would engage me, aged eighteen, in elaborate discussions on Toqueville's *Souvenirs*. This sort of endorsement of my curiosity at such an early age and on a topic as specialised as this meant the world to me. The most exquisite moments I had with him, with his joy of life, with his superb intellect, were in the summer weeks at Interlaken. There I would have him almost to myself, and I emerged from this great vacation almost a different person, with the resolve to become as much like him as I could. Another cherished memory was a trip to Venice, which he somehow subsidised entirely in his generous, almost absent-minded way, and during which turned me into an addict of that magical place – it seemed he knew every nook and cranny of it.

There were scores of such letters. I myself loved being in his company and loved the atmosphere which surrounded him, although I was acutely conscious that whatever I could do he could do better. He was good at not making this too obvious, and I gathered that, although he knew that my gifts did not include intellectual brilliance, he felt that I had a fortunate ability to cope with whatever life threw at me. He described me as a *Lebenskünstler*, which I suppose just about translates as a life artist.

In any event, as I bade my last farewell to him and thanked him for the enormous amount he had done for me, he told me that I was the best gift that anyone had ever given him. I was pleased to hear these words from a dying man whom I much admired. In our garden in Kent we have a rose named after him.

## Kathleen

Kathleen looked after Werner during his last eight months in Freiburg and took on herself the burden of almost twenty-four-hour nursing. She became practically a prisoner, never leaving the house for fear that Werner might need her. She was determined to outlive him. Typically, after his death she tidied up the Freiburg flat with my sister-in-law Patricia's help and then returned to London.

As I think of her setting the flat in order, I am reminded that Werner, when well, told me that one day he was feeling rather awful and had said to her, 'I think I am going to die,' to which she had replied drily, 'Well go upstairs and tidy up your study first.' Werner said he laughed and immediately felt better.

She was someone to whom I owe a lot. As my grandfather makes clear in his letters, which I have quoted, my arrival in 1946 was a substantial burden that she willingly took on at a difficult time. Part of her success was that, at the time, her adoption of the place of my mother seemed to me the most natural thing in the world. I don't think that it occurred to me as a boy to be consciously grateful, still less to express my gratitude.

Whereas my failing, as Werner had observed, was that I was too inclined to fit in with received views, my brother Martin's was that he took a delight in doing everything he could to annoy the establishment, down to refusing to wear the school cap. Since we often went to or from school together, this was embarrassing for me, because I was expected as a prefect to enforce school rules and not to wink at their non-observance by my brother.[69]

Kathleen rallied to his side by asserting that the rules were idiotic and that I should ignore them. I now understand her position much better than I did at the time. She, after all, had accepted this outsider into her family, and here he was bossing about her eldest son.

When she said to me *sotto voce*, 'He is going through a difficult phase,' I remember replying quietly 'the trouble is that he is always going through a difficult phase'. I fear that, although in my view this was a fair comment at the time, it increased rather than diminished the tensions of that afternoon.

When I was in the army in 1957–8, Kathleen wrote a whole string of loving letters to me. It was a time in her life when she was in general happy and not in pain, as she was in later years. She wrote happily about buying dresses, travelling by train, parties and guests, and going back to visit her father in Wem. She and others kept on writing that my letters were amusing and interesting but they have all been tidied into the universal dustbin. Indeed, as the year progressed, she lost much of the fondness for me which she clearly had in earlier years. It saddened me, and I never really understood why.

---

[69] Years later I was shown something like the following in the card game Trivial Pursuit. 'Who irritated the judge by being improperly dressed?' 'Martin von Simson, who addressed the judge in a West Country County Court in jeans.'

I realise now that I was strange to her in a way that I was not strange to Werner, who had been very close to my father, whom evidently I closely resembled. I remember Werner telling me that when they were both undergraduates, Helmuth had been passenger in a car driven by him when they were stopped by the police. They accused Werner of driving too fast. He hotly denied it. Helmuth was asked what he thought. He stated that he had no doubt that Werner had indeed been driving too fast. Werner thought this an eccentric way to treat a close friend. Helmuth, open-eyed, said, 'Surely you would not wish me to lie.' My critics would claim that I have inherited what some would describe as his priggishness.

Kathleen died unexpectedly some weeks after Werner. She had been in pain for years and was not enjoying life. I went round to see her one evening after my brother Piers' second wedding, and suddenly our relationship slipped back to what it had been years earlier and she started looking back on her life. I came home full of joy at this reconciliation and shared it with Elisabeth that evening.

Kathleen died during that night. At her funeral her brother Paul read Hardy's elegy on the death of his mother, 'After the last breath'. Her youngest son David reminded us of the splendid dinner parties which she and Werner gave. In her old age, Kathleen worked for Writers in Prison. One of these was a prisoner of conscience to whom she regularly wrote. I quote David both for what he said and to illustrate the way in which he expressed himself.

The prisoner was an opposition writer who had been imprisoned by Lee Kuan Yew. Kathleen discovered that a guest of hers had been honoured by Her Majesty with the Order of the Bath, a distinction which had also been conferred on Lee Kuan Yew. So she badgered her dinner guest into writing to President Lee, as one holder of the Order to another, to explain that imprisoning innocent people was not really the done thing. The writer duly got released and wrote Kathleen a most moving letter explaining that in the fifteen years that he had been incarcerated, he had never been allowed out into the sunlight, and this simple human pleasure had now been restored to him – along with his liberty – thanks entirely to her.

Her energy was prodigious. First in Birmingham, then in Luxembourg and finally in Switzerland, she created homes for her large family of boys and brought them up almost single-handedly. Nannies and cleaning ladies were what other people needed. She would do it herself. And no matter how Werner prospered, her frugality and self-denying habits were those of a lifetime. Not until arthritis and rheumatism had taken their terrible toll would she consent, on rare occasions, to make use of taxis or planes.

I interpose to say that in her younger years she would take us camping all round Europe and sleep in the car herself with her feet sticking out of the window while we were in tents. If by any chance Werner was in evidence at all, he would be in comfort at a local hotel. I recollect driving back from one of these holidays on the Mediterranean with the others, all of us pretty dirty. We turned up at the Hotel Georges V in Paris, where Werner was staying. She went up to the desk, asked for Dr von Simson and insisted on being given his room number and phoning him. She then made us all fetch our sleeping bags from the car and carry them up to his room. The concierge looked on open-eyed and open-mouthed. I still recall my embarrassment as a sixteen-year-old. Werner regarded it as one of the funny things that happen in life.

In her letter of condolence on Werner's death, Veslemöy Lunt wrote:

Werner was fortunate to have such a patient and loving wife as you. The demands made on you were, I feel, sometimes superhuman. I remember particularly your kind hospitality in Interlaken one Easter a very long time ago, when you were feeding and looking after at least twenty of us, providing two lunches/dinners every day singlehandedly.

This was indeed our practically daily existence, and those meals with several conversations going on in various different languages, sometimes simultaneously, were what typified our life at that time.

In Freiburg, she and Werner gave evening concerts and fed innumerable students who adored them both and admired her silent conducting of these evenings.

Martin was at Kathleen's funeral. I was moved to hear him read Hazlitt's *Thoughts on the Fear of Death*:[70]

Perhaps the best cure for the fear of death is to reflect that life has a beginning as well as an end. There was a time when we were not: this gives us no concern – why then should it trouble us that a time will come when we shall cease to be? …

There is nothing in the recollection that at a certain time we were not come into the world, that 'the gorge rises at' – why should we revolt at the idea that we must one day go out of it? …

---

[70] Hazlitt had lived in Wem. I recollect Kathleen pointing out his house.

There follows a passage which seemed of particular relevance to me who regularly worships in the Temple Church:

> Ye armed men, knights templars, that sleep in the stone aisles of that old Temple church, where all is silent above, and where a deeper silence reigns below (not broken by the pealing organ), are ye not contented where ye lie? Or would you come out of your long homes to go to the Holy War? Or do ye complain that pain no longer visits you, that sickness has done its worst, that you have paid the last debt to nature, that you hear no more of the thickening phalanx of the foe, or your lady's waning love; and that while this ball of earth rolls its eternal round, no sound shall ever pierce through to disturb your lasting repose, fixed as the marble over your tombs, breathless as the grave that holds you!
>
> … It is not wonderful that the contemplation and fear of death become more familiar to us as we approach nearer to it: that life seems to ebb with the decay of blood and youthful spirits; and that as we find everything about us subject to chance and change, as our strength and beauty die, as our hopes and passions, our friends and our affections leave us, we begin by degrees to feel ourselves mortal!

A beautiful passage chosen by one who knew that he was going to follow his mother before long.

## Martin

Martin died a month later. He too had been at the Bar, and many spoke of him with affection. His was an unusual combination of general affability and a penetrating intelligence of which I was in awe. He talked with ease to whoever happened to be around – man, woman, boy, girl, or passing dog – and left them the happier for having had a chat. He might be very clever but he nonetheless had a genuine interest in what other people thought and did. Although not usually dressed for the part, he walked around Dungeness like a benevolent squire inquiring after the welfare of his tenants, and people loved it.

As a boy and a young man he was strikingly handsome, but my favourite picture of him is, somewhat older, beaming in a steaming kitchen in London or Interlaken to which he used to bring, or more often persuade someone else to bring, vast turkeys at Christmas time. He and Patricia, following the path trodden by Kathleen and Werner, set an example of hospitality which it was difficult to match. Anyone who wanted to invite himself or herself or the whole family to Sunday lunch was a welcome guest. Such a visitor could then sit in the kitchen and watch the master prepare various sauces which complemented his carefully cooked meat.

He saw himself as a Rumpole and shared Rumpole's deep humanity.

He differed from many clever men in that he did not throw everything aside in the pursuit of power or wealth. Nor did he think it appropriate to consort with the high and mighty of this world. These things were not what he coveted. Martin was never remotely jealous of anyone else. Nearly all his life he was, so far as I know, at peace with himself and with the world. He had achieved his aims: to remain in the company of the wife who had been his companion since his teens, whom he adored and who adored him. To watch, with her, the growth in the life of his children as they in turn grew up and founded families. To enjoy the company of his many friends. These were the things he enjoyed.

Martin was the first of my younger brothers to die. He was two years younger. Although David did not die until fifteen years later, it seems appropriate nonetheless to mention my youngest brother here before returning to the 1990s.

## David

David was fifteen years younger than I. He wrote in October 2011 that he had been diagnosed with pancreatic cancer. A year later he died.

He was much the most amusing of the five of us and had a wry sense of humour, which I greatly treasured. When he left his Luxembourg village school, he went to a prep school in Sussex. I drove him there once. As we passed through a village, where there were some lads hanging about, he remarked with an assumed stiffness but in his treble voice 'the youths of Penshurst, I presume'.

I remember being in Bertrange and looking for the first time at a book containing some of Picasso's cubist paintings which left me puzzled. The twelve-year-old David looked over my shoulder and said, 'That's interesting. He is showing the man from the front and from the side at the same time.' I am ashamed to say that he understood what he was seeing well before I did.

On being asked to describe his best friends at prep school he said drily, 'I only have one friend and I don't like him very much.' Yet as he grew older he gathered more and more friends, all of whom I think remained faithful to him and he to them. Many drove to the West Country in winter to be at his funeral and then attended a memorial service in London.

After New College Oxford, where he was with our brother Piers, he went for what I think was a year's holiday in France and then returned to England and became a merchant banker. But he had something of a desire to shock and at one point wore blue eye make-up and dungarees. Once, when inviting him to dinner, Werner asked him to put on proper clothes for the occasion. David responded by turning up in white tie and tails, much to Werner's amusement. They agreed he should let the guests in. When they arrived and were somewhat taken aback at the white tie, David said hesitantly and pretending to be surprised, 'Oh ... Oh ... Erm. Don't worry. I am sure Werner won't mind. Just relax.' Which I suppose they did when they found that David was the only one in white tie.

When as a young man he thought that his bank was not paying him enough he asked for a rise in salary and was summoned to the chairman, who denied his request. David asked whether they were dissatisfied with his performance and was told: 'Not at all. You are doing very well. But we always test the sense of commitment to the Bank of our young men by keeping them waiting for an increase.'

David said he understood. Could he suggest that they install a bucket of cold water over his door because that would really test his commitment? 'But you will forgive me if I leave you with thanks.' He had, of course, taken preliminary steps to secure a better paid position with another bank.

He was an accomplished linguist and was working for Swiss Bank Corporation in 1995 when it merged with Warburgs, for which our brother Piers had worked all his professional life. Like many in the city, including Piers, he thought the Euro was a disaster and its adoption showed that the time had come for the United Kingdom to leave the Union. We corresponded amicably about this until his death.

He spent his last week with his family on horseback in Petra and in a gondola in Venice. Typical of his style.

## Gitta

Elisabeth's mother, Gitta, led an eventful life described in her own memoir, *The Red Thread*.[71] The daughter of the Schubert Scholar O. E. Deutsch, she left Vienna in 1938, when the Germans entered, came to England, was interned like her father as an enemy alien on the Isle of Man and then moved with him to Cambridge, worked as a secretary for the philosopher Wittgenstein, married and gave birth to Elisabeth. She remains in my memory as strikingly elegant and beautiful. Elisabeth told me recently that our marriage had been effectively arranged by Gitta and Werner, who thought that we would be good for one another. If so, they were right. When her last husband, John Holroyd-Reece, died, she went back to Vienna, worked for the United Nations Industrial Development Organisation (UNIDO) and both wrote and translated poetry, for some of which she received the Auden Translators' Prize. She died in Vienna in March 1998.

My friend the late Adrian Head wrote of Gitta at her death: 'To get to know Gitta and her poetry and prose, to enjoy our correspondence and her telephone calls was like bringing a shooting star into one's own earthbound existence.'

He himself also wrote poetry in English and German and, like me and many others, valued her many gifts.

We decided to move some of her furniture and other effects, much of which had come from the keep, to England. However, we had no spare space in our Campden Hill house, and the cost of finding a secure repository was quite substantial. We knew that Juliet and Ben were looking for a place in the country for times when they were not in London and so hit on the idea of taking a lease of a

---

[71] Ariadne Press, 1996.

property which we could furnish with Gitta's furniture and to which both they and we could escape. Ben found part of a manor in Dorset, and there we stayed for a few years until we moved to Luxembourg and they moved to a place in Kent.

*Juliet and Ben's wedding in the Temple Church*

# XXII

# *The Family's Future*

But future generations take the place of the dead. We had the joy of seeing Juliet get married in the Temple Church in April 1997 to Ben Bevan. He was the fifteenth child of his parents, Roger and Molly, and one of the challenges which Juliet had to meet was to learn the names of the fifty-two grandchildren then in existence.

Ben's brother David played the organ; one of the hymns composed by Roger's brother Maurice was vigorously sung. Many of Ben's family and his and Juliet's friends made up an orchestra and choir.

Juliet had decided that she would process down the aisle with me while the Sanctus from Bach's B-minor Mass was sung. I had raised my eyebrows at this and pointedly asked her whether she did not think that Sanctus should be feminine. 'Oh, Daddy!' is her smiling reply on such occasions. In fact, I was hugely moved as we processed at a stately pace.

Since then, she and Ben have blessed us with two grandchildren. They may well write their own memoirs in due course.

*Granddaughter Anna in Kent 2022*

*Grandson Leo in Germany 2022*

# XXIII

# The Court of Appeal

My appointment to the Court of Appeal was announced in 1995. It is customary for lord justices to be made members of the Privy Council, and on 17 May 1995 I was duly sworn in. This was an occasion I found emotionally moving. I thought of my forebears who had taken similar oaths to the Emperor on being made Privy Counsellors in Germany.

A year or so after I went to the Court of Appeal, Lord Bingham, then Master of the Rolls, asked me to keep an eye on all the cases in which there had been a reference by the English courts to the European Court of Justice and to help to ensure that things were proceeding in the appropriate way and with appropriate dispatch. I had the nerve to ask whether, in return for my doing this, it would be possible to relieve me from doing the criminal work in the Court of Appeal which I had found particularly time-consuming because of my inexperience in this branch of the law. To my surprise he agreed. I was grateful for the advice I had received from Lord Woolf in his congratulatory letter that I should not work too hard. I didn't.

One of the congratulatory letters on my appointment referred to a rumour that a pacemaker now went with the job. I am relieved to say I did not require this.

*Lord Justice of Appeal. Photograph taken by Christan Courrèges*

It was Lord Woolf who had first suggested that I might enjoy the judicial life, and I am hugely grateful to him for this and much else. He and I went to various meetings in Europe with other judges. I sat with him when he was Lord Chief Justice in a case known by lawyers as *Factortame IV*. Following ECJ case law, we ruled there that, in certain circumstances, damages could be awarded against a member state of the EU, in this case the United Kingdom, who had acted in breach of EU law. The government's appeal was, to their astonishment, unsuccessful. Like the earlier *Factortame* cases it was a landmark case which shocked traditional political opinion. I reflect now that it might have been one of the causes of the virulent hatred of the ECJ which was in evidence in some parliamentarians during the Brexit debate.

# XXIV

# *The Freemason Controversy*

Just before the beginning of the summer holidays in 1998, all members of the judiciary received a form to fill in from the Lord Chancellor's department headed 'Register of Freemasons'. This asked each judge to declare whether or not they were a freemason or to declare that they were not prepared to disclose this information. A press release indicated that the Lord Chancellor, Lord Irvine of Lairg, thought that there was a level of public concern on the issue of judicial membership of the Freemasons which might serve to undermine confidence in the justice system, and that this must be avoided, if at all possible. The Lord Chancellor stated that he hoped that the public register would go some way towards doing this.

I myself, notwithstanding my love of Mozart, have never to this day been, or aspired to be, a Freemason. Nevertheless, I was horrified to receive this request from a government minister. It seemed to me to threaten the independence of the judiciary. I contacted some continental legal friends for their reactions. They were flabbergasted. So I decided to refuse to make the declaration sought.

I pointed out that I had left Germany at the age of nine. I had spent much of my life reflecting on how it had come about that that a civilised nation had slipped into barbarism. One of the relevant factors had been that many judges had let important constitutional changes pass without comment and without warning of their implications. Those judges who sought to alert the public had been silenced.

The official representatives of the judges had taken the view that it was inopportune to make a fuss. I however felt that there was no legal obligation to make such a declaration, and it was wrong for the government to put pressure on judges to do something which they were not legally obliged to do. The Lord Chancellor had publicly emphasised his faith in the integrity of the judiciary and firmly rejected the view that some judges might have been wrongly influenced by their Masonic membership in deciding cases.

Thus the basis of the request was a belief that the public *wrongly* suspected improper Masonic influence in the judicial decisions. It was illogical to rule out eligibility for judicial office because of an unwillingness to declare one's position in relation to a matter which was regarded as irrelevant to suitability to that office. If one went this far there was no logical stopping point.

This position met with considerable support, and in 2009 the then Lord Chancellor, Jack Straw, finally announced that the practice had been discontinued.

However, there were those who said (jokingly I think, but Germans are accused of not always understanding the English sense of humour) that I would be sent off to the ECJ as a punishment for making a public fuss.

# XXV

# *The Inner Temple*

The Inner Temple has been an important part of my life ever since my call in 1962. For decades I regularly lunched there, first with my fellow students and junior barristers and later with Queen's Counsel and judges. I also became a member of Gray's Inn when my chambers moved there, and that also became a regular lunching place. In 1985, I was elected a bencher by the Inner Temple. Partly in thankfulness for the grant of a pupil studentship of 100 guineas to me in 1962, I joined the Scholarships Committee whose chairman I became in due course.

My life in the Temple has been affected by my German origins, but by no means adversely. I did not at the time know that my mother had worked with him, but in 1998, sixty years after the call to the Bar of Count Helmuth James von Moltke, I suggested to the then Master of the Temple and to the Treasurer of the Inner Temple, Elizabeth Butler-Sloss, that we might arrange a service of commemoration of the Count. They were both enthusiastic. I gave an address[72] which

---

[72] See Appendix p.375.

was heavily influenced by letters he had written to his wife during the Nazi years[73] explaining how he had used his skills as a lawyer to fight against the creed and practices of Nazism. The letters concluded with one written on the eve of his execution in January 1945. At the service the church was full and contained members of his family, including the then German ambassador to the Court of St James, his cousin Gebhardt von Moltke. I was very touched to receive a letter from Helmuth James' widow Freya[74] in which she wrote:

> It was deeply moving for me to read [the address] and to find Helmuth James understood, admired, remembered and shown for the first time as a Christian lawyer, as a fine, bold lawyer. This makes me feel very thankful. No lawyer had done this so far; only a lawyer, however, could do this for him. And you did it so well, so beautifully and so movingly … How pleased he would have been! You made Helmuth James part of your life by studying him so carefully … Only relatively few Germans know that he belonged to those that helped to save the soul of the German people. Those who do love him.

When I was treasurer of the Inn in 2003, I referred to his example when addressing the students on call night.[75]

Two years earlier, on the initiative of a German lawyer, Volker Heinz, who had also been called to the Bar at the Inner Temple, the Temple Gift Foundation was founded with my full support. Its aim

---

[73] *Briefe an Freya 1939–1945* (C. H. Beck, 1988). The English version is *Letters to Freya: A Witness against Hitler* (Collins Harvill, 1991).

[74] *The Times* of 14 March 1947, under the headline 'The royal family at Lady-smith', records that the Queen sent for Freya and gave her a seat at the royal table and spent some time talking to her.

[75] See Appendix p.375.

was to establish and provide finance for some von Moltke Fellows in both Germany and the United Kingdom. We wished to enable young lawyers from each country to study in legal practice for six months in the other country so as to broaden their outlook. Volker had secured a considerable amount of funding from German donors on the basis that we in the United Kingdom would secure an equal amount and that the same number of fellows would go from the United Kingdom to Germany as from Germany to the United Kingdom.

Unfortunately the Foundation, after a few successful years, spluttered to a halt. There was no shortage of German lawyers wanting to come here but only a very limited demand from UK lawyers to go to Germany. Each had to have a sufficient command of the language of their destination to be able to benefit from their sojourn there, and this I suspect was a major discouragement for those from the United Kingdom. So I fear was the widespread, if unjustified, view that nothing was to be gained by familiarising oneself with German law. Things were different in the nineteenth century. A few years later I wrote an article setting out my views on the desirability of seeing things from different perspectives.[76]

In 2003, I secured that four stone benches were placed just outside the Temple Church. In the centre of Church Court there is a plaque recording that the two courts which had been there were destroyed by enemy action in 1941. At the dedication of the benches on 17 October 2003 I said:

> Behind us is the site of Lamb Building destroyed by enemy action. Thus also was much destroyed in Berlin, where some of us grew up. I cannot say, with Wilfred Owen, 'I am the

---

[76] 'The Judge as Comparatist', *Tulane Law Review* 80 (November 2005).

enemy you killed, my friend.' But my father was one such. In front of us are benches to mark a fervent wish for peace. Whether you walk from East to West or West to East, whether you speak English or German, these benches will bring that fervent wish to mind. The inscription behind us speaks of the past. May the inscription before us speak of the future.

The inscription on the ends of the benches reads, in English and German, 'Peace be with you'.

The Inn kindly placed at my disposal for the year of my treasurership a small flat, in which we discovered the delights of having a flat in the Inn. It is rather similar to living in a cathedral close.

When I ceased to be treasurer, I became a tenant of a flat in Temple Gardens, opposite what had been the site of my chambers when I joined them in 1963, overlooking the Inn's gardens, the Thames and St Paul's. We found it delightful and we remain there to this day.

2003 was an eventful year for me, both because I was treasurer and because the year ended in my resignation from the Court of Appeal and my departure to Luxembourg.

When I was elected treasurer, someone asked me, 'What reforms are you planning to bring in during your year?' I replied that I was hoping to keep the ship afloat but envisaged continuing much as before but perhaps making some minor improvements. To my joy, for I felt that this reply was hardly inspiring, he breathed an audible sigh of relief and said, 'Thank heavens for that.' People always prefer the familiar, and if one is inherently lazy then the most instantly attractive course is to do nothing.

As treasurer one is surrounded by people on the various committees who make recommendations in their respective fields of operation. I found that I learned from them and, with the help of the excellent sub-treasurer Peter Little, it was very easy to secure agreement.

Apart from making speeches, I did a lot of entertaining on behalf of the Inn, which was often both agreeable and informative. For instance, I entertained a dozen or so Chinese judges who were in England to have a look at the operation of our criminal law and who came to lunch after a fortnight at the Central Criminal Court. I asked them what they had found helpful. Their answers were revealing. One of them said that he had found the discussions on sentencing very similar to what he was used to and very helpful but that they had all been astonished by the amount of time and care which was devoted to the trial process itself. 'At home it is only people who are guilty who are prosecuted.' It occurred to me that von Moltke would have found that judicial approach familiar.

I tried to capture life in the Inn in an article I wrote for its Yearbook.[77] The atmosphere of the Inn twenty years ago is happily captured by the speeches made on the appointment of Lord Falconer as Lord Chancellor.[78] The government of the day had, without consulting the senior judiciary, insisted on making a number of reforms which included the departure of the existing Lord Chancellor, Lord Irvine, and his replacement by Lord Falconer. In the course of my speech at a dinner which the inn gave to Lord Falconer to mark his appointment I said:

I can, of course, think of a number of reasons which may have caused you to suggest the Day of Atonement would be a

---

[77] See Appendix p.375.
[78] *Inner Temple Yearbook* 2004/5, p. 72.

suitable date upon which to hold this dinner. A consciousness of the need for repentance so early on in office? Anyhow, we acceded to your wishes. It has, however, the sad consequence that Master Woolf and Master Rix, who would have wished to be here, have asked me to send you their expressions of regret and good wishes ...

I reminded Master Irvine earlier on this year of Lord Acton's dictum that there is no worse heresy than that the office sanctifies the holder of it. Rest assured we are no heretics. We don't, all of us anyhow, think of you as a saint ...

There is no doubting the fascination exerted on all by a man who sees himself as a sculptor and the Constitution much as Michelangelo must have regarded the block of marble out of which he intended to carve his monumental David. As he put it in one of his sonnets,

> *The marble not yet carved can hold the form*
> *Of every thought the greatest artist has,*
> *And no conception ever comes to pass*
> *Unless the hand obeys the intellect.*

You certainly don't do things by halves. In relation to the Constitution you follow the advice of the man whose mother-in-law died in Brazil. When asked how the remains should be disposed of, he replied, 'Embalm, cremate and bury. Take no risks.'

Life is always exciting for the reformer – be he Luther, Cromwell, Robespierre, Napoleon, Lenin, Mao Tse Tung or Margaret Thatcher. It must be hugely exciting for you. There are indeed all sorts of things in our society which are not for the best in the best of all possible worlds. And of course it is more exciting to be part of a process of change than merely to patch up an outworn system.

And yet ... Was it pure coincidence that on the day of your appointment the Master at Matins used Reinhold Niebuhr's famous prayer: 'Give us the serenity to accept what cannot be changed, courage to change what should be changed, and the wisdom to know the one from the other ...'

In your hands at this moment is a rare treasure – the legal system of this country, with a long tradition of courage, honesty and technical competence in barristers, Queen's Counsel and judges and a long tradition of politicians willing to accept that courageous and strong judges are needed to blow the whistle when, as will always be the case from time to time, the political temptation to oppress the minority of the moment is strong. I think I know you well enough to be able to say with confidence that you are conscious of this fact as much as I am. For me and many others this tradition has motivated whatever good we have done in our professional lives. You of course know that there are many, both within this Inn and outside it, who are desperately afraid that these traditions – some of them major political achievements of this country – may be unwittingly destroyed ...

I believe that if you were to abolish the Inn, the country would lose more than it would gain. Sometimes one must realise what one can *not* do, and that's sometimes more important than what one *can* do. You cannot legislate for courage and honesty. You cannot in a short period of time create a tradition of fearless honesty and competence in the courts. You cannot easily create a civilised society such as an Inn of Court in which there is happiness and respect for the views of others, and barristers and judges can relax and tease each other about their failings. Fortunately, all these things are available to us now. They are of huge benefit to society. Please, don't pull the house down. It won't be easy to rebuild.

Lord Falconer made an elegant speech in reply, which included the following:

I should say it's not a matter for me, but I've got absolutely no intention of abolishing the Inns of Court. Working in the Temple, eating in the Temple, drinking in the Temple, playing table tennis in the Temple, lying in the garden in the Temple, always with people who completely share a view and a recognition of the importance of the law, the importance that the law be dispensed impartially and independently and with people in every case recognising that the process involved in court was seeking to come to the best and the fairest view ...

We are, as Konrad has referred to, in a period of change, with the Judicial Appointments Commission, a Supreme Court and the abolition of the role of Lord Chancellor. These are mighty constitutional changes. I very much recognise the great anxiety that those expected changes cause, but I believe the time has come for these changes. My department tells me the story of the visiting East European delegation who hear goggle-eyed of a system where a cabinet minster appoints all the judges, is head of the judiciary, runs all the courts and legal aid, and if the going gets rough can chair the final court of appeal himself. Even Ceaucescu, they cried, at his most extravagant would not have tried that.[79]

In making the changes which I have referred to, I think it is important to stick firmly to three principles. First of all, the independence of the judiciary must be preserved, and strengthened. That is what we all believe in. Secondly, the quality of the judiciary must stay as high as it always has, and there is nowhere in the world that one goes where people do not respect the English judiciary as the best in the world. And thirdly the partnership between the government and the judiciary must continue as it always has. We have done it in the past by sleight of hand, the role of the Lord Chancellor. We need to be much more straightforward and direct about the close relationship between an independent judiciary and an effective executive ...

In the event we still have the office of Lord Chancellor, but only in vestigial form. The other reforms have been enacted.

---

[79] I remember that when I was sitting as an ad hoc judge in the European Court of Human Rights I mentioned that I understood that the compatibility of the position of the Lord Chancellor with the European Convention of Human Rights might well come before that court one day. One of the judges said to me something like that and added, 'I gather that works well in your country, but in mine if we were to adopt it then we would be straight back to dictatorship. In this court we have to declare a law which works for all the member states. Can you not quietly give up your system for the sake of the rest of us?' This is a typical European approach to a problem for which I have much sympathy. But many in this country simply say, 'Why should we all have the same rules?'

# XXVI

# *Sovereignty*

In my fifties and sixties I watched developments in Europe with particular interest. I regarded the concept of state sovereignty as partly responsible for all those horrors which surrounded my childhood. My German background has alerted me to dangers which are perhaps not so obvious to those who have lived a quieter life. After the war the received view in England was that, for reasons embedded in their history, the Germans were uniquely susceptible to state-organised evil. There is no doubt that they were susceptible. But uniquely? Hardly.

The sovereign state has a huge grip on people's imagination throughout the world. Who in Africa, China, the Americas, etc. does not stand up proudly when they hear the words 'this is a sovereign state'? It seems to give us a certain importance and dignity which we acquire by being associated with a long history. The Nazis found a ready audience in Germany for their myth that Germans were innately superior to all other races. When I was at school in England the map was still painted red and I soon became sufficiently English to join my contemporaries in taking it for granted that it was the English who were innately superior to lesser breeds without the law.

As I reflected, it became clear that absolute sovereignty brings its problems. It is an ineluctable fact that human beings have mutually conflicting desires. The fact is that we are different. Yet no doubt the vast majority wish to live in harmony and avoid bloodshed. This is most easily achieved under a polity which enables the *minority* on any issue to live at peace with the fact that the majority takes a different view and that this view should prevail; and which enables the *majority* to accept that the minority is made up of fellow human beings to whom one also owes certain duties which limit what can legitimately be inflicted on that minority.

The territorial state has proved a useful tool for describing the boundaries of such a polity within which everyone accepts the democratic discipline that the minority is content to yield to the majority. For the majority to demand obedience from a minority which does *not* regard itself as belonging to the same people is usually regarded as oppressive. So it seems to me that the challenge is to widen people's conception of who is part of the same people. This is easier said than done. In any event it only comes gradually over time.

The concept of sovereignty was indeed a useful conceptual tool in ordering society at the time of the wars of religion in the sixteenth and seventeenth centuries. At that time most European states were in effect aristocratic dictatorships. One recalls the phrase *cuius regio; eius religio*. The ruler was responsible for choosing the religion of all those who lived in his territory. If any subject was not prepared to fit in, he could, in theory at any rate, move to the territory of a more congenial ruler. So the word *sovereign* entered political discourse.

However, the concept of the sovereign state has in my view been stretched far beyond sensible limits. In part this expansion of the use of the concept of sovereignty is because the historical image of the European state has been transformed from an *empirical fact* that has shaped life in Europe from the Thirty Years War onwards into a *metaphysical entity* with its own soul and volition which is taken for granted as the prime actor in political discourse. And this, not merely in Europe but around the world.

From 1789, the idea of the nation became a powerful metaphysical focus of social identity, and social purpose, something to live and die for collectively. Millions did. The idea of the nation could set the identity, unity and purpose for all human effort – not merely the practical framework but also the ideal, aspirational framework. The economy of the nation could harness the overwhelming power of collective energy in the self-developing of a society, in competition and conflict with other societies which had undergone the same kind of development.

Sovereignty as a concept in popular parlance has now grown to comprehend an alleged right of a state to organise affairs within its borders as it pleases and an alleged right of the rulers of each state to be free from interference by other states.

I think this is not a good way to organise political life. Whether this be right or wrong, what is clear is that the more power we ascribe to the state the more difficult it becomes to enlarge the number of those prepared to submit to the democratic discipline.

It seems to me that the concept of a sovereign state should be criticised from three independent standpoints.

## What makes a people?

The first of these is that there is no self-evident answer to the question 'To what entity should sovereignty attach?' Anyone who lives in a modern state, which is the result of innumerable wars and migrations, must ask, 'What makes a people? Who has the right to consider himself part of the people? Why today's borders not yesterday's?'

Problems can and do arise when the boundaries of the state do not coincide with the boundaries of any particular group which sees itself as a national entity. That group may be a group within the state which wants to break free – many Irish, those in the Balkans in the early part of the last century, many Scots now – or a group which overspills the boundaries of the state – the Germans in the Baltic States would be a historical example, some persons in parts of the former USSR and Hungary would be contemporary ones.

Hitler confronted these questions in a German context by saying that, so far as he was concerned, the people consisted of Aryans as he defined them; and that the borders of the Aryan state should be what he called the Greater Germany, which *included* land which as a matter of fact was at the time not controlled by Germans but which he considered was required in order to accommodate and feed those Aryans. He added a further problem by seeking to *exclude* from his German state people who regarded themselves as members of that state but whom he considered not to be worthy of that status – Jews, Romanies, homosexuals, the physically or mentally handicapped, etc.

To put it unduly mildly, as a principle for ordering political life in the world the uncertainties underlying the concept of a state have produced sources of conflict.

## No state is in fact omnipotent

It is simply a fact of life that what *one* state wants is frequently inconsistent with what *another* state wants. So they cannot both be free to do what they want. This has always been true but the point has gained in force as a result of modern technical and commercial developments. Moreover, the people in any state are profoundly affected, not only by the decisions of the *governments* of other states, but by decisions made by *people* over whom it has no control and by *events* over which it has no control.

These events can take a whole variety of forms. Armed conflict and events produced by climate change and migrations; a nuclear explosion, whether as a result of an accident or deliberately induced; an economic depression in a country to which we want to export; the view taken by individuals of the prospects for sterling; what is happening in cyberspace; and so on. These are examples of things which no nation can control. For such matters the slogan 'Take back control' is misleading – first because we never had control over such matters and second because in practice we cannot get control. The same point can be made about state action. Germany had no control over the bombs dropped on Berlin when I was a boy; the UK had no control over the bombs dropped on London by the Germans or those exploded by the IRA when I was a man. Because I have heard and seen the effects of both, the point is vividly present to me.

'America First' caught the imagination of many – at any event in the States. But since states want conflicting things, it is obvious that not every state can successfully pursue a policy of putting itself first.

I myself felt unease when both sides of the referendum debate in the UK started from the same premise: we must do what we think best for *us*. It seems clear that this approach is only sustainable as a principle of international order if, in arriving at an answer, one takes into account a number of considerations and adopts a very broad view covering a long period of what is 'best for us'. To concentrate solely on financial effects – apart from all the difficulties attendant upon trying to guess the future – seems to take for granted that achieving financial prosperity trumps all other considerations. None of us would happily accept this in our personal lives. Is it not possible that selfishness is the problem not the answer?

The way ahead, and what the wise politician seeks to do, is surely to see how we can *influence* those in a position to cause us harm. The EU is an attempt to construct a framework for securing such influence for each member state.

## No state should be omnipotent

But I would go further and maintain that no state *should* think itself omnipotent, even within its own borders.

One great desideratum of political life is to provide order and prevent the mayhem which can result from each person being in a position to give free rein to their private passions. The state is a useful tool in this context.

However, one must be conscious that the state sovereignty version of popular sovereignty can itself be an enemy of other desirable goals.

In most of Europe, including this country, in general people want society to be so organised that the exercise of state power does not result in unnecessary inhibitions to the free development of everyone's personality; or, to put it more graphically, does not result in torture, and the suppression of any freedom of thought and expression considered by the ruler to be dangerous.

What we saw in Germany in the 1930s and 1940s was precisely this form of oppression. We can still see it in many parts of the world, often accompanied by whipping up the populace to a frenzy by means of lies and terror so that they forget what it is to be human.

In Western Europe and America there is currently no immediate prospect of a state suddenly becoming a dictatorship totally
devoted to suppressing dissentient views. But I have I think a greater
a horror of mass rallies being incited to action by political oratory
than most Englishmen. I am worried when passions are deliberately
whipped up against political opponents, against the rich, against
homosexuals, against the people who disapprove of homosexuals
and so on. I do understand that for a politician addressing a large
crowd, nuance and subtlety are hardly options. But surely deliberate
lies designed to persuade people to adopt goals which you regard
as desirable cannot be acceptable. Whipping up hatred is never the
answer. Politicians within the state cannot be relied on always to
behave in a manner which democracy requires. It can be useful to
have an oversight given to others away from the national pressures.

# XXVII

# *The European Union*

## The choice before me: England or Luxembourg

Early in 2003, when I was in the Court of Appeal and while I was treasurer of the Inn, applications were invited from those interested in being nominated by the United Kingdom for the post of judge of the ECJ in Luxembourg. It was suggested to me that I volunteer, and for reasons which will by now be apparent I did. Applicants were asked to state their reasons for their interest in the post and the strengths they would bring to it. This I did as follows.

> I hugely enjoy what I am doing at the moment and think myself fortunate to be doing it. However, it has repeatedly been suggested to me over the last twenty years that, because of the personal family background which I have outlined, I might have a useful contribution to make in Luxembourg. If I had not put my name forward on this occasion I would have regarded that as something which I would regret.

The next few years look set to be ones of great interest for the Union. Enlargement is something with which I am in sympathy – binding Poland and Germany together will be as important as binding France and Germany together has been. I have for the whole of my life had an interest in the tension between law and politics and in international relations. To play a part as a member of the Court in building the larger community infused with respect for human rights and democratic values is an exciting prospect. Most problems are perennial. I enjoy learning how others approach them. I generally enjoy the company of foreign judges and have the impression that they enjoy mine.

So far as the Court is concerned, clearly a necessary skill is the ability to work in committees and maintain harmony. A major challenge in the Court must be, I imagine, to be willing to be overruled without getting unduly upset and to be able to work with those whose confidence in their own judgement is such that they find it difficult to abandon their first positions. These skills I think I have acquired over the years in the various committees and organisations in which I have taken part and over which I have presided, most notably perhaps as a presider in the Court of Appeal and as treasurer of the Inner Temple.

Clearly it is an advantage to be at home in English and German and to have some knowledge of French, Italian and Dutch. My French is not as good as it will need to be for maximum effect in the Court and if I am chosen then I would wish to attend a total immersion course sometime in the autumn as suggested by David Edward so as to be up to speed by January.[80] I am reasonably sure that this is within my reach.

I have no doubt that the pragmatic British approach to solving questions is something which is a useful counterbalance to that based on the logic and intellectual rigour which results from a French schooling. Possibly because of my background, I often have an acuter perception of where a continental is coming from than is common amongst those who have worked exclusively in this country. This enables me to appreciate the force of the points which they seek to make and also to formulate my points in such a way that they can more easily be taken aboard by those brought up in a different tradition. To be able to make a deferential or light-hearted reference to another country's literary or social traditions smooths away suspicions. I have found this a strength in discussion with continental judges at conferences and so on.

I think it will be an advantage to be perceived by other judges, especially those from the new member states, as a senior judge in his own national system who has considerable experience of that system and yet whose knowledge extends beyond that. I suspect that the need in the Court of Appeal to master different fields of law at some speed and to get on with producing a judgement in conjunction with colleagues is also good training for the task which faces a judge in the ECJ.

In principle, none of the candidates was supposed to know who the others were. In practice, as tends to happen, news seeped out.

---

[80] In fact it proved impossible to arrange this.

It is typical of the spirit of the profession that I received letters of congratulation from others who I now believe were interviewed.

22 May 2003 was a very hot day. I had been summoned to an interview at the Foreign Office at 2:45 p.m. to be preceded by an assessment of my French three-quarters of an hour earlier. This assessment, made by a charming French lady, was a nightmare for me. I was asked to translate at sight an EC directive on dentist widows' pensions or something equally abstruse and to translate French spoken in various different French accents and to chatter away in French.

Years later, I invited the lady to come to the ECJ and see what went on. She did and came to dinner with us afterwards. After a glass or two I asked her whether my French had been the best that she had encountered amongst the various applicants. 'By no means', she replied with refreshing honesty.

The fact is that a fluency in social discourse in a language, while useful, is not adequate for drafting legal texts in that language or having a discussion about such drafts. Until the day I left the Court I had some difficulty in concentrating sufficiently for hours at a time on others speaking *their* French. Finnish, Portuguese, Polish, Irish, and Czech French all sound very different. It is not just a question of different accentuation. There are different 'false friends' in each language which the outsider may not recognise. On top of that, the judges all had different legal backgrounds and thus different self-evident truths of which each of their fellow judges might not be aware

The interview panel was presided over by Sir Hayden Phillips, the permanent secretary to the Lord Chancellor, and consisted of Lord Cullen, Lord President of the Court of Session in Scotland, Lord Justice Simon Brown, Mr Ian Hendry, Deputy Legal Adviser at the Foreign Office, and Ms Joanna Foster CBE, lay member and, so

I was informed, chair of the BT Forum. At the end of the interview, which took a fairly predictable course, I was asked whether I had any questions. I said I only had one, to which they probably would not know the answer: I wished to know when the Court took its summer holidays. Had I been asked for more detail I would have explained that I had a part-share in a house in France, and the shareholders were on the point of allocating slots for the following summer.

On reflection, this light-hearted remark was not an intelligent question for me to ask at that interview, and I suppose it might have cost me the job. But, perhaps because I was happy in the Court of Appeal, I was surprisingly relaxed. When I was asked, I think by Ms Foster, why I thought I was the best person for the job, I replied, if I remember correctly, that I did not think I was the best person for the job, did not even know who the other candidates were, and hoped the panel could find someone better. But memory is deceptive. This may be what I wished I had said. I honestly don't know.

In any event, in due course the UK government put my name forward, and it received the common accord of all the member states. The securing of common accord was generally regarded as a formality in those days, although it in fact took months, and in the event my appointment was announced in October 2003. Since my appointment, but not I hope because of my appointment, a panel of distinguished judges has been set up by the Union to give an opinion on candidates' suitability to perform the duties of judge and advocate general of the Court.

## Chateau on the Moselle

On arrival at the ECJ I was warmed to receive from Professor Ulrich Everling, a former member of the Court, a letter in which he wrote that 'Werner von Simson would have been very happy to see you follow in his footsteps in the endeavour to forward European integration and to be able to contribute as he did to the overcoming of the chasms which still persist between peoples, sadly including between the English and the Germans.'

I was also greeted by the Swedish judge who knew of my aunt Elisabeth's friendship with his aunt, Lise Meitner. In remembrance of my Baltic ancestors and as a sign of welcome to the incoming Baltic judges I took a delightful Latvian, Aleksandra Melesko, who had been recommended by my predecessor, as one of my legal secretaries. The Latvian judge greeted me as a relation of Paul Schiemann, who was a hero in that part of the world.

Elisabeth and I then set about finding a suitable place to live in Luxembourg. We decided to rent out our house in London and use the income to finance the taking of leases of a house in Luxembourg and of a flat in the Inn for our London stays.

Most of the other judges lived in flats in Luxembourg City, but this had not been the choice made by my UK predecessors, who recommended that we live in the country. This we also decided to do. Elisabeth had always wanted to live in the country. Although I enjoyed the country when the sun was shining, I had wanted to live in London on the basis that I did not wish to spend a significant part of my life commuting and yet wanted to live with her. She had accepted this without demur but now she could have her wish. I was in the fortunate position of being provided by the Union with a car and a chauffeur so that I could work during the journey. I recollected that Geoffrey Lane had done the same for years in England when he was Chief Justice.

We had in mind a converted farmhouse, of which there were plenty around, and so we tried a local estate agent. This profession in

*KS signing the Court's Register on appointment*

Luxembourg was, at the time, simply not set up to be of much help to the buyer. The descriptions of the houses in the written material were perfunctory, few if any photographs were available, and if you asked for details of the layout or of plumbing and heating you were told that they could arrange for you to have a look. Fortunately, we had been invited to dinner by old friends who had settled in Luxembourg, and someone at the dinner suggested that we contact an American lady who made it her business to find houses for foreigners in our situation. This we did. She asked us what we had in mind, and we produced thirty or so photographs of converted farmhouses which we had photographed while looking around and trying to decide whereabouts we wished to live. She said she could find something suitable but continued browsing through our photographs. On one of our tours we had seen a nineteenth-century chateau in Remich.

We climbed up to look at it and spotted that over the door were engraved the letters 'KS': my initials.

That photograph got mixed up with the photos of farmhouses which we showed the American lady.

'Would you like to live there? The owner wants to sell it.'

I was very firm.

'It is not for us. First, we are looking to rent and not to buy. Second, there are only two of us who will be in permanent residence. It's far too large.'

*Our chateau in Remich*

'Would you nevertheless like to have a look at it?'

Simultaneously I said no and Elisabeth said yes. So of course we went – just to have a look.

When we got there, we went inside looked around and both immediately felt at home. We met the owner's agent, who told us the price of the freehold, which was far more than I was prepared to pay. She explained that the property would rise in price and that in ten years – which was the length of time I envisaged staying – it would be worth double.

'In that case, why do we not lease it, keep it in reasonable condition, leave after ten years, and the owner can have the benefit of the price rise. I gather he is rich enough not to need the money in the meantime.'

She said she would put that suggestion to him. To my shock and surprise, he agreed in principle, and we came to terms on the rent.

Some people are lucky enough to live in houses which have been inhabited by their forefathers for generations. War and life's chances have denied me this pleasure. I cannot point to a property which has been the centre in the life of our daughter and grandchildren, and I regret this. The plus side has been that we have lived in several very agreeable places. The chateau was one of them.

It was situated on a hill overlooking the Moselle and vineyards, in which we walked for miles. It had a garden in which we gave parties for friends or staff from the Court. The building consisted of a large cellar in which we could give dinners for sixty or so and in which the grandchildren could play. On the ground floor were a large kitchen, a study for me, a drawing room and linked dining room. There we regularly gave dinner parties for less than thirty and, quite often, concerts. If the concert had a large audience, we would eat afterwards in the cellar. The first floor had five bedrooms, the second a further three, and so we were able to and did put up many people at the same time. On the third floor Elisabeth had a huge room largely for herself, where she practised her flute and recorders and where she drew and painted. From there one over-looked vineyards and the Moselle all the way to Schengen. On the top floor was a room which could be used for making things and storage. Elisabeth had collected a large number of dresses over the years. She hung them on racks there. Gradually some of them were coming back into fashion, as they do to this day. Now, one by one, she gives them to the next generations.

*KS in his room at court wearing ECJ robes*

*Elisabeth and Paul Heim, a former Registrar, at a court function*

I had a fulfilling time at the court during the day,[81] and Elisabeth spent much of her time happily reading and discussing books, drawing and painting, and making music. All this apart from actually running the house. We had a very full social life – not chiefly among the judges but rather among Luxembourgers and foreign diplomats, bankers and musicians. Although, clearly, London has more to offer, it is so spread out and there are so many fascinating people around that somehow it seems difficult to see one's friends and acquaintances regularly. We found Luxembourg's social life rather more concentrated and intense than we had anticipated.

Both of us were very happy there.

---

[81] I describe my first impressions in an article I wrote for the Inn's Yearbook reproduced in the Appendix p.390.

## The work of the Court

The principal function of the Court is to interpret and apply the provisions of the treaties under which the EU operates and of all the subordinate legislation made under them. It has to decide who has power to do what and decide whether what they have done is lawful and what the consequences of any illegality should be.

Typical questions are: did the Council, the Commission, or the Parliament or some European functionary have the power to do what was done?[82] Has a member state infringed its duties under EU law?[83]

Sometimes those questions arise in so-called direct actions, where a litigant, usually the Commission or a member state, brings a defendant, often another member state or a European institution, before the ECJ. More often, these questions arise before a national court, which usually can decide them on its own. But the national court, faced with a question of EU law, can, and in certain circumstances must, refer the question to the ECJ to provide an answer.

When I joined the Court there was general dissatisfaction with the length of time taken to produce the answers to questions posed by national courts, which at that time was around two years. This dissatisfaction was strongest in those countries, such as the United Kingdom, where national delays were below the European average, and weaker in those countries such as Italy where the law's delays had simply been accepted as inevitable.

---

[82] For instance, to refuse to reveal the legal advice given by its lawyers as to whether it was lawful to pass a particular measure without consulting the Parliament, or to engage someone as an employee without going through the prescribed procedures.
[83] For instance, by giving an industry an unlawful subsidy or by not enforcing a provision of EU law which prescribes the minimum size of the holes in fishing nets.

The primary reasons for the long delays by the European Court in deciding cases are the fact that the member states use more than a score of languages and the need to consult them in their various official languages as to how they think the Court should respond to the case. Such a case had, in all probability, been conducted so far in different languages by lawyers from different legal traditions. Such translations are difficult and take time. Consultation is desirable because a decision as to what EU law is will, in many cases, have implications which go way beyond the parties to the litigation. Each member state wishes to consult its officials and ministers and does not routinely expect them to speak any language other than their own. Pretty well every attempt to cut down the need for consultation, translation, or to reduce the time of consultation, met with strong opposition from several member states.

In order to achieve a reduction in waiting times, it proved necessary to reduce the Court's vacations and speed up procedures within the Court – the time taken by the administration, by translation, and the time taken by members of the Court in doing their work. Helped by the increase in member states and thus of judges, we managed to reduce the waiting time to about fifteen months. Sometimes the price that was paid was that some members of the Court did not have as much time as they would have liked to give of their best. There were occasional complaints that the quality of the judgements suffered as a result. I could not possibly comment.

When I first joined the Court, the thing that struck me was that, because of the procedures of the Court, one revisited the case many times over many months between first reading the papers and signing the judgement. One often read 100 cases in a month. Perhaps because I was one of the older judges, I often lost time when revisiting a case in getting myself back to where I had been a couple of months earlier. In England in general the process was very much shorter, seldom exceeded three weeks, and I tended not to have more than a few cases on the go at any one time.

The procedure which was in operation when I was at the Court depended on the particular type of proceeding but to get a feel of what happened one needs only look at the procedure when a question was referred by a national court for a preliminary ruling by the ECJ. This question was circulated to the member states in their respective languages. The important papers from the national court and the replies from the member states were translated into French, the language in which the Court worked.[84] [85]

These translations were then sent to the reporting judge who had been nominated for the case by the president of the Court. The reporting judge would remain with the case until judgement. He

---

[84] It is often asked, and not just by the English, why the working language was not English – a language spoken as a second language by far more Europeans than French. The answer is that when the Court was first constituted French was an official language of three of the six member states and English of none. In consequence, the case law of the Court was expressed in French and used French concepts. To change into English after other countries whose citizens preferred speaking English had joined the Community would have been a major task. When I was at the Court I did not think it appropriate for the judge nominated by the UK formally to suggest that English be adopted as the working language. After I left I wrote a chapter ('La Langue de Travail de la Cour') in *La Cour de Justice sous la présidence de Vassilios Skouris* (Bruylant, 2015), pp. 563–74, suggesting that the change should be made and should be proposed by the judge nominated by France. The French judge did not, so far as I know, put forward this proposal. In any event this suggestion has not been adopted by the members of the court – who had been chosen for qualities which included the ability to communicate in French. The current president, Judge Lenaerts, speaks excellent English as well as French but is a Belgian coming from the Flemish community. For him to approve such as suggestion would I suppose have gone down badly with the French-speaking ministers in the Belgian government.

[85] I discussed the advantages and disadvantages attendant upon a change to English in *Arnull, Eeckhout and Tridimas: Continuity and Change in EU Law* (Oxford University Press, 2008), pp. 3–19.

prepared a preliminary report in French containing a summary of the issues and arguments and a recommendation of what should be the formation of the court – how many judges were needed to compose the court which would decide[86] – and what further procedural steps if any should be taken. The reporting judge might give an indication as to how he thought the case should be decided. Then he would send his draft report to the advocate general who had been allocated to the case, would study the reply and try to agree with the AG as much as possible before finalising the draft.

The reporting judge would then circulate his preliminary report to all the other members of the court. Any other judge was at liberty to circulate a note indicating his disagreement with all or any part of what was suggested. The reporting judge would in general write a reply indicating his reaction to any note. Once a week we would have a meeting attended by all the judges and advocates general and there we would decide how many judges were needed to decide the case and whether they should have the assistance of an advocate general. The case would, save in the very rare cases where it was decided that the Grand Chamber of all the judges was needed, then be allocated to a chamber of which the Reporting Judge was a member.

After contacting the parties, the Registry then fixed a date for the hearing. Judges from the formation to which the case had been assigned were allocated to it on a strict rota basis, no account being taken of any judge's nationality or expertise. If I was not in the formation I then tended to forget the case unless it was particularly interesting.

---

[86] What appeared to be the simplest questions to answer only needed three judges; the most important might need all the judges in the Court, or one could suggest something in between.

The date of the hearing was then announced, and if you were involved you reread the case. You heard oral argument from counsel. This was sometimes excellent but quite often unsatisfactory for one or more of a number of reasons. The advocate might have come from a country which had no tradition of oral argument and might just be bad at it. Or he simply was not on top of his case.[87] Simultaneous translation of legal argument is often not easy to follow, perhaps because the advocate is speaking too fast, perhaps because the argument does not appear to make sense to the interpreter, which is not necessarily her fault.

In general, only twenty minutes were allowed to each advocate. Some criticised this, but there were genuine time pressures. One's ability to concentrate for any length of time on an argument which is being simultaneously interpreted is limited. Moreover, the longer cases went on, the fewer cases could be decided, and the longer were the consequential delays. Further, there is no doubt that forcing lawyers to concentrate the oral argument led to fuller written argument, which did not need to be interpreted simultaneously and is easier to follow if well done. Inevitably, judges' power of concentration and speed of thought will vary from judge to judge, and also from day to day.

During my time at the Court the number of questions posed by members of the Court to the advocates increased. This irritated

---

[87] I recollect one case when the advocate asserted some fact. I asked what was the basis of this assertion. He said it was in the bundle of case papers. I asked him where in the bundle. He did not know. I said he should tell me when he gave his reply later in the day. I checked over lunch but could not find it. When he replied he made no mention of it. I asked for the reference. He said, 'In the bundle.' 'Page, please.' He just shrugged. I said rather crossly that I must warn him that I would assume that he was misleading the court unless he gave me the reference. He shrugged again. I got the impression from some of my colleagues that they thought I was being rather hard on the poor chap. That would not have been the reaction in the United Kingdom. Almost certainly the barrister would have been sanctioned.

some members, who were not used to this way of testing the argument. Some will have had no practice at framing such questions, which is not as easy as it looks when well done. I recollect one such occasion when one of my colleagues posed a series of tangled questions which rested on a variety of legal propositions and lasted rather more than five minutes. The extremely competent English advocate said very politely, 'I am sorry. It is my fault. I did not fully understand your Lordship's question. Could I ask your Lordship to repeat the question?'

I had every sympathy with him and found it difficult to keep a straight face.

After the hearing, one waited for the advocate general's opinion, which could well take more than a month, especially if it needed translating into French. This was delivered to every member of the formation. The reporting judge had then to get on and prepare a draft judgement, which might or might not agree with the conclusion or the reasoning of the advocate general. Since the Court was anxious that all the Court's judgements should evince a stylistic unity, the draft was then submitted to one of a number of *lecteurs d'arrêt* educated in the traditions of the Court. It was their task to make sure that the legal French was correct and elegant. They occasionally made suggestions of substance, perhaps drawing attention to some earlier judgement, as to what might be incorporated in the reasoning, but these were suggestions only, often good, and I never found them offensive.

I found that having my judgements placed in this stylistic corset was annoying, the more so since I was no admirer of the corset. When judging in England I liked preparing my judgements in my own style. Here is the start of one of them – *Awwad v Geraghty & Company [1999] EWCA Civ J1125* – which would have been incon-

*KS painted by Emily Patrick for the Court*

ceivable in the ECJ, although the problem with which it deals is one which could equally well have arisen there.

St Yves of Brittany, patron saint of lawyers, used in the thirteenth century to act for nothing for the poor. Many lawyers still do. At the other extreme are those who will only act in return for payment. In the middle are those who would be prepared to act for nothing or less than usual if their client loses but wish to be paid if their client wins. One such is the appellant Miss Geraghty. After a trial, Rougier J found that, prior to her carrying out the work in question, the solicitor and the client orally agreed on 20th September 1993 that she would charge him at her normal rate if he won the litigation and would charge him at a lower rate if he lost the litigation. These appeals are concerned with the enforceability by her of that particular type of conditional fee agreement entered into by her with her client, Mr Awwad, in relation to libel litigation brought by him against Mr Gustavson.

One can contrast this with the ECJ Case C-539/09 *European Commission, applicant, supported by European Parliament, The Court of Auditors of the European Union, interveners v Federal Republic of Germany*. I was the reporting judge in that case and so responsible for the drafting of the judgement of the Grand Chamber, which started with these words:

By its application, the European Commission asks the Court to declare that, by objecting to the conduct by the Court of Auditors of the European Union of audits in Germany concerning administrative cooperation under Council Regulation (EC) No 1798/2003 of 7 October 2003 on administrative cooperation in the field of value added tax (OJ 2003 L 264, p. 1) and the provisions for its implementation, the Federal Republic of Germany has failed to fulfil its obligations under Article 248(1) to (3) EC, Articles 140(2) and 142(1) of Council Regulation (EC, Euratom) No 1605/2002 of 25 June 2002 on the Financial Regulation applicable to the general budget of the European Communities (OJ 2002 L 248, p. 1) and Article 10 EC.

Reading this now, drafted in the Court's habitual style, I still shudder. However, I entirely accepted that there were undoubted advantages in a court such as the ECJ producing judgements laid out in a uniform manner which could, after a while, be absorbed by lawyers from a score of different legal traditions who knew what to look for and where in the judgement it was to be found.

The draft judgement was then circulated for comment to the other members of the formation. Their notes in reply would vary from dealing with merely stylistic points to root and branch disagreement. You studied those and decided, if you were the reporting judge, whether or not to amend your draft. If it was clear from the notes that I was in a small minority, it was my practice, unless I felt that there were serious dangers in doing so, to explain in a short note why, although I disagreed with it, I had accepted a particular suggestion. The amended draft was then circulated and a meeting of the formation arranged.

There one learned of the views of those who had not circulated any note, and the arguments were tested in discussion. Sometimes the disagreements persisted, and we arranged another meeting, thus giving the reporting judge the chance to test the ground with a different draft. Eventually a draft was agreed. This would then be submitted to the *lecteur d'arrêt* for the final *toilette du texte* and then translated into all the languages, a process which sometimes revealed an ambiguity in the French draft which needed to be resolved.

Occasionally human error found its way into the process. I remember one occasion where, at the end of the judgement, costs were awarded to one party in the French draft but in the definitive judgement in the language of the case, which was (I think) Danish, the costs were by mistake awarded to the other party. The parties wrote to the court and asked what had happened. My first instinct, as president of the chamber, was simply to ask the translator to correct the Danish text so as to make it correspond with the French text, since the judgement had been drafted and discussed in French. However, this degree of informality understandably offended at least one of my colleagues, who insisted that the corrected text in Danish be submitted to the Chamber (none of whose members spoke Danish), be approved by them and then sent to the parties. So that is what we did.

The insistence on formality was different from what I had been used to back in London. I remember that when I was presiding in the Court of Appeal, I suddenly had placed in front of me a patent case, although none of the three of us who were supposed to decide it knew much about patent law. I phoned one of my colleagues who was presiding over two other Court of Appeal judges, one of whom was a very knowledgeable patent judge, to ask him whether he would be happy to send that judge over to me in return for one of mine. It was arranged in a minute. In Germany this would have been grossly illegal. Those who had lived through a time when courts were packed by the government of the day[88] were understandably insistent that these sorts of things could not be arranged informally.

In England one often heard it as a criticism of the ECJ that not all of the judges had been judges before they joined the Court. Indeed, there were academics, former civil servants and former ministers in the Court. Yet I thought this criticism misplaced. Because the Court works as a body, we each, in my view, in general gained from the others' experience. Judges would concentrate on what they regarded as justice, civil servants more on whether a particular solution would work in practice, academics on where a solution fitted into the intellectual framework of the Treaties and past judgements, and politicians on how a judgement might be received by members of the public. The particular qualities required of a UK judge when conducting

[88] In Germany, the Nazi Party, and see also the speech of Eduard Simson quoted above at page 18. But the problem has not in history been confined to Germany.

oral hearings in which the parties must respect his instant decisions are not so essential in the slower processes of the ECJ.

One of the things which became clearer to me as time went on was that the received truths and the received way of doing things elsewhere were often different from the received truths and ways of doing things in my country. Not merely was this a fact, but I was always conscious that it might just be that others did a particular thing better than we did. Of course, this receptive frame of mind comes more naturally to someone who does not merely have one country which he thinks of as 'my country'.

Another criticism which was made was that a judgement was either obscure or merely stated what was not in dispute and avoided deciding what appeared to be the crucial issue. Occasionally this criticism was justified. Sometimes the process of drafting the judgement led to a paragraph being excised from the draft because it was not crucial in itself and because it did not seem worth further debate. Securing agreement was the priority if we wished to get on. The danger is that if you do this too often then you can be left with the sausage casing but no meat.

But the fault did not in general arise from a failure by the Court to consider the point which it failed to resolve. Often the point had indeed been debated at length in the pre-judgement notes and discussions without agreement being reached. In those circumstances, in important cases in the larger formations if the formation was fairly evenly divided we tended not to press matters to a vote. This was because we all recognised that if the formation had contained different judges then the majority might have gone the other way. This led to a situation where we felt that we should not at that stage crystallise EU law on the point. But nonetheless we had to produce a judgement. So we left the point to be raised in another case after the academics and the profession had thought about it further and produced some new ideas and perhaps consensus. If the point was really felt to be immediately crucial by a national judge he could, and very occasionally did, raise it by a further reference to the Court.

The possibility of altering the rules so as to permit dissenting and concurring judgements was much debated in academic circles, and there were strong opinions on either side. In some countries the idea that the court was the mouth of the law had as its consequence a feeling that the court should not reveal to a wider public that opinions had been divided and that a choice had to be made. Some felt that it would be better for the independence of a judge (who might wish to be renominated for a further term) if his personal view were not published in his native country. Moreover, it was felt that to leave national courts to wrestle with producing the *ratio decidendi* of a case from judgements delivered by several judges in the Common Law manner would lead to increased difficulties and uncertainties. Moreover, if each member of the Court had been at liberty to produce his own judgement then the process would have taken longer. As it was, each judge had more than enough to do. Yet I was conscious of the danger of judges being attracted to agree with the majority simply because they lacked the energy to disagree and have an argument. I can see that dissenting judgements can help in developing the law and, when in England, I occasionally produced one.

Personally I had no very strong views on the subject of dissenting and concurring judgements and was content to let the wisdom of the majority prevail.

From time to time, I would make a suggestion for an improvement in the working of the court as I saw it. Some were welcomed, others not. I was introduced by the Greek president to a new technique for rejecting suggestions: a huge smile and 'Ah, the British sense of humour.' I was disarmed, and the discussion was closed. A rejection of what Schiemann thought would be improvements was not new to me in my judicial life. When I was an English judge my suggestions for reform, some of which may well have been the same as suggestions by others – establishing sentencing guidelines in criminal cases, allowing academics to become judges in the superior courts, providing written directions to the jury are examples – were rejected in the 1980s as being impracticable but were then adopted years later.

## The Brexit debate

On the whole, while at the Court I kept to the approach which I had signalled in the application letter which I have set out earlier. I felt that it was part of my job to try to persuade outsiders to the Court, particularly, but not exclusively, in the United Kingdom,[89] of the value of what the European Union and the Court were doing. In part I did this through lectures, the most significant of which were, I think, the Thomas More lecture in Lincoln's Inn,[90] a lecture I gave in the University of Southampton[91] and the Mackenzie-Stuart

---

[89] I wrote articles and gave a number of lectures in Germany and some in France, The Netherlands, Hungary and the USA. See, for example, 'Aktuelle Einflüsse des Deutschen Rechts auf die richterliche Fortbildung des englischen Rechts', *Europarecht*, 38(1) (2003), pp. 17–35; 'Vom Richter des Common Law zum Richter des europäischen Rechts', *Zentrum für europäisches Wirtschaftsrecht*, 145 (2005), pp. 1–16; 'Das Zusammenspiel der Grundrechtsordnungen und ihre Interpreten', *Zentrum für europäisches Wirtschaftsrecht*, no. 200(2) (2013), pp. 1–22; 'A Response to the Judge as Comparatist', *Tulane Law Review*, 80(1) (2005), pp. 281–97.
[90] 'Europe and the Loss of Sovereignty', *International and Comparative Law Quarterly*, 56(3) (July 2007), 475–89.
[91] *Yearbook of European Law*, Oxford University Press, vol. 19: 1999–2000, pp. 205–16.

*Meeting of the ECJ and the USA Supreme Court*

Lecture in Cambridge.[92] In part I did it by inviting UK judges to the Court and engaging with them there. Elisabeth and I used to give them a dinner in the chateau afterwards. I still meet people whose faces I can no longer recall but who assure me that we met at one of those dinners.

After I left the Court, I considered what part if any I should take in the debate on whether the UK should remain within the EU. I found myself being asked by parliamentary committees concerned with Brexit to give evidence, which I hope I did in a totally dispassionate way.

Judges in England were expected to keep their party political allegiances if any to themselves and to refrain from public controversy. This seemed to me a wise general rule, and instinctively I was inclined to keep to it even after retirement. So far as the Brexit debate

---

[92] 'The EU as a Source of Inspiration', *Cambridge Yearbook of European Legal Studies*, 14 (2012), pp. 325–6.

was concerned, my position was, however, a rather special one. I had resigned from the English judiciary ten years before and had at the instigation of the UK government served on the ECJ. That Court has its own rules of conduct for serving and past members of its judiciary. These presented no obstacle to my taking part in the Brexit debate so long as I did it with integrity, dignity, loyalty and discretion. With these restrictions I was of course happy to comply.

So I did what I could to enlighten people as to the facts and identify the underlying problems.[93] I did not feel qualified to contribute to the economic debates. This had the enormous advantage that I was not forced to speculate as to various possible economic futures. I could confine myself to clarifying what went on in the ECJ and setting out the political problems which the EU was designed to overcome and the mechanisms it had devised to this end. I could also point out the undoubted practical difficulties which would be caused both to the UK and to the European Union by the UK leaving.

My own background led me to believe that I knew more about these things than does the average voter or MP. As it seemed to me, I was one of a relatively small minority of people who – by reason of the time at their disposal, their health, education and experience – were better placed to understand Europe's complex problems and come to reasoned decisions on them. The majority, whose jobs require their attention all day, are unlikely to have had the time to read the relevant material or the ability to concentrate on and reflect in depth on such questions.

Many will say that this shows that I think I am a member of an elite. So I do, but not in the way they imagine. I do not think

---

[93] Typical was my participation in a debate in 2014 on judicial review by judges of governmental action for the Constitution Society: https://consoc.org.uk/publications/judicial-review-and-the-rule-of-law-who-is-in-control/.

of myself as belonging to *the elite of society as a whole*. That seems to me so vague as to be a useless concept. I use the term 'elite' as defining those who are the best *in a particular society in a particular field*. In this sense there are many elites in our society: those who are regarded as top footballers are elite footballers, top surgeons are elite surgeons, top singers are elite singers, and so on. In this sense there is nothing strange in having elite judges or elite politicians. I am perfectly content to accept that others are much better placed than I to come to valuable decisions on most matters. In relation to those matters – how a national health service, rail or road system ought to be organised, what is an appropriate interest rate to achieve full employment, by what rules various sports should be governed etc. etc. – they are the elites, not I. But in relation to matters appertaining to the European Union I hope that it will not be thought unreasonable if I consider myself as a member of an elite.

Of course, I accept that, so far as political choices are concerned, those who cannot reasonably claim to be in the relevant elite may nonetheless reasonably claim to have a voice because they are affected by the ultimate decisions. Whether that voice should take the form of participating in referendums is disputed. Personally, I prefer the voice to be articulated in other ways and not to amount to actually making the decision on complex issues with which voters are not familiar. But I totally accept that the decision to subject to a referendum of all or a subset of voters the question whether or not to leave the European Union is one that under our constitution Parliament can take.

While I have a strong love of history and am by nature cautious of change, I accept that clearly politics must involve more than the application of the brake pedal to prevent any undesirable change. Not everyone wants everything to remain the same. Indeed, most desire some changes. Inevitably there is disagreement on when and what changes should be made. Faced with this, politicians wishing to get elected understandably seek to find out what appears to be the majority view in their area. They often adopt this view as their own. This is also understandable but undesirable as an invariable rule. I prefer Burke's approach in his Speech to the Electors of Bristol[94] which I had also adopted in relation to the European Court of Justice.

Politicians often concentrate their speeches on objections to the current system, promise change without being precise as to the nature and details of this change, or when it should be carried out, or what its likely cost will be. As to those matters the voter is left unguided. I recognise but regret that this has proved an effective policy for the purpose of winning an election.

I was saddened that the leaders of both sides of the referendum debate apparently agreed that the question 'What is best for the United Kingdom?' was the only relevant one. Its precise meaning was obscure, since the United Kingdom is an abstract concept. Things cannot be better or worse for abstract concepts. Precisions are required. This formulation of the question led some to treat the root question as capable of being answered by calculations based on the anticipated financial loss or gain for each currently living individual in the UK.

In the event, much of the European debate in this country was focused on the question: 'What is best for us?' So the preliminary question arose: who are 'we' in this context? Those born in England,

---

[94] 'Parliament is not a Congress of Ambassadors from different and hostile interests; which interests each must maintain, as an Agent and Advocate, against other Agents and Advocates; but Parliament is a deliberative Assembly of one Nation, with one Interest, that of the whole; where, not local Purposes, not local Prejudices ought to guide, but the general Good, resulting from the general Reason of the whole.'

or the UK? Those *now* living in England, or the UK? European citizens? Future generations?

There is no objectively *right* answer. Lots of answers are possible. When considering 'Who are we?' in the context of mass migration, global warming, the dangers of nuclear war or global food or water shortages both a practical judgement and a moral judgement are involved. The practical judgement involves considering what groupings can usefully contribute to the provision of an answer and what groupings will be affected if these problems are not satisfactorily resolved. The moral judgement is concerned with the question whether there is any moral obligation on a particular grouping to do something towards the resolution of the problem.

'We' in this context are for me the citizens of the member states of the EU both as individuals and as groups of individuals. Some would say this is too narrow a group and that we should consider the whole of mankind. On the other hand, many would answer the question 'Who are we?' with a much narrower circle: 'the English', 'the Scots', 'the Welsh', 'the Northern Irish' or 'citizens of the United Kingdom'.

To me, the crucial political question is what practicable political actions can help to bring about a situation where the world becomes a better, safer, more tolerant place, where the selfishness of the strong does not make life a misery for the weak?

In all polities there is a tension between the desire to have an efficiently functioning political system and the desire to prevent abuses of power. Given our long and disparate political histories, there is also in Europe a tension between the desire to have for the whole of Europe a functioning political system and the desire to let each historical entity retain its customs and way of life. But it was and is common ground that we must build a community or communities governed by law rather than force. There was and is also a realisation that lack of economic prosperity has brought about wars in the past and that to avoid such wars it is essential to have a functioning economic system.

I tried to point out that to try to resolve these tensions the structure adopted by consent in the EU is a rather complicated mechanism involving various European institutions – a Council of Ministers appointed by the member states according to their own democratic procedures, a directly elected Parliament, and a Commission of members appointed by each member state, again through its own democratic procedures, and then approved by the European Parliament, and finally a court, the ECJ, whose job it is to resolve disputes. These institutions are tasked with making, administering and interpreting laws.

This is a totally new type of international political organisation born out of the need to create something functioning after a war which had destroyed the old systems. So political leaders deliberately created a polity with its own rules interpreted by its own court. Many feel strongly that English political genius has consisted in creating law and constitution piece by piece and feel that a conceptual construct can easily become the master rather than the servant and is alien to English instincts. I tend to agree.

Many in this country feel that the Continent's problems and ways of thought are not ours: we are different from all the others and less aggressive. Well, up to a point … Over the past few hundred years England has effectively taken over Wales, Ireland and Scotland. A hundred years ago, part of the island of Ireland managed to break free again from England. The Scots and the Welsh have recently been moving in the same direction. The growth of the empire was not entirely without an element of aggression and bullying of other countries – ask the Indians, the Americans, the Africans.

What one can say is that England's borders have for hundreds of years not been diminished and may have given many of the English the feeling that they are immune from happenings elsewhere. I find this puzzling in the light of our history – most recently the two world wars – but I think this feeling exists. A foreigner is thought of as foreign and not really 'one of us', notwithstanding the fact that among England's rulers and its general populace many have over the centuries come from abroad.

Nevertheless, it may well be that the fact of being an island and a difference in histories have played some part in making the English insensitive to what was and still is a widespread desire on the Continent, namely, to make a success of being a part of a larger, communal endeavour to regulate conflicting national desires and to bring peace and prosperity.

There are indeed problems with political constructs. The unforeseen always occurs. Yet the result of the English piecemeal approach of eschewing political constructs and living day by day is also not wholly satisfactory. To the astonishment of continentals, the UK government was apparently certain that it could validly separate the United Kingdom from the EU on whatever terms it chose without Parliament enacting legislation. The Supreme Court decided to the contrary; but what is important in the present context is that the uncertainties surrounding the UK constitution are such that the government evidently believed that parliamentary authority for the process of separation was legally unnecessary.

The fact is that the UK constitution is remarkably uncertain and incomplete. It leaves substantial imbalances between the power of the three devolved administrations and the power of English MPs. It leaves a House of Lords with a bizarre system of appointment. The first past the post system of elections to the House of Commons leaves a lot of people disenfranchised – especially when those who share their view are in the majority among the voters but can only muster a minority of members of Parliament who cannot form a government. The constitution leaves an enormous amount to the good judgement of MPs with no ground rules.

The basic problem in the relations between human groups is a magnified version of the basic problem in relations between human individuals. People's desires are often mutually incompatible, and the problem is how to continue a friendly and peaceful relationship notwithstanding incompatible desires.

The EU was in its origins, and still is in my eyes, an attempt to provide a workable answer to the problem of conflicting desires and priorities. Over the past sixty years it has functioned reasonably well, although, unfortunately in my view, much of the original idealism and feeling of fellowship has been diminished, mainly as a result of a Gaullist, nationalist, self-centred view of politics – of late shared by UK and some other governments – and partly because the larger the Union has grown the more difficult it is to find any policy which receives approval from everyone.

Because of the broad success of the European Union there has been a stream of states wanting to join it. In this country there is a widespread feeling that the sole purpose of the EU was and is to increase national wealth by trade. That, as a matter of history, is not why the European Community came into being. The Community was founded to achieve peace and make the world a better, safer place. The financial arrangements were seen as valuable in themselves but also as a means to an end: peace. It is this which explains why repeated treaties, signed on behalf of every member state, have stated that the signatories desired 'an ever-closer union of the peoples of Europe'. What, however, is arguably true is that, at the time when the UK joined the EU, politicians stressed economic rather than political advantages, and that this may have influenced the earlier referendum in favour of continued membership.

I saw the treaty commitment to the ever-closer union of peoples as a vow, at the state level, akin to marriage at the individual level. Non-performance of such a solemn commitment requires justification. To my mind, having willingly signed the treaties which recited this desire for an ever-closer union of the peoples of Europe, we owed obligations to the other member states and their populations to live up to this commitment.

The commitment is one of the reasons why the member states, including the United Kingdom, when faced with half a dozen ex-Soviet Union countries with no tradition of stable democracy, worked hard to welcome them to the Union and why they joined the Union. It seemed to me a breach of faith then to leave the Union absent major and totally unforeseen circumstances.

When you agree to marry, you know that in all probability there will in the next fifty years be differences of view on a whole variety of matters – some foreseen, some not – but you are determined to work together towards the same broad aim of living happily together while yet retaining your two personalities. There is a commitment to a common life leading, one hopes, to the interweaving and enriching of two separate personalities, thoughts and gifts, just as when musicians play a piece of polyphonic music one hears different tunes being played or sung simultaneously and notices that this interweaving can lead to something more beautiful than one person insisting that his will must prevail and his tune be the only one.

The member states signed up to a status involving unknown obligations in the future but yet a commitment to a common life. A very bold thing to do, but capable of producing something which is more than the sum of its parts. Where the EU differs from most marriages is that from the beginning a mechanism was set up, policed by the Commission and the Court, for reaching agreement, for the enforcement of what had been agreed and for resolution of differences.

I think that gradually many people realise that exclusively seeking the best for oneself and to hell with the others is a no more admirable policy for a state than it is for an individual. I was brought up to think and still think that selfishness is the problem, not the solution. It is commonplace in the United Kingdom for the richer areas to use their money to help alleviate poverty elsewhere in the kingdom. But there seems to be a feeling here that helping a poor area in, say, Scotland is desirable but helping a poor area in, say, Italy is in principle a misdirection of taxpayers' money. I regret this.

Throughout my life I have been very conscious of being part of the first European generation to have lived the whole of their adult lives without being personally exposed to war. Peace amongst the member states has substantially followed the creation of the European Communities. More people in each country are closer to more people in other countries. But is this *because of* the Communities or merely chronologically *subsequent to* the creation of the Communities? Clearly there have also been other factors involved, but the Communities have played their part.

However, to my disappointment Parliament decided that the United Kingdom should leave the EU at the end of 2019.

**The development of my views on the EU**

Since my student days, no doubt influenced by my German background, I have felt that the EU and the European Convention on Human Rights were promising attempts so to organise political life as to minimise the chance of slipping back into war or barbarism. Like all forms of national governments they have not been not wholly successful. Like most governments in sovereign states the centre has sought to regulate more and more. Then a large number of new states with a dictatorial past joined the enterprise, which made it all more difficult. The larger it got and the more it sought to regulate, the more difficulties arose.

For much of my life I reacted to these difficulties by saying in exasperation that if only the UK, France, Italy, Hungary or whoever was being difficult would throw themselves into the enterprise with more enthusiasm all would be, if not well, at any rate much better. But I have come to see more clearly that it takes time to create that feeling of brotherhood with those whom one thinks instinctively of as totally different. So, this is work in progress. It may be that Covid and the invasion of Ukraine have given it a jolt.

I see now that I gave too much weight to a number of factors. One was my own background among European thinkers with their own intellectual framework stretching back to Kant and their books. Another was that I did not give sufficient weight to the fact that for many of the people who wished the UK to leave the EU the question of whether to do so was determined, not by the painstaking analysis of so-called experts, but by an instinctive feeling that they wished to be governed by their own kind, not by someone who was not 'One of Us'. Although I think of myself as English as well as German, many, both there and here, would certainly because of this regard me as not One of Us. Naturally I regret this.

For all my enthusiasm for European citizens working together for the common good, and for the mechanisms which are laid down in the treaties intended to achieve this aim, I have increasingly come to recognise that, at the moment, the European Union simply does not engage the heart and soul of many, perhaps most, of its citizens. Over the centuries there has grown up in the citizenry of most of the European states a sense of loyalty and attraction to their own state which they do not feel to any other state or to the Union.

Here we differ from the United States of America, although its citizens are also composed of people with links to other countries. Those who moved to America did so in general in protest against what was happening in their country of origin and their own prospects there and were wanting to make a new start in a new country. In consequence, they were content to embrace actions designed to advantage the United States even if they disadvantaged their country of origin.

The prerequisite of political life as we understand it is to establish a system of government which, as a system, meets with the unspoken instinctive consent of the governed. This, if it is to succeed at all, can only succeed over time so that it seems natural to those involved.

This instinctive consent the EU has to a significant degree failed to achieve as yet. In part this is the result of the institutions of the EU running too fast too soon. People in general dislike the new and need to be persuaded to embrace it. This takes time. In part it is the result of the continued expansion of the original six so that in a sense one was regularly starting anew even in the existing member states, which were required to have a feeling of loyalty to the new members. In part it is the result of politicians not wishing with enough fervour the good of people living in other states and not even trying to persuade their own citizenry to embrace the good of others as part of their life's mission. In part it is the result of politicians encouraging the electorate to blame 'outsiders' for whatever goes wrong.

# XXVIII

# *The Things That Matter*

I have said much about European politics and the development of my thoughts on the subject. I confess that neither the law nor European politics are now at the centre of my reflections. As I look back, I see that my personal values and perceptions have evolved as well as my political ones.

My reason for writing this book was to share my understanding of the family background and also my own thoughts with my family. So I may I hope be forgiven if I conclude with personal and intimate thoughts not usually shared with strangers. The English will find this very strange, the Germans less so.

What dominates is the banal reflection that life, both in a personal context and in the context of society as a whole, is best lived centred on love and respect for others.

I recollect being told at the time of my confirmation that prayers should start with thankfulness, then contrition for my failings, then prayer for others and finally prayer for myself.

Thankfulness is always what I have found easiest, and I was delighted a few years ago to come across a saying by Meister

Eckhard that, if the only prayer you say in your entire life is 'thank you', it will be enough.

What has changed is the things I am thankful for.

As my childhood letters show, in my early years it was chocolate cake and the like. Now, good health, comfortable surroundings and above all the affection of family and friends have replaced food, although my Ugandan experience has made me give thanks for water when I brush my teeth etc. in a way I never did before I went there.

What has remained constant is a feeling of thankfulness, in particular thankfulness that I was being looked after by others. More recently this has intensified, not because, as yet, I have required more looking after, but because I no longer have the distractions of work and so have had more time to reflect on more important things.

I am now more conscious of how for most of my life, in the manner of a child, I have simply taken for granted that those around me should look after me. I have not thought much about the price they were willing to pay. My conscious thankfulness has markedly increased as I have grown older. I see now that I was hugely blessed in having my uncle's family who were willing to take me as one of their own when I was left an orphan in a war-torn land. They did it so well that it never occurred to me in my youth that they might have done otherwise. I am now consciously grateful for the almost total absence of anti-German feeling directed at me personally. I might so easily have been bullied at school but I was not. I recognise now how much I have owed to various mentors who have held out a helping hand as I tried to find my way around the world. My head is filled with agreeable memories and thanksgiving.

I am fortunate that I have never wavered in my love of my wife over more than half a century. But I have become increasingly conscious of all that she has done for me throughout my life, which I simply took for granted for most of it. The only credit we can claim is that I arrived at this awareness without her or anyone else having pointed it out.

So much for thankfulness. As for contrition, I recollect the school chaplain drawing our attention to the words in the Confession before Holy Communion in relation to sins: 'The burden of them is intolerable.' He added 'If it's not, it jolly well should be.' I am sure he was right, and it is clear to me that I have left undone those things which I ought to have done and that I have done those things which I ought not to have done. While consciousness of this has from time to time caused me to try to rectify what was omitted or done amiss, I have never lost sleep over it. Nor is this the place to rehearse my shortcomings. Fortunately, I have led a life of sufficient obscurity never to have had the commentariat feel it was their duty and delight to expose them.

Intercession I have found instinctive so long as I don't try to analyse in terms of cause and effect what I am doing. The best that analysis has produced has been, first, the awareness that praying for others might actually cause me to do something about their problems and, second, a realisation that some of those prayed for have found strength in the fact that others are praying for them. Further jejune reflections I can spare the world.

Praying for myself is rather similar. I do it instinctively but find it hard to analyse what I am trying to achieve by what means.

To conclude, I slip into the philosophical analytical mode which comes so easily to some of my German countrymen and which I have shared with my family. I notice that for a long time I have received a double measure of happiness: happy that I am happy, and happy that I know that I am happy.

# *Appendix*

## Confirmation Speech by my grandfather Hermann

*Delivered at the celebratory lunch following my mother's confirmation.*

It is the custom in the course of a speech after a Confirmation to add something to the profession you have made on such an important day. I shall depart from this custom, because I have nothing of my own which I wish to add. After such an outstanding and sagacious sermon as you have heard from your pastor I do not wish to add anything similar of my own, less felicitously expressed. But I would like to read an excerpt from a judicious letter[95] which a very clever Jew wrote to his daughter 108 years ago at the time of her Confirmation.

---

[95] The whole text of the letter is set out in Sebastian Hensel: *Die Family Mendelssohn 1729–1847*. Published by Verlag Karl Alber, Freiburg 1959.

'You have, my dear daughter, taken an important step in your life. At this time with a father's heart as I wish you happiness for your future life I feel compelled to speak seriously of things of which we two have never before spoken.

'Does God exist? What is God? Is a part of us eternal, living beyond the time when the remainder of us has disappeared? And where and how? I do not know the answers to any of these questions and so I have never attempted to teach you anything in this regard. But one thing I know – that there is in me and in you and in all mankind an eternal tendency towards the good, the true and the right; that we have a conscience which warns and leads us when we stray from it. I know this, believe it and live in this belief, and it is my religion. These things I could not teach you, and indeed no one can learn this from someone else. Everyone has such a conscience who does not deliberately and knowingly deny it.

'We have brought you and your siblings up in Christianity because this is the belief of most civilised men and contains nothing which will lead you away from the good. Instead it shows you the way to love, obedience and resignation – if only by the example of its author, recognised by so few and followed by fewer.

'In making the confession of faith you have done that which society requires of you and are called a Christian. Now you must be what your duty as a human being requires: truthful, loyal, good and unceasingly attentive to the voice of your conscience, which allows itself to sleep but not to be seduced by enchantment. If you do this, you will inherit the greatest happiness which life on earth affords, a unity and contentedness with yourself.'

As often as I read these words of Abraham Mendelssohn to his daughter Fanny I wonder at the simplicity of the definition of the concepts of 'religion' and 'Christianity'. I hope that it will make the same impression on you and that it will give to you the same open-mindedness to overcome the doubts which arise from time to time and that it will give you the ability to recognise the high ideals of Christianity and to seek after them. You will not always have such a pastor whose human qualities you treasure as Pastor Kurz. I wish that you do not need sermons to awake in you a religious sensibility, that you are not dependent on the power of speech, but that you carry your religion in your heart and that it will give you that direction to what is good, true and right.

## Address by KS on Helmuth James, Count von Moltke

*On the sixtieth anniversary of the call to the Bar of Helmuth James, Count von Moltke, 15 November 1998, the Temple Church.*

'Ye shall be holy: for I the Lord your God am holy.' So God spake to Moses.[96] 'Be ye perfect as your heavenly Father is perfect.' So said Jesus to the multitudes.[97] The challenge seems impossible – in part because of the high standard set by the concept of holiness or perfection, and in part because we are required to strive for holiness and perfection in all areas of our life. So we look around for examples to follow.

The Church, recognising this, encourages us to look at, and meditate on, the lives of holy men and women in the past. Many of these lived long ago in environments far removed from our own. We learn from them, yet we ask: where is the twentieth-century lawyer in a grey suit who may serve as an example to us in the Temple as to how we can use our gifts as lawyers in the Lord's service? The

---

[96] Leviticus 19:2.
[97] Matthew 5:48.

practice of the law does not seem to us a natural breeding ground for sanctity.

One whose life can help us and whom we honour today was Helmuth James, Count von Moltke. His father was German; his mother the daughter of Sir James Rose Innes, Chief Justice of South Africa and a member of the Inner Temple.

Helmuth James grew up in Germany. He was twenty-six when Hitler came to power. He qualified and practised as a German lawyer. Nonetheless, he was also called to the Bar by the Inner Temple, in the Michaelmas Term of 1938, sixty years ago this month. He was a pupil in John Foster's Chambers at 2 Hare Court and thought of practising here. However, he came to the conclusion that it was his duty to return to Hitler's Germany. Five years later, he was imprisoned. On the orders of Hitler his name was removed from those who were entitled to practise as lawyers in Germany. Thereafter he was tried for treason by a court, created by the Nazis, named the People's Court. Its president, Roland Freisler, proclaimed the following legal principles: 'It is already a preparation for high treason to arrogate to oneself any judgement on a matter which it is for the Führer to decide.' 'Anyone who objects to acts of violence, but prepares for the eventuality that another, that is, the enemy, removes the government by force, thereby engages in preparation for high treason.'[98] Freisler asked rhetorically, 'From whom do you take your orders? From the Beyond or from Adolf Hitler?'[99] Helmuth James was not one of those who plotted the death of Hitler. His crime in essence was merely that he used his intellectual gifts and powers of leadership, not in the service of Hitler, but to expose evil and make plans for the governance of Germany once the Hitler regime had been

[98] *Letters to Freya*, p. 400.
[99] Ibid., p. 409.

defeated. In January 1945 he was condemned to death and executed whilst still a member of the English Bar. For the moment, perhaps the last Inner Templar to suffer that fate.

Here was a man who thought it morally wrong simply to ignore what the politicians were doing. He was a doer as well as a thinker. He was conscious of the dangers of failing to confront reality by submerging oneself in detail. Losing sight of the wood by reason of concentrating excessively on each tree is a well-known failing amongst lawyers. So is taking no notice of anything in the world other than their daily case load. Helmuth James refers to the matter thus in a letter to his wife:

'It is our duty to recognise what is obnoxious, to analyse it, and to rise above it in a synthesis which enables us to make use of it. Whoever looks the other way for lack of the ability to recognise it or of the strength to surmount what he has recognised is indeed putting his head in the sand. The rage for detailed information leads to attaching excessive importance to detail and neglecting the equally important task of sublimating the facts and bringing them into proper perspective. If one chases after details, one won't have the strength to prevail over them. It is certain that this strength is greater in a calm atmosphere than in a hectic one, and anyone able to spread this atmosphere of peace around himself is a live support and driving force in the right direction. Peace is not complacency. Whoever lets black be white, and evil good, for the sake of outward calm does not deserve peace, and is putting his head in the sand.

'But whoever knows at all times the difference between good and evil, and does not doubt it, however great the triumph of evil seems to be, has laid the first stone for the overcoming of evil.' [100]

---

[100] Ibid., p. 73.

Here was a man who was conscious of the attractions of shutting his eyes to what was painful and of becoming callous. That is a danger to which we at the Bar and on the Bench are much exposed professionally. The professional and personal challenge is to remain objective without losing the capacity to feel the other person's pain. Because we do not wish to get hurt ourselves, we find ourselves taking care not to feel the other person's pain, using euphemisms for sending others into jail or bankruptcy. This is dangerous, not only for others, but also for ourselves. We must learn to use pain. The part of us which feels suffering is, I suspect, the same part as that which feels joy. If we let that part shrivel up, we will not be perfect, as we are commanded to be perfect. Moreover, if we are untouched by the pains and joys of others, we may find that the pain which inevitably at some stage life will inflict upon us is a pain which we cannot absorb and use. Perhaps this is what the Psalmist had in mind when he sang 'Blessed is the man who walking through the valley of dryness uses it for a well.'[101] Helmuth James referred to the attractions of protecting oneself from pain in a letter which he wrote in the context of seeing the remains of relatives who had been killed in bombings of Berlin:

> You ask how one can stand it all. That isn't so hard. To avoid getting callous is much harder. I am always catching myself at it … I overcame my emotion and horror, and then it was quite easy. But that is a false reaction. One should overcome this defensive indifference, one should not put on an armour, one must bear it. In order to endure death and horror, one tends to kill off one's own humanity, which is a much greater danger than not being able to bear it.

---

[101] Psalm 84:6.

So in Helmuth James we see a man who remained sensitive to horror even in times filled with horror. Of the shooting of hostages he wrote in 1941:

In one area in Serbia two villages have been reduced to ashes. 1,700 men and 240 women from among the inhabitants have been executed. That is the so called 'punishment' for an attack on three German soldiers. In Greece 220 men in one village have been shot. Certainly more than a thousand people are murdered in this way and another thousand German men are habituated to murder in this way. May I know this and yet sit at my table in my heated flat and have tea? Don't I thereby become guilty too? What shall I say when I am asked: and what did you do during that time?

But here was a man who did not just sit back and agonise. His example to us is that he employed his courage and legal skills to do what he could in the situation which faced him. Having, through calm reflection, recognised evil, he then accepted his duty to expose it and fight it. This he did fearlessly. He was a public international lawyer in a unit whose function it was to advise the supreme command of the German military forces on legal matters. The task of the unit was to issue written opinions on paper. He wrote boldly and clearly. Moreover, time and time again he managed to attend the meetings of senior officers for whom those opinions had been prepared. The effect of his personality and courage on them was sometimes, at any rate, to shame them into following his lead.

Here was a man who simply put aside all thoughts of personal safety, let alone advancement, in order to articulate publicly what he

379

thought was right. He put the following draft before his superior for the latter to sign:

> I understand that the chief of the Department for Commercial and Economic Warfare Measures has suggested the murder of the British Ambassador to Switzerland. The department for counter espionage has apparently refused to do this, and so it is now being suggested that the Gestapo should be asked to do it. I ask for permission to enter an absolute veto against any further attempt to murder the British Ambassador to Switzerland. In particular it seems to me untenable that requests of this sort should be made by the Army to the Gestapo.[102]

For a junior officer to write like this in Hitler's Germany took a formidable amount of courage.

One of the matters on which he expressed himself was the position of those persons who had been in the armies of countries defeated by Germany, such as Poland and France. Many such persons then took up arms as part of the army of a country still fighting Germany, such as the Soviet Union or Great Britain. When such persons were subsequently captured by the Germans, were they to be treated as civilians bearing arms – for which the penalty was death – or as soldiers who had become prisoners of war? He persuaded the authorities that the proper legal analysis of the situation was that these persons were to be regarded as soldiers. Here is how he did it. Again I quote from a letter to his wife:

---

[102] Ger van Roon, *Helmuth James, Graf von Moltke* (Siedler Verlag, 1994), p. 238.

There was a big row and I wonder whether they will try and throw me out at last. Once more I was defeated in the large group ... When the meeting was over I went to Weichold [his superior] and said I had been left in a minority of one. But I remained unconvinced and asked permission to exercise the right of every official to have his dissenting opinion put on record. Big row: I was an officer and had no such right but simply the duty to obey. I said I was sorry but this was a question of responsibility before history, which to me had priority over the duty to obey. The matter came before the Adrniral [Schuster] and after five minutes he endorsed my opinion. He obviously had shared it all along, at any rate had wavered, and my resistance had strengthened his courage. Result: the Admiral will represent the opinion of the Sections officially but will have his personal dissent recorded on the minutes and will also speak to these minutes before the Führer.

[The Admiral] succeeded finally in getting Keitel [the Field Marshal] on to my line and at 6.30 came a Führer Order with my conclusion and with my arguments ... a great disaster has been averted and despite everything it gives me great satisfaction to think that many non-German women have your husband to thank for the continued existence of theirs.[103]

Note the firmness. Note the openness. Note the result of his leadership, although he was a junior officer and those whom he was leading were his seniors. One can lead even though formally one is not the person in charge. The Christian is at times under a duty to lead his superiors not just to follow them.

---

103 *Letters to Freya*, pp. 60–61.

Perhaps I may allow myself here to recall that he mentions a few days after this letter that he dreamed he went to his chambers in the Inner Temple. It was a pleasant dream – save that at the end everything went wrong and he had to choose between the alternatives of being shot as a spy in England or as a traitor in Germany.[104]

The treatment of prisoners of war frequently occupied his energies. Let me quote the following from a draft which he prepared for his superior Admiral Canaris in relation to the treatment of Soviet prisoners of war:

> The legal position is as follows. The Geneva Convention on Prisoners of War is not in force between Germany and the Soviet Union. Therefore it is the rules of international law concerning the treatment of prisoners of war which are in force. These have established, since the 18th century, that captivity is neither revenge nor punishment, but essentially a security measure whose sole purpose is to prevent the prisoners from taking any further part in the war. This approach has arisen from the view, held by all armies, that it was contrary to military conceptions to kill or harm the unarmed. It further is consonant with the interests of each combatant nation to save its own soldiers from harm when in captivity.[105]

Here we see the Christian lawyer making use of his legal and persuasive skills to persuade his superiors that maltreatment of enemy prisoners is both against the law and against self-interest.

He became privy to what was happening to the Jews. Listen to his thoughts and actions:

---

104 Ibid., p. 66.
105 Van Roon, *Helmuth James*, p. 258.

Yesterday I was at a meeting in the Foreign Ministry about the persecution of the Jews. It was my first official contact with this question. Against 24 men and quite inflexibly I attacked a decree [one of the Nuremberg Laws against the Jews] which already had the approval of all ministers and the chief of the OKW [the top military command] and for the moment have halted its course. And when I returned, the official in whose competence it really fell asked me: 'Why did you do it? You can't change a thing although of course these measures are catastrophic.'[106]

'In fighting the latest decree against the Jews I have succeeded in getting the three most important Generals of the OKW to write to the fourth that he must immediately withdraw the approval he gave on behalf of the chief of the OKW. The next stage is to see whether he does so. Only after that will the real battle be joined.

'My self-appointed representation of the interests of the Wehrmacht has been endorsed by [Admiral] Canaris and by [General] Thomas. I dictated letters and both were visibly pleased when they signed them. Which proves the general rule, that as soon as one man takes a stand a surprising number of others will stand too. But there always has to be one to go first: otherwise it does not work.'[107]

Surely there is here a lesson for all of us. We are called to set the tone and then at least some others will follow our lead. We must use our legally trained brains to help us to identify the important issues. He draws our attention to the fact that there are times in our lives

---

[106] *Letters to Freya*, p. 171.
[107] *Letters to Freya*, p. 183.

when our willingness to be counted and to assert the just may be of much greater significance than we ourselves at the relevant time perceive. He once reflected in these terms:

> Strange how infinitely many things suddenly depend upon a single decision. Those are the few moments when one man can suddenly count in the history of the world. Everything before, everything that follows is based on mass, anonymous forces and men. And then suddenly one feels that all these forces are holding their breath, that the gigantic orchestra that has played so far has fallen silent for one or two bars, to let the soloist set the tone for the next movement. It is only one heartbeat of time, but the one note, which will sound out alone and solitary, will establish the next movement for the whole orchestra. And all await that tone.[108]

His activities during the war will have saved some lives. However, to his contemporaries he will have seemed, as Jesus must have seemed, unsuccessful. By and large the Nazis went their way, and he did not stop them. But he is an example for us. Like our Lord he emerges the ultimate victor. True, like our Lord, he was imprisoned and executed because he would not renounce his vision of holiness, his vision of perfection. His earthly life came to an end. But who is the inspiration now? It is not Judge Freisler, who presided over the people's court. It is Helmuth James, Count von Moltke whom we commemorate today as one whose life may serve as an example to us lawyers in the Temple.

---

[108] Ibid., p. 259.

## Call Night Address 2003

*Address delivered on the occasion of the call of students of the Inner Temple to the Bar.*

On behalf of my fellow benchers and all the other members of the Inn I welcome to the Bar and as full members of the Inn those who have just been called. A welcome also to parents and other admirers who have joined you and us for this important occasion. Exams are over. Life now starts in earnest. The task of shaping the law is now in your hands. You take over at a particularly exciting time. Reform is in the air. Reform of our domestic legal system and reform of the European Union. Watch this space. But don't just watch. Play a full part in all that is going on.

This Inn, as you know, is a place where one can eat and drink together. I have found it a happy place for as long as I can remember. It is an inn. What distinguishes it from inns round the country is not the food – though that is good – but that here you can be certain of finding interesting and pleasant people who will want to talk to you and with whom you will have much to talk about. Here we tease each other about our failings. Here we share our joys and perplexities. Not just at table, but walking in the garden, listening to concerts, watching plays, taking part in debates or moots, attending church, or just having a drink of coffee and, just occasionally, something stronger. And when we want to work then we can go upstairs and work in the library. Those of who have our place of work here regard ourselves as outstandingly lucky.

The place exudes peace, giving us the possibility of thought and reflection. In its time it has been the centre of many reforms. The church is over 800 years old: it is said that a draft of Magna Carta itself was there debated by the barons who forced King John to sign it. The roses after which the Wars of the Roses were named were plucked in the gardens of the Temple. Ecclesiastical reforms were hotly debated in our church in the seventeenth century. The Master, Hooker, preached in the morning. In the afternoon, his number two, the Reader, preached and told an eager audience that the Master's views would take them straight to hell. Many of our buildings stretch back for centuries. You will find it a joy to invite your friends and relatives from time to time to share in the pleasures of this place. When you get older you will get happiness, as I constantly do now, from seeing new faces light up with the excitement of the life that is opening up in front of them.

What is so wonderful about our profession is meeting and advising people from all walks of life – the foolish professor, the wise dropout, the unhappily married, the government minister, the businessman, the doctor, the patient, the thief, all manner of men and women. This broadens your own experience of life after a while. Your clients are conscious that in a very real sense their lives, prospects and happiness are in your hands and if you make a mess of it their lives may very well be ruined. Each of those persons will be inclined to look at the world from his personal perspective. What you should be able to give them – even without their asking for it – is the perspective of the other side and the perspective of a judge who is not personally involved in the tragedy which has resulted in the law suit. Now that's an absorbing and rewarding thing to do.

Now you cannot do this job well unless you apply yourself. Effortless superiority is an attractive concept. Lack of effort is easy to achieve. Superiority is more difficult but not impossibly so. But superiority combined with lack of effort is all but unattainable. I have been trying for years to play the piano beautifully without practising. Achievement of this goal has eluded me as it has eluded everyone else who tries this way to success. You owe it to your client and yourself to get on top of the facts and papers in any case and to listen to what your opponent and, if you are in court, the judge are saying. You owe it to your client and yourself to be alert and on top form not just when you are in court but also when you advise in chambers or in your office at work. It is irresponsible to drink too much or sleep too little.

So, be diligent and be honest. But then take time to reflect and formulate your thoughts in as few words as possible. Few of us who make our living by talking fight long-windedness with sufficient vigour. Think. If you have thought, then it is sheer laziness not to compress your thought into a reasonable space. Remember that words are precious and that using words purposefully is your business. So whether you are writing or speaking, be precise and concise.

The law has over the centuries rightly had a reputation of being very slow to change. That is not today's problem. A danger which faces us all arises from the increasing *speed* of change and the absence of time for reflection. Television and radio are media in which, at any event by present convention, there are no pauses for thought. Every thought must be contained in a sixty-second formulation or the speaker will either be cut off or interrupted. He is lucky if, in the sixty seconds of speech graciously allowed to him, his words are not accompanied simultaneously by noises of one kind or another which do not aid concentration. The shallower the idea, the more quickly it spreads, because it requires no brains for its absorption and no time is allowed for reflection.

This is where you come in. What your university life will have done with luck is to teach you to think about the underlying substance of issues. It is this skill which you must now share with the world. Where we go depends on you, how you think and how you behave. You should have the advantage over most of mankind of having been taught to think clearly and broadly. Cultivate this skill by reading and reflection. If one thinks only in one language and lives only in one culture, and has no sense of history, then it seems natural to accept as self-evident truth whatever the fashion of the day dictates. That seems to me the greatest danger of the present era. One of the things which those with a university education must do is to recognise when they come across them phrases which need a bit of thought before one can adopt or reject the ideas which they seem to contain.

Let me give you an example. Some years ago, at a political meeting, I heard the speaker say that it was a scandal that many people earned less than the national average income. He implied that if his party came to power he would ensure that this was no longer the case. Everyone applauded. Now if you had been there you would perhaps have asked, 'Does your party promise that when it comes to power everyone will earn more than the average at that time? If so, how can that logically be? Does not the concept of an average imply that some will be below it? Or are you promising that at that time in the future they will earn more pounds sterling than the average which is presently being earned? If so, are you promising that the purchasing power of the pound sterling then will be the same or greater than its purchasing power now?' Unless the speaker gives clear answers to such questions, you will recognise him as either dishonest or muddle-headed.

Let me give you another example. It is common for politicians to say that everyone is entitled to the best education, the best health-care and so on. Because of your education you will want to reflect on what is meant by the statement 'everyone is entitled', what is meant by 'best healthcare' and 'best education'. But you will also want to reflect whether entry into this paradise will ever be open to us. Will there not always be better teachers and worse teachers, better doctors and worse doctors? If one takes time to think, it is obvious that not everyone can have access to the best.

That is a fact of life. You can seek to improve the less good; you can argue the merits of how those should be chosen who are enabled to have access to the best – money? membership of the party? brains? beauty? But no system can secure the best for everyone. It is important that one realises the limits of what can be achieved and does not pretend otherwise. If people believe falsehoods, they will be vicious when they are undeceived.

There are times when your ability to think clearly will make you unpopular and you will be under the strongest of pressures to stop thinking. It is the easiest thing in the world just to accept the values which happen to be current in the place and at the time in which one happens to find oneself. Particularly if they can be expressed in a word or a phrase which is easy to remember. 'Liberté, Egalité, Fraternité.' 'We hold these truths to be self-evident, that all men are created equal, that they are endowed by their Creator with certain unalienable rights, that among these are life, liberty and the pursuit of happiness.' These are seductive phrases which have hugely influenced the course of history.

But equality can be an elusive concept. You will recollect Anatole France's acid comment: 'The law, in its majestic equality, forbids the rich as well as the poor to sleep under bridges, to be in the street and to steal bread.'

You have learned and will continue to learn to unpack these phrases and to ask, 'What values is the speaker trying to persuade me to adopt? Do I think it right to adopt those values?' It is hugely important for us all that you recognise these questions, answer them wisely and have the bravery to bear what may be the unpleasant consequences of your answer.

Some citizens, while delighted to find it generally accepted that they have rights, give no sign of having understood that they will in practice lose these rights if they do not accept some duties. If I wish you to respect my right, then I must accept it as my duty not to interfere with your right. If I wish society to come to my help when I am ill or old, then I must accept that it is my duty to try and earn an income and pay tax when I am young and healthy. Fortunately you will find that there are many things which one enjoys doing which it is also one's duty to do.

This is an important night in your life. Savour it. Enjoy what remains of the evening. Take pride and pleasure in your calling as a barrister and make this place your home.

## A Day in the Temple

*A description of life in the Inner Temple in 2003 written for the Yearbook.*

When I became Treasurer, Elisabeth and I moved into a flat in Hare Court. We discovered a new life. This beautiful little corner of London is a bee-hive of activity for most of the hours of the day.

I wake to the sound of the bells of St Clement's. One of our porters – Roger, David or Dennis – is already doing his rounds just checking that the place is as he left it the night before and opening up various locked doors and gates. Chambers are being cleaned by ladies from all over the world. Dustmen come and remove the rubbish bags left by those who have cleaned. The milkman and the paper man leave their offerings at the bottom of each staircase. Food is being delivered to the kitchen. A light can be seen in chambers here and there, illuminating someone with his nose in a pile of papers or some learned tome.

Quite often, one of the Inn's many committees has a meeting arranged for 8 or 8.30, which everyone involved knows will be over at the latest by 9.30. The Finance Sub-Committee will discuss whether to give its blessing to the sale or purchase of some property; or whether or not the bid by the Library Committee for more books or by the Scholarships Committee for more scholarships should be financed; or whether the price of lunches should be enhanced so as to enable both desires to be met. These morning tasks are made the more agreeable because the inner man has not been forgotten – Charles or Vicky have arranged for one of their staff, many of whom have been with us for years, to make some coffee and produce some fruit and croissants.

Meanwhile, outside the church, a notice board appears telling the outside world that 8.30 every morning is when a twenty-minute Matins is said by the Master and whoever else feels that this is a good start to the day.

In the Hall the staff are clearing up the debris from a 21st birthday party the night before and making everything spick and span for lunch. Out in the garden Les is tending the Inner Temple Rose. He has won the Riverside Trophy presented by the Worshipful Company of Gardeners in each of the last three years. So walking round the garden is always a joy.

I go to my room to find a full in-tray. There will be cheques to sign, suggestions by committee chairmen to consider, minutes of committee meetings to note or approve, agendas for forthcoming meetings to decide, letters to read, draft or sign and so on.

In all this my task is made infinitely easier by help from various quarters. The cheques will already have been approved by the head of department or his deputy and by the Sub-Treasurer, one of whose many gifts is anticipating by a note the very question that I wish to ask; the letters may well have been drafted by the chairman of the relevant committee or by the Sub-Treasurer. When I come across something where I have any doubts which the Sub-Treasurer does not put to rest, I can discuss it with the appropriate Head of Department, the relevant committee chairman, or the Reader and the Reader-designate or indeed put it before the Executive Committee or Bench Table. The sense of working together as part of a team of barristers, judges and staff is undoubtedly satisfying.

The number of things done by one or more members of this team is astonishing. When I was chairman of the Scholarships Committee, I thought I had some idea of what the Education and Training Department under Yeshim were involved in. I did not know the half of it. Not merely do they work weekends marshalling scholarship candidates but they are also spending evenings and weekends supervising and organising events at Cumberland Lodge, Highgate House, Latimer House and the Inn itself, seeing that students and the younger barristers learn from their elders the gentle arts of examining witnesses, preparing skeleton arguments and dealing with difficult judges. The staff do far more than they are contracted to do, and scores of barristers and judges regularly give of their time to teach others and serve on committees. The Inn owes them a lot – but I hope and suspect that they get as much out of it all as they put in. The end result is that we have a sense of community which I think is stronger than it used to be when I joined the Inn.

To work surrounded by graceful buildings and spaces is a privilege and a joy. Of course, all those buildings need maintenance. The Surveyor's Department, in addition to planning and supervising large building projects, has a highly skilled staff of plumbers, electricians and carpenters, each with an apprentice, who turn out to deal with the routine tasks and inevitable emergencies and challenges to which such an estate as ours gives rise – not just during working hours. Many of them have been here for years; at least one is working with his father. We can be proud of them.

To many of you the human face of the Inn is the Sub-Treasurer's deputy, Charlotte Bircher. She is responsible for the front office and generally acting as his aide. Her vocation, however, is organising social occasions galore with whatever talent is around – dinners, lectures, parties, barbecues, Easter egg hunts and even all-night vigils. She's brilliant at it, and Monsieur Michelin would say that any one of her parties *vaut le voyage*. So whilst I go across to the Court of Appeal, that is what she's up to.

At my desk in the Law Courts there is a number of e-mails waiting to be answered, and then I can get down to concentrating on the latest piece of litigation. Whilst I am quietly exchanging thoughts with counsel, back at the Inn things are moving in the kitchen.

On a typical day this is just part of what we get through: 50 ducks, 200 salmon cutlets, 10 legs of lamb, 100 kgs of potatoes and vegetables, 100 eggs accompanied by 200 rolls and 12 loaves of bread. The kitchens are modern and spotless. Each of the staff has his appointed task, and everything moves in a preordained rhythm towards lunch. The staff eat before barristers and judges come across from the courts and then greet us with a smile and with food which is the envy of the other Inns. Martin, our head chef, will tell you on exactly which tree in what field the cow used to scratch her back before she gave her all to grace our tables. Like everyone else, so far as I can see, he takes a justified pride in his work. I enjoy lunch so much that I usually miss the concert which is taking place in the church whilst organ enthusiasts eat their sandwiches there.

Food and conversations over lunch with friends or perhaps a distinguished visitor set me up for an afternoon in court or doing papers of one sort or another. Just time to have a quick word with anyone who has a problem which they want to discuss with me whilst we're there. Occasionally I'm five minutes late for court because of this but hope I'm forgiven.

Meanwhile, in the library they are poring over some new piece of software and helping some barristers in a hurry find what they want; and Clare Rider the archivist is busy answering a query about the history of the Inn. In the garden, manure is being delivered for the roses. In the kitchen the washing-up is proceeding apace. A leaking roof is being mended and somewhere else a tap stops dripping. Rooms are being prepared for two or three committee meetings taking place at 5 o'clock. Potential staff are being interviewed.

The Collector is explaining pension arrangements to someone about to retire. Sounds of singing can be heard from the church. All around us conferences are taking place. Between 6 and 6.30 the place gradually gets emptier and then starts filling up again, perhaps with those who have been to a memorial service, perhaps with diners or party-goers or those attending a Bar Music Society concert. Sometimes I'm amongst them, sometimes I'm working, sometimes I'm at a concert elsewhere and return to an Inn temporarily hushed.

As we stroll around in the darkness there is the reassuring figure of Denis and his dog Floyd guarding this jewel in the centre of London.

## A Letter from Luxembourg

*A description of my life in the European Court of Justice written in 2004 for the Inner Temple Yearbook.*

The sun is shining through the blinds which are intended to shield me from its rays. The twin spires of the cathedral are seen in the distance. In front of me: a computer which through the Court's intranet can access a vast amount of material. Behind me are books and reports in several languages and the files from the cases in which I am the 'juge rapporteur' who oversees the case from the moment it enters the court until it leaves it in judgement form, usually more than a year later. Next door, shielding me from intrusions by the outside world, is the friendliest Cerberus you have ever seen – Cliona, a secretary from the Emerald Isle. With her are Gabrielle and Nathalie, two French secretaries who keep some 150 files in order and ensure that my infelicities in French are not inflicted on unsuspecting third parties. Across the corridor, each with a room, are my legal secretaries – another Inner Templar and former chairman of the Students Association, Carsten Zatschler, a member of Gray's Inn, Deok-Joo Rhee, and a Latvian lawyer, Aleksandra Melesko. The first comes of German parentage, was educated in Belgium and has collected degrees from Cambridge, Paris and Berlin; the second is of Korean origins with a degree from Oxford; the third has Russian parents, with a degree from Riga, and worked awhile in Brussels for an American firm dealing with Community law. These six make up my so called 'cabinet'.

As often as not at least some of us lunch together in the canteen downstairs and then take a walk – at as brisk a pace as the others are prepared to tolerate round the area of the court. Sometimes we go over to the buildings of the European Parliament or of the Commission – buildings of, to my mind, no architectural distinction – and eat or shop there. Sometimes we walk through more open areas and woods in which the blackbirds happily vie with the cuckoo. I miss the splendour of the law courts and the comfort of the benchers' rooms, but these are more than compensated for by being surrounded by a gifted team of lawyers significantly younger than I, full of the vigour of youth and moreover sometimes more experienced than I in the details of the relevant corner of Community law and the practice of the Court. We spend most of our time at lunch laughing and teasing one another, having spent the morning drafting or discussing. The subject matter of the drafts and discussions can vary from something as important as breaches of the Stability Pact to something as banal as the proper classification for duty purposes of tracked vehicles used off the road for dumping builders' rubble. Many of the other judges have much older legal secretaries – ex-judges or academics – with more experience than mine and they tease me about my youthful team, but I hope that we do as good a job as the other cabinets. Anyhow, if we miss something through inexperience, there are older heads around who will not hesitate to put us right. I hope that our enthusiasm and dedication make up for not having spent years drafting reports, notes and judgements in French.

So what are we up to? Well, the others are all working hard. Carsten and Gabrielle are preparing a draft report for me and my fellow judges on a dispute which has arisen between the European Commission and five contractors, several of whom have gone bankrupt in different Community jurisdictions, in relation to a contract drawn up in English but governed by German law. Deok-Joo is preparing a draft judgement in a case where the Dutch High Court has asked for our view as to what taxes Community law permits in relation to someone who had been employed in Austria and wants to bring his car back to the Netherlands. Aleksandra is getting ready to discuss with me a case in which it is alleged that the Greek government failed to comply with a directive which governs the right of architects from one country of the European Union to practise their avocation in another country of the Union. In each of these cases we have to get on top of not just Community law but also the national law concerned. I get teased because I still have the English judge's habit of also wanting to know the facts before laying down the law which is to be applied to them. My Scottish predecessor, Sir David Edwards, had, I am told, the same shortcoming.

As for me, I am just taking a break before going to the weekly meeting of all the judges and Advocates General in which we discuss every case which comes to the Court with a view to deciding whether it is to be heard by three, five or a larger number of judges and also discuss other matters upon which a common policy is desirable. I expect to be finished shortly after seven, but we have been known to go on till after eight. Almost certainly at least one of the legal secretaries will still be beavering away when I return.

I have now come back from the meeting and all three are still there, but chatting after a hard day. I will try and finish this piece which I have promised the Editor. Apart from having to skim-read every case that comes to the Court for the purposes of the weekly meeting and every judgement emanating from the Court, I'm currently the juge rapporteur in some forty cases and part of the constitution in another 100 or more. Every case which comes to the Court is allotted by Deok-Joo to one of the three legal secretaries, each of whom thus has a third of the number of cases with which I have to deal but spends at least three times as long on each of them.

For me it's a very different life from that in the Court of Appeal, firstly because I am assisted by the cabinet and secondly because here the judge fulfils not only the function of a High Court Master, suggesting how a case should be dealt with procedurally, and of a judge of first instance, making findings of fact and of law, but also of the House of Lords, endeavouring to provide a satisfactory way of solving the cases which come before the Court without giving a ruling which will be unsatisfactory in the context of different facts on a future occasion.

The Court's judgements tend to be short when seen from an English standpoint, though long by some countries' standards. A judgement on a Denning model would be laughed at. The lengthy consideration of policy choices which you can find in English judgements, which considerations are equally behind our judgements here, are frequently not found expressed. By contrast, the opinions of the Advocates General do often expressly consider policy choices. However, what is discussed in the Advocate General's opinion may well not be what exercises the judges in their discussions which the Advocate General does not attend. You will not find sixty or more pages of judgement.

Sometimes the task of securing agreement amongst judges from so many different national and professional backgrounds is indeed arduous, and every sentence potentially gives rise to disagreement. This encourages brevity. So does the fact that most of us are working in a foreign language. Something lapidary tends to be the result.

The whole process is not made easier for those of us who are not native French speakers, which of course is the vast majority, by the fact that all judgements are drafted and discussed in French and by the fact that the form of judgement which the court has adopted owes something to traditional judicial French styles. Although the judgements are short, the tradition is to use one very long sentence to say what most people would find easier to understand if the sentence were divided into three or four. So you may find sesquipedalian words in sentences of inordinate length. It will be interesting to see whether the style of judgements will alter now that ten new judges have all joined at once.

But it's all fascinating: the legal and political issues, the differing sensibilities and gifts of the judges, the techniques of securing agreement, the working with legal secretaries to produce judgements. The atmosphere is a very happy one, and I enjoy going to work every morning. But now I'm taking the twenty-five-minute drive home to our house overlooking the Moselle and the vineyards, whose produce I shall shortly pour down an expectant throat. Some of my colleagues in the Court of Appeal thought I was mad to be going here. I think that I'm a lucky man to have been given the opportunity.